Ivy League Prep

An Innovative, Strategic Approach to College Admissions

Samuel B. Silverman

Ivy League Prep, An Innovative, Strategic Approach to College Admissions

Copyright © 2018 by Ivy League Prep, LLC

Published by Ivy League Prep, LLC

To my family and to Tracy Li for always being
in my corner—no matter what.

Contents

Preface

College admissions, especially to the nation's top schools, is becoming increasingly competitive. I wrote this book to give you and your child actionable advice and a strategic way to approach college admissions. The chances of being admitted to highly selective colleges is slim—but if your child develops a strong, cohesive theme and a compelling personal narrative, his or her chances of being admitted can be significantly improved.

This book draws largely upon my own experience: I was a non-minority, non-athlete, non-legacy applicant admitted to several top colleges including Yale, the Wharton School at the University of Pennsylvania, Dartmouth, Cornell, Georgetown, and Duke. I enrolled at Yale, and my experience there and the resulting opportunities that followed have significantly shaped my life.

While a student at Yale, I founded Ivy League Prep, and since then I've personally helped over 100 clients gain admission to their top college choices. I've worked as a management consultant for The Boston Consulting Group, one of the world's foremost strategy firms, and I gained experience working in China as the Director of Corporate Strategy for professional golfer Jack Nicklaus. I currently serve as the Director of Scholarships of the Kantner Foundation—a national merit-based scholarship foundation—and I'm the Managing Partner of EB5 Affiliate Network, an EB-5 regional center operator and consultancy firm I founded.

In short, I know what matters in a college admissions profile, both from the perspective of a recent applicant and as an experienced consultant, and I have a track record of helping students gain admission to the nation's most selective schools.

For me, careful strategy paid off. The focused time and effort I expended on activities that mattered resulted in successful admission to top-tier schools, and attending Yale provided me with several key opportunities. Careful strategy can pay off for your child, too. If your child invests his or her time and energy in the right ways, he or she can greatly improve his or her chances of being admitted to the nation's top colleges. Attending a top college will provide your child with unique opportunities, an amazing network of peers and alumni, and a great foundation for a highly successful career.

In this book, you'll be introduced to today's increasingly competitive admission landscape and why fighting for a spot at a top college is worthwhile. We'll walk through what a successful admissions profile looks like, at each step identifying strategies for showcasing your child as a compelling applicant. We'll discuss the admissions process holistically, working through each stage of your child's education—specifically identifying what your child needs to do as a freshman, sophomore, junior, and senior. Additionally, the book includes strategies for selecting colleges and reveals several common mistakes your child needs to avoid throughout the admissions process.

My sincere hope is that this book will help you and your child better understand the admissions process and provide the insights you need to approach college admissions confidently and strategically.

I wish you and your child all the best.

Samuel B. Silverman

Section One:

Introduction

Chapter 1:
Why Top 25 Matters

While a college education has become something of a basic requirement for career success, not all colleges grant the same benefits to their graduates. The college a person attends acts as a gateway to the future—which gateway your child will go through depends on which college he or she attends.

Graduating from a top college will set your child on an upward career trajectory that is, statistically, difficult to replicate for those who attend a lower ranked school. And while it's possible for graduates of lower ranked colleges to achieve a high level of success, those that do are exceptions to the rule.

The distinction of graduating from a top school isn't just bragging rights—it's leverage your child will be able to apply throughout his or her career. The school's reputation and network, the education your child obtains, and the experience he or she gains will all serve to propel him or her toward success. The stakes are extremely high, and as a result, so is the competition.

Brand Recognition

The name of the school your child attends isn't ultimately what matters. What that name gives your child—the doors it opens—that is why attending one of the top 25 colleges is so valuable.

Graduating from a top school gives instant credibility. The school's brand is transferred to your child as a graduate, and he or she will be able to trade on that brand the rest of his or her life. In fact, the real-world value of your child's education is largely dependent on the strength and reputation of his or her college's brand.

Your child's first job opportunities after graduating will be shaped by where he or she attended college. Only so many top finance, consulting, and tech positions are available each year, and an overwhelming number of these jobs are given to students who graduate from the top 25 schools.

Similarly, only so many graduate school slots are available in a given year. Graduates from the top 25 colleges have strong admissions results at the highest ranked graduate schools because the top graduate schools are looking for applicants with experience at the top firms and best undergraduate programs. Where your child goes to college and what jobs he or she gets after graduating will directly impact which graduate schools will admit your child. Brand matters.

Network

Successful careers are often built on who a person knows—not just what a person knows—and so the network your child gains through the college he or she attends is vital. The better the network, the greater the opportunities.

Attending a top college means becoming part of a professional network. Your child's network of classmates (who are the future leaders in their respective fields), professors, and alumni living around the world will be one of the driving forces behind the opportunities to which your child will have direct access.

For example, while I was a student at Yale, I took a class called Study of the City. The course was taught by Professor Alexander Garvin, who at that time had been teaching it for more than 30 years. I told him I was interested in pursuing a career in real estate and asked him if he knew any developers in Florida. He told me of a local firm he was working with—located 20 minutes from my house—that had developed the Bears Club for professional golfer Jack Nicklaus. Professor Garvin made the introduction, I got an interview, and I landed a coveted summer internship working for this developer. This was an exceptional early experience for me—I was a sophomore at the time, and most firms don't hire interns until their junior year.

That's the kind of impact having a strong network makes. Fewer and weaker connections mean fewer and weaker opportunities. But close connections to influential people with strong networks can mean early opportunities and a jumpstart to your child's career and his or her own network.

But the college your child attends affects more than just his or her professional life. Your child's spouse and lifelong peers will likely be classmates. And so the school your child attends significantly impacts what kind of people he or she will surround him or herself with along the way.

Education & Experience

The top 25 schools offer strong academics, a variety of interesting programs, opportunities to study abroad, and more. While each of the top 25 schools has its particular strengths, specific majors, and distinctive study opportunities, all of these colleges offer strong academics and opportunities that prepare students for exceptional careers.

One of the ways in which Yale prepared me for my career, for example, was the opportunity to take part in a Yale-Beijing University Joint Program. One of only 11 students given this incredible opportunity, I traveled to Beijing and studied for five months. This experience had a significant impact on my future and is representative of the many valuable opportunities available to students at top universities.

In addition to these kinds of special opportunities, attending a top college means learning under the best professors and having access to research grants, funding, and facilities that simply aren't available for students at lower ranked schools.

Lasting Impact

Taken together, the reputation of a top school, the network it offers, and the education and experiences it provides will have a lasting impact on your child's future. Attending a lower ranked school places a ceiling on a person's professional advancement—a ceiling that is incredibly difficult to break through.

Attending a top college, however, is an investment in a high-trajectory career—one that would be unlikely apart from the leverage given by such a school.

Consider the following statistics from Yale's "First Destination Report: Class of 2016."[1]

Starting Salary	Class of 2016
< $20,000	3.5%
$20,001–$30,000	7.9%
$30,001–$40,000	10.9%
$40,001–$50,000	17.0%
$50,001–$60,000	9.4%
$60,001–$70,000	14.8%
$70,001–$80,000	13.8%
$80,001–$90,000	11.4%
$90,001–$100,000	4.1%
$100,001+	7.2%

According to the most recent data from the U.S. Social Security Administration,[2] the median individual income is estimated at $29,930. This places 88.6% of Yale's Class of 2016 at a higher level of compensation in their first job out of college than the median individual income of all wage earners in the United States.

Beyond that, 51.3% of the Class of 2016 earned more in their first job out of college than the median household income, which is $55,775 according to the U.S. Census Bureau.[3]

In other words, the majority of Yale's Class of 2016 made more as individual earners than the U.S. median household income—which includes households with multiple earners.

And how did the Class of 2016 find these high-paying jobs? According to the Destination Report, 59.4% of the graduates indicated they found their positions through a Yale Career Strategy resource, faculty referral, Yale alumni and peer networking, On-Campus Recruiting (OCR), or other Yale resource.

The Yale "First Destination Report" demonstrates the kind of lasting impact attending a top school has on a person's life. One opportunity leads to another and creates a chain of events that becomes a career.

For me, as a senior at Yale, I applied to numerous management consulting firms through the Yale On-Campus Recruiting platform. I received offers from two: The Boston Consulting Group and Oliver Wyman. These were the job opportunities attending Yale unlocked.

For context, the year I applied to The Boston Consulting Group, the firm received more than 100,000 résumé submissions nationwide, about 200 of which were from Yale students. The firm hired just over 100 people nationally, 9 of whom were from my class at Yale. So, the overall job offer rate was about 0.1% (100 out of 100,000), but of the students who applied from Yale, the offer rate was 4.5% (9 out of 200). This means that the Yale students who applied to The Boston Consulting Group were offered jobs at 45 times the rate of other applicants.

I accepted the offer from The Boston Consulting Group and went to work in their Miami office. There, I met one of my current business partners when we were assigned the same consulting case.

After two years, I received a call from the real estate developer I had interned with while a student, and based on his strong recommendation and my experience studying in China while at Yale, I was offered a job working in Beijing as Director of Corporate Strategy for Jack Nicklaus, the professional golfer. And while in Beijing, I met another of my current business partners at a Yale Club Beijing event.

You see, getting a great job out of college wasn't the end of the impact that attending Yale had on my career. The connection I made with the Florida real estate developer through a professor and my experience studying abroad in China both had lasting impact.

From China, I applied to several business schools. I was admitted to Stanford (6% acceptance rate) and Wharton in Round 2 (12% acceptance rate) and chose Stanford.

The specific events of my journey are unique to me, but my story is representative of the kind of lasting influence the school a person attends has on his or her life.

I can think of no other investment that will have as meaningful and long term a payoff as attending a top school. Despite the efforts required to gain admission, despite the costs, the tangible benefits of attending such a college are priceless and irreplaceable.

Chapter 2:
Current Admissions Landscape

The current trend in top-tier college admissions is increasing application rates and decreasing acceptance rates. This has created an incredibly competitive admissions landscape. Students who want to attend top colleges absolutely must set themselves apart from the massive pool of applicants.

General Statistics

The Ivy League, for example, now has an average acceptance rate of approximately 8%—nearly half what it was a decade ago. And this trend is not isolated to Ivy League Schools. Institutions across the United States have seen increasing levels of competition.

The competition is even greater among non-legacy, non-minority, and non-athlete applicants. While about 70% of the U.S. population identifies as white or of European descent, only 30% of Ivy League students identify as white or European (not including any athletic recruits or legacy students).

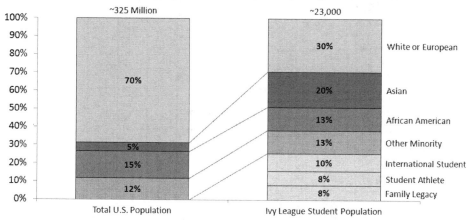

Estimated Demographic Breakdown of Ivy League Admissions

Of the roughly 195,000 applicants who identify as white or of European descent, only about 7,000 are accepted to Ivy League schools. This means the acceptance rate for such students is actually about 3.6%.

Academic Factors

Top colleges have high academic standards, and many students whose applications to top-tier schools are rejected have phenomenal academic records. In fact, the majority of applicants to top schools are academically qualified to be admitted. The most selective colleges reject valedictorians and applicants with perfect exam scores. For these colleges, admission depends on more than just grades and scores—but GPA, class rank, and entrance exam scores do matter.

For reference, consider some test statistics[4,5] for the incoming freshmen at Harvard, Yale, and Duke, three of the most selective colleges:

ACT Composite		
University	25th Percentile	75th Percentile
Harvard	32	35
Yale	31	35
Duke	31	34

SAT Reading & Writing		
University	25th Percentile	75th Percentile
Harvard	740	800
Yale	750	800
Duke	730	800

SAT Mathematics		
University	25th Percentile	75th Percentile
Harvard	730	800
Yale	740	800
Duke	750	800

So, if your child wants to gain admission to a top school like Harvard, Yale, or Duke, he or she will need to aim for an ACT score of at least 31 or SAT section scores at least in the mid-700s. In order to have even an average SAT score, your child would need a composite of 1540 (the maximum is 1600).

Early Decision

Generally speaking, students who apply early decision have a higher statistical likelihood of gaining admission than if they applied regular decision. One school with a large increase to admission rates for early decision applicants is University of Pennsylvania, with an overall acceptance rate of 9.2% but an early decision acceptance rate of 22.0%. Similarly, Dartmouth College has an overall acceptance rate of 10.4% but an early acceptance rate of 27.8%. In general, early acceptance rates across top schools demonstrate a significant increase in the odds of acceptance through early decision and early action programs.

So, if your child knows he or she wants to attend a particular school, applying early decision significantly increases his or her chances of admission. (We'll talk in greater detail about regular decision, early decision, and early action applications in Chapter 33.)

Chapter 3:
About Sam & the Ivy League Prep Approach

So, now that you have a better understanding of why attending a top college is so important for your child and what the current admissions landscape looks like, I want to briefly explain more about myself and the Ivy League Prep approach to college admissions.

I was a non-minority, non-athlete, non-legacy applicant who was admitted to four of the eight Ivy League schools, including Yale and the Wharton School at the University of Pennsylvania. After graduating from Yale, I worked at The Boston Consulting Group and then for Jack Nicklaus in Beijing before returning to the U.S. to pursue my M.B.A. at the Stanford Graduate School of Business.

While at Yale, I founded Ivy League Prep to help students gain admission to their dream schools. And I've written this book to provide clear examples and actionable information to help your child do just that—to improve his or her odds of being admitted to a top college.

Is there still chance involved? Absolutely. But getting into a top-tier college does not happen by accident. Your child must engineer the results he or she wishes to attain, and doing so takes long-term planning, a custom strategy, and careful execution.

This book is based on my personal experience, not only as a recent undergraduate and M.B.A. applicant, but as a professional admissions consultant and business strategist. I have consulted with more than 100 families through the college admissions process and serve as the Director of Scholarships of the Kantner Foundation—a national scholarship foundation that has awarded millions of dollars to outstanding college-bound high school seniors. I've also been a management consultant at The Boston Consulting Group, one of the top-ranked strategy firms in the world, which was ranked #3 on the Forbes Best Companies to Work for list in 2017.

Experience-Based Advice

At Ivy League Prep, our methodology is modeled after what works—and is a proven, data-driven model for giving an individual his or her highest chances of getting into a top school. Our method emphasizes tactical decision making, creative strategy, and a focus on spending time in such a way that the student gets the most value per hour developing his or her admissions profile.

Having strong academics and excellent test scores is not enough. Most of the applicants to the top schools have strong academics and great scores. Your child has to have a hook that distinguishes him or her from all the other applicants. In short, if your child wants to get into a top school, he or she must stand out.

The more your child stands out, the more competitive he or she becomes, and the higher his or her chances are of being admitted. So, developing a successful admissions profile is more than simply pursuing challenging academic courses through high school and excelling—it's more than getting perfect scores on the ACT and SAT. A successful admissions profile involves being academically diverse, community-minded, innovative, and highly focused in one particular area of interest—and unifying all of these elements into a clear, focused theme and compelling personal narrative.

So, what did I do to stand out?

The linchpin of my profile was a passion to combat illiteracy, which began as a project I created—Children's Books on Tape—and later evolved into a nonprofit. That organization became the theme around which I built my profile.

Children's Books on Tape is an organization I founded to help bring literacy to English as a Second Language (ESL) learners by recording children's level books onto cassette tapes and then donating the recorded tapes along with the books and tape recorders to Title I elementary schools—schools with high numbers or high percentages of children from low-income families. Each donation is comprised of four tape recorders and multiple listening libraries that consist of fifty recorded books on tape in library storage bags. Through these listening libraries, disadvantaged elementary students who are having difficulty learning English as a second language—often because they do not have an English-speaking parent at home to read to them—are able to take books and recordings of those books home. These listening libraries give ESL students additional exposure to English and help them improve and reinforce their reading skills outside of the classroom.

My efforts founding and rapidly expanding this organization demonstrated the kind of ingenuity, leadership, and ambition that college admissions officers want to see. I took an idea and created something that made a difference, growing it from a one-person operation to a 501(C)(3) not-for-profit corporation.

I built my application theme around this organization. For example, I took a graduate-level course on childhood psychology and learning. I also volunteered as a teacher in a summer reading course for 4th graders in an ESL program—donating a Children's Books on Tape listening library to the program as well.

We'll take a more in-depth look at my successful admissions profile in the next chapter.

More About Sam

In addition to my work with Ivy League Prep, I serve as a trustee and Director of Scholarships on the Kantner Foundation, a not-for-profit national scholarship foundation that has awarded millions of dollars in merit scholarships to outstanding high school seniors across the country. In this role, I review thousands of scholarship applications, so I have a lot of exposure to student profiles and know what makes students stand out. Since the Kantner Foundation sends scholarship funds directly to colleges, I know what student profiles were successful at the top schools and which were not.

I am also the founder and managing partner of EB5 Affiliate Network ("EB5AN"), a leading EB-5 regional center operator and EB-5 consulting firm. The EB-5 Program is a U.S. visa program administered by United States Citizenship and Immigration Services (USCIS) that awards visas to immigrant investors whose investment capital helps stimulate economic development and create jobs in areas of high unemployment. EB5AN owns and operates one of the largest networks of USCIS-approved EB-5 regional centers in the country and is considered a national leader and pioneer in the regional center affiliation model. Visit EB5AN.com to learn more.

For my work with Children's Books on Tape, the Kantner Foundation, and EB5AN, I was named a member of the Forbes 30 Under 30 Class of 2018 for the social entrepreneur category.

Data-Driven Approach

Ivy League Prep employs a data-driven approach to college admissions. We carefully examine the current admissions landscape and refine our methodology based on what a student needs to demonstrate in order to be admitted to a top college.

We understand that while every college application involves several factors, not all factors are weighted equally. In fact, extracurricular activities and third-party recognition take on added significance for top-tier schools when compared to low-and mid-tier schools. Also, while having high standardized test scores is essential for getting into a top college, extracurriculars and recognition are given more weight than standardized test scores and the written components of the application.

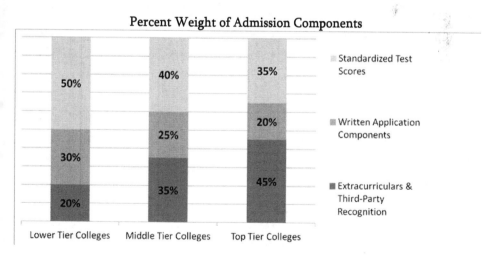

Percent Weight of Admission Components

For school-specific data, see Appendix II: Admissions Statistics.

Unbiased, Straightforward Guidance

Unlike school guidance counselors, who want to keep all parents happy and are prone to playing favorites or giving a select few students all of their attention, Ivy League Prep offers its clients total commitment without conflicts of interest or a misalignment of expectations.

We offer each student unbiased, straightforward advice to help him or her develop the most competitive admissions profile possible. We don't sugar coat anything.

Our goal is to give students the best information—the knowledge and direction they need to get into top colleges.

Gaining admission to a top school requires a student to focus on what truly matters for admissions success. And so we prioritize certain activities over others to ensure that the limited number of available hours are spent strengthening the competitiveness of the student's profile.

We help students leverage time spent on particular activities or interests to augment their profile in multiple ways (e.g., awards, recommendations, etc.), thereby maximizing the return on the hours they invest. Instead of using a laundry-list approach, we guide students to develop a handful of high-impact activities. By working smarter and focusing their time, students don't fall into the trap of blindly throwing hours away—they pursue activities that actually strengthen their chances of being admitted.

Long-Term Strategy

The overriding philosophy at Ivy League Prep is to encourage an early, diligent focus on pursuing what matters most for a successful admissions profile. College preparation ought to begin long before the senior year of high school, and many of our clients begin conversations with us while their students are in middle school.

You should invest time in developing your child's interests outside of school. If your child really enjoys math, then pursue a summer program that allows him or her to advance a level in math—which is much easier to accomplish before high school. If your child loves to read and write, consider working with a tutor to help your child write a book.

The key is to draw upon what interests your child and expose him or her to that subject outside the classroom. Give your child opportunities to pursue areas of interest and provide opportunities for him or her to explore.

One of the biggest mistakes we see is students getting straight As in middle school while taking classes that are too easy. The problem is when such a student starts high school, he or she is on the wrong track. Advancing to more challenging course is much easier in sixth, seventh, and eighth grade than it is in high school. If you want your child to finish his or her senior year with the most advanced math, science, or language courses offered by the school, you must ensure your child is on track in middle school.

In his book, *Outliers*,[6] Malcolm Gladwell discusses how the majority of elite hockey players are born early in the year. He explains that because the youth hockey leagues determine eligibility by calendar year, players born earlier in the year tend to be physically larger and more mature than those born later in the year. During the key years of a child's development, the physical and mental advantages of being 11 months older are significant—which, in this case, often means more attention and coaching. In turn, the extra coaching and advancement over a multi-year period increases the likelihood that a player will be able to pursue the sport at a professional level. The key is that an early competitive advantage, no matter how small, can compound over time and significantly impact long-term outcomes.

The same concept applies to college admissions. Helping a child identify and pursue an innate ability or interest early on will compound over time and increase the odds that the child will be at the top of that field or interest when it is time to apply for college. The key to maximizing the impact of this compounding effect is to start early with the right guidance and the goal of differentiation during the admissions process.

Chapter 4:
Example of a Successful Profile

A successful profile consists of a strong academic record, a highly focused personal narrative, and accomplishments that affirm an applicant's value to a top college.

In this chapter, I hope to use my own experience to illustrate what a successful profile looks like. Beyond academics, the key to my profile's success was that it showcased the unique narrative surrounding my project, Children's Books on Tape—which was an accomplishment in itself. But with third-party recognition in the form of a grant and other awards, I demonstrated to admissions officers that I would bring to their schools valuable leadership experience and an ability to find innovative solutions.

My Academic Record

As important as the extracurricular component of my profile was, the foundation of my application was a competitive academic record, without which I wouldn't have likely even been considered by top colleges.

I took one of the most demanding schedules available at my high school, taking a total of nine AP classes and scoring 4s and 5s on all AP exams but one. My GPA was a 3.95.

My ACT composite score was 34. I scored 800 on both the Writing and Math sections of the SAT and a 730 on the Reading section for a composite SAT score of 2330 (the maximum score was 2400 at that time). I took three SAT Subject Tests (U.S. History, Math IC, and Writing), scoring 780 on each.

Children's Books on Tape

Children's Books on Tape was born out of an experience I had early in my teen years when I went with my mother to the elementary school where she worked. There, I encountered a problem: elementary school students struggling to learn to read because their parents did not speak English.

That experience inspired me to find a solution. Children's Books on Tape was that solution. As I've already mentioned, Children's Books on Tape is an organization that donates listening libraries to Title I elementary schools in order to help students struggling to develop their English reading and writing skills.

By itself, founding and leading Children's Books on Tape definitely had a significant impact on my admissions success at several top colleges. But what made me an even more desirable candidate was the recognition I had already received for my efforts in the community. I was able to present a unique narrative of a community project that had successfully raised funds—not just from relatives and friends, but from local merchants and the local branch of a major bank.

I was able to demonstrate my success using numbers: tripling my budget and delivering 150 books on tape during the project's first year. And I was able to showcase how my leadership, determination, and ingenuity resulted in a partnership with a local university.

All of the work I put into this project culminated in a $5,000 unrestricted grant from the Dwight Allison Fellows Program awarded to me by The Community Foundation for Palm Beach and Martin Counties. This recognition validated that my project was making a real impact on the community.

Ideas that solve old problems in new ways, measurable success, affiliations and partnerships, third-party recognition, and real impact— these are the kinds of elements that make an admissions profile stand out to top colleges.

With that overview of what made my admissions profile successful, I want to transition now to some of the actual elements from the admissions process: my personal statement and several of my acceptance letters.

My Yale Personal Statement

Following is the essay I submitted with my application. Notice how it uses my major extracurricular project to demonstrate my leadership and innovation while tying in my love of learning, my desire to help others learn, and my language skills. My theme is obvious. My narrative is compelling. And the value I'd add to the college is clear.

"¡Bienvenido a los libros para niños en cinta!"

In English, this is, "Welcome to Children's Books on Tape!" This is a project that has been the focus of my life for the past 5 years. It began on a "take your child to work day," when I accompanied my mother to the elementary school where she taught reading. I quickly noticed that several students experienced difficulty with a round robin reading lesson that my mom organized. When I asked one of the kids why he was troubled, his response was quite a revelation. "Mis padres no hablan íngles," he said. "My parents do not speak English."

On the ride home that day, it occurred to me with startling clarity that the secret to learning a language is constant exposure. This concept spawned an original idea; I could record children's books on tape and donate them to the elementary school library to enhance the learning process. To do this required the formulation of a business plan, which included the creation of a budget, raising of necessary capital, the choice of business entity, and the manufacturing and marketing of our product – the transmission of knowledge and learning.

Before long, I was not only making the recordings, but also fundraising and seeking support from local merchants. I asked for donations of tape players and other supplies. In response to my solicitations, Wachovia Bank, for example, helped by funding a large supply of new books, and a community benefactor donated hundreds of dollars. My budget for taped books more than tripled, while I was able to keep my expenses the same. As a result, in the program's first year, we were able to deliver nearly 150 Children's Books On Tape to Warfield Elementary School, a low-income Title 1 School with a large student base consisting of migrant farm workers' children.

Recently, we have established a working partnership with the Florida Atlantic University's College of Education which will produce over 450 Children's Books on Tape each year to be distributed to sixty-four low-income schools. For my work with the project, I was honored to receive an award ($5,000 unrestricted grant that I used as seed money for my project) from the Dwight Allison Fellows Program given by The Community Foundation for Palm Beach and Martin Counties. The best reward, however, has been the knowledge that these tapes have really helped children to gain one of the most important tools for success in their education, and throughout their lives - - the ability to read. 1 This has been hugely gratifying for me, and I intend to study ways of bettering minority education while attending Yale.

I am excited by the prospect that at Yale, I will be able to become part of the Tutoring in Elementary Schools (TIES) organization and contribute to their strategy to improve literacy and utilize my Children's Books on Tape project to reach even more students. I am confident that by bringing Children's Books on Tape to TIES, an organization that teaches people to "read, write and think critically", Yale volunteers will not only be able to teach students during day time hours, but each student will have their own personal storyteller - - a Yale student's voice recording of a story - - to provide constant exposure to the English language and build pronunciation skills through auditory reinforcement.

I am also excited by the prospect that while at Yale, I will be able to interact closely with world-renown professors and culturally diverse classmates. Just as importantly, I will be able to explore classes in a myriad of areas of study besides the humanities, while continuing to develop and expand my Children's Books on Tape project in New Haven and beyond.

[1]"The single most important activity for building the knowledge required for eventual success is reading aloud to children." – Anderson et al, Becoming a Nation of Readers (1995)

My Acceptance Letters

I've also included some of my acceptance letters below. What I want to drive home is what got me accepted to Yale. It wasn't necessarily my grades or test scores—though those certainly mattered. It was my work with Children's Books on Tape.

Consider the following comment from the Yale admissions officer for my area:

"I was truly inspired by your work with immigrant families. Your dedication to service and your innovation & leadership make you a Yalie through and through. I look forward to meeting you in person!"

On the following pages, I've included my Yale acceptance letter, a letter from the Yale admissions officer for my area, my acceptance letter from The Wharton School at the University of Pennsylvania, my likely letter from Dartmouth, and my acceptance letter from Dartmouth.

Yale University

Office of Undergraduate Admissions
P.O. Box 208234
New Haven, Connecticut 06520-8234

Campus address:
38 Hillhouse Avenue
Telephone: 203 432-9316
Fax: 203 432-9392

March 30, 2006

Mr. Samuel B. Silverman
███████████
Jupiter, FL 33477

Dear Mr. Silverman:

Congratulations on your admission to Yale College, Class of 2010! It gives me great pleasure to send you this letter, and you have every reason to feel proud of the work and aspirations that led you to this moment.

On the folder that holds your admissions materials, you will find the words of the late George Pierson, a professor and official historian of the university: "Yale is at once a tradition, a company of scholars, and a society of friends." In evaluating candidates for admission to Yale College, the Admissions Committee seeks to identify students whose academic achievements, diverse talents, and strength of character will make them feel at home in this remarkable community. We look forward to your becoming a vital contributor to the university's life and mission.

To notify us of your decision, you may use the enclosed reply card. While the final reply date is May 1, we would love to hear from you before then.

Also, on April 17th, 18th and 19th, most of your future classmates will come to the campus for some portion of Bulldog Days, our program for admitted students. We hope you will join them! To register for Bulldog Days and also to connect with other admitted students, please visit our new website <www.admits.yale.edu>.

Finally, if you have any general or specific questions about Yale, feel free to e-mail us at bulldog@yale.edu. I am delighted, both for you and for the College, at the prospect that you will join us next fall. Welcome to Yale!

Sincerely,

Jeffrey Brenzel
Dean of Undergraduate Admissions

JBB/an
Enclosure

Yale University

April 6, 2006

Office of Undergraduate Admissions
P.O. Box 208234
New Haven, Connecticut 06520-8234

Campus address:
38 Hillhouse Avenue
Telephone: 203 432-9316
Fax: 203 432-9392

Samuel B. Silverman

Jupiter, FL 33477

Dear Samuel,

As the admissions officer responsible for your area, I would like to add my personal congratulations on your acceptance to the Yale College Class of 2010. It was a pleasure to present your application to the Admissions Committee, and I am as delighted with the Committee's decision as you are.

Being a Yalie is about belonging to an exceptional community, one that is defined partly by the incredible people who teach and study here, and partly by the amazing visitors who come to campus each year and further enrich our community life. Among hundreds of eminent visitors to campus this past year alone were NBA all-star Dikembe Mutombo, who spoke about his humanitarian efforts in the Democratic Republic of Congo; Pulitzer Prize-winning authors Jhumpa Lahiri, David McCullough, and Marilynne Robinson; former Secretary of State Madeleine Albright; primatologist Jane Goodall; actors and filmmakers Sam Waterston, Sofia Coppola and David Lynch; violinist Sarah Chang; activist and performer Harry Belafonte; and the heroic Paul Rusesabagina, whose story was depicted in the Academy Award-nominated film *Hotel Rwanda*.

Campus is a beehive of activity right now. Trumbull College is currently being renovated, the seventh of the twelve residential colleges to undergo this process. Students and faculty alike are excited by the incredible new facilities at the Daniel L. Malone Engineering Center and the Class of 1954 Chemistry Research Building. In the fall, our women's soccer team advanced to the third round of the NCAA College Cup for the first time in the team's history, while our women's squash team captured its 3rd straight national title this winter. Under a new Yale program, you and your classmates will be among the first to have the option of studying for a semester at Peking University in Beijing.

Yale is truly a place where you will learn and grow as a person and a scholar. Having read your application, I know that your energy and talents will play a tremendous role in continuing to make Yale such a vibrant and exciting place. I encourage you to come to campus for Bulldog Days on April 17th, 18th and 19th to get a taste of life as a Yale student. Please feel free to contact me by telephone at (203) 432-9316 or email at jose.roman@yale.edu if you or your family members have any questions.

Once again, I want to offer my warmest congratulations, and I look forward to seeing you this fall in the Yale College Class of 2010!

Sincerely,

Jose Roman
Assistant Director

I was truly inspired by your work with immigrant families. Your dedication to service and your innovation & leadership make you a Yalie through and through. I look forward to meeting you in person!

28

Office of Admissions

March 30, 2006

Mr. Samuel B Silverman

Jupiter, Florida 33477

Dear Samuel,

Congratulations! It gives me great pleasure to invite you to attend the University of Pennsylvania as a member of the Wharton School.

The members of the Class of 2010, the 254th graduating class since Benjamin Franklin founded the University in 1740, are an outstanding group of individuals. After carefully reviewing nearly 20,500 applications for our class of 2,400 students, we are pleased that every admitted student will have the opportunity to contribute to our heritage of academic excellence, social leadership, and cultural advancement. We offer you world-renowned faculty, nationally recognized academic departments, and an unparalleled freedom of intellectual exploration.

While we are eager for you to join the Class of 2010, we realize fully the importance of the decision you must make in the next few weeks. If there are questions that you or your parents have, or if you have not yet visited Penn and would like to do so, please let us assist you. The enclosed Penn Preview invitation provides visitor information, schedules, maps, and telephone numbers for your convenience. When you reach your decision, please return the reply card and acceptance deposit to us by the first of May.

On behalf of the Penn community and the admissions staff, congratulations again on your outstanding achievements. We look forward to welcoming you to our campus in September.

Sincerely,

Willis J. Stetson, Jr.
Dean of Admissions

Dartmouth College

Office of Admissions • 6016 McNutt Hall • Hanover • New Hampshire • 03755-3541
TEL: (603) 646-2875 • FAX: (603) 646-1216 • E-mail: admissions.office@dartmouth.edu

February 10, 2006

Samuel B. Silverman

Jupiter, FL 33477

Dear Samuel,

Greetings from Dartmouth. I hope your senior year is going well and that you are enjoying your courses and activities.

My purpose in writing is very simple--we have reviewed your application and think you are an outstanding prospect for Dartmouth. I recently read your folder and was exceedingly impressed with your academic accomplishments and intellectual potential. There is no question that when we mail our final decisions at the end of March, you will be offered admission to the College.

I see no reason to delay letting you know about the status of your application, and I hope this early indication will "ease your mind" a bit. The college admissions process is unnecessarily long and anxious for many students. So, relax, get back to that book you meant to read, and use this time to reflect on your plans and goals for the next phase of your education.

If you have any questions about Dartmouth, please let me know. In the meantime, best wishes for the remainder of your high school career.

Sincerely,

Karl M. Furstenberg
Dean of Admissions
and Financial Aid

Dartmouth

Office of Admissions

March 30, 2006

Samuel B. Silverman
███████████████████
Jupiter, FL 33477

Dear Samuel,

Congratulations! It is with great pleasure that I inform you of your admission to Dartmouth College as a member of the Class of 2010. You were selected from an accomplished and academically talented group of nearly 14,000 applicants. The admitted group, of which you are a part, is outstanding in its achievements, interests, and potential. We are enthusiastic about the prospect of your attendance and are confident that you and Dartmouth are an ideal match.

The faculty and staff join me in inviting you to attend Dartmouth. This is a particularly exciting time at the College; the opportunity for personal involvement in all facets of your education here is significant. The College continues to be distinguished by the commitment of its faculty to combine excellence in teaching with exceptional scholarship and research. New initiatives undertaken in recent years, including a reaffirmation of the commitment to a diverse student body, an expansion of the financial aid program, and a major expansion of academic and research facilities, will each enhance Dartmouth's national leadership in liberal arts education.

All of us at Dartmouth hope you will visit campus during the month of April and take the opportunity to meet students and faculty, attend classes, and stay overnight in the dorms. During the period from April 19th to April 22nd, we will sponsor a series of special programs to introduce admitted students to the academic and extracurricular life at the College.

Again, congratulations on your acceptance. Please let us know if we can be of any help to you in the next few weeks. We would appreciate confirmation of your matriculation plans on the enclosed form by May 1st. I hope you decide to become a part of the Dartmouth community.

Sincerely,

Karl M. Furstenberg
Dean of Admissions
and Financial Aid

Section Two:

The Successful Profile

Chapter 5:
The Admissions Process

In this chapter, we'll take a look at what happens once your child's application is received by a school. This may seem like a strange place to start since we haven't discussed any specifics about developing a compelling application yet, but the purpose here is to show you how the application will be read so that you and your child can strategically approach the college admissions process.

Overall, applications are read in a short period of time. For all of the hours your child will have poured into his or her application, the admissions officer may spend 20–25 minutes with it. So, your child needs to carefully craft his or her application so that in this brief introduction through a limited amount of content, the admissions officer will be struck with your child's unique narrative and academic credentials, all knit together nicely by a clear and compelling theme. Your child's application will need to quickly and clearly show an admissions officer— through exam scores, awards, recognition, and other evidence—that your child's application deserves further consideration.

Following are the key questions we'll address in this chapter.
- Who reads applications?
- How do they score an application?
- When does this all happen?
- What exactly are they looking for?

Who Is Involved?

While the application reading process differs from one school to another, the key people involved typically remain the same. First, your child's application will be read by the admissions officer for your region.

Next, the application may be read by another admissions officer, professor, or other trusted third-party reader—or, depending on the first read, it may be sent to the associate director of admissions to confirm a rejection or to the director of admissions to confirm acceptance.

Assuming the application was not accepted or rejected outright and it gets a second reading, it may then proceed to a third reader: the associate director for likely rejection or the director of admissions for likely acceptance.

If the application has not yet been accepted or rejected and remains somewhere in the "possible" category, it will be sent to the admissions committee for further consideration.

Regional Admissions Officer

After all the buckets of mail have been alphabetized, processed by systems technicians, and turned into a file for each applicant—a process that often takes the better part of a month—the regional admissions officer will receive, read, and score the application.

Upon receiving your child's file, the admissions officer for your region will spend roughly 20–25 minutes reading the application. During this short period, the officer will attempt to understand who your child is and what he or she has accomplished. To do this, the admissions officer will examine your child's academic credentials, essays, extracurricular activities, awards, third-party recognition, and recommendations.

If your child's application has a strong, clear theme, the admissions officer will pick up on it. And if the application is disjointed, the officer will not likely develop an image of who your child is. Similarly, if your child's application lacks any kind of narrative, it won't likely be very memorable. We'll discuss theme and narrative in detail in Chapter 7.

Regional admissions officers are expected to have a good sense of the context from which a student has applied. Regional officers should be familiar with your child's high school, and as a result, will be able to consider your child's application in light of the opportunities your child had and the resources he or she had access to.

For example, the courses your child takes in high school will, typically, be considered in context. If an honors class is more challenging at your child's high school than the equivalent AP class, the regional admissions officer is likely to know that and keep it in mind. Or if the grading policies of your child's high school are very strict, this is likely to be noted.

After working through your child's application, the admissions officer will assign scores based on your child's academics and extracurriculars and then return the folder for further processing.

If, however, the regional admissions officer is particularly impressed by an application, he or she can mark it for acceptance and send the folder directly to the director of admissions. The director will then assess the application and either offer a final decision to accept the applicant or send it back for a second reading. Generally speaking, fewer than 10% of successful applications are accepted after only one reading.

If, on the other hand, the regional admissions officer determines an applicant's academic credentials or some other issue makes it almost certain that his or her application will be rejected, the officer can mark the folder for rejection and send it directly to the associate director of admissions. The associate director will then assess the application and either offer a final decision to reject the applicant or send it back for a second reading. A large number of applications will be rejected after only one reading—perhaps as many as 25% or more, depending on the school.

Second Reader

If your child's application is passed on to another reader, the process basically repeats itself—only this second reader won't be an admissions officer familiar with your area. Instead, the second reader is generally another admissions officer or professor, and in some cases a third-party whom the college trusts to read and score applications.

Because the first reader has already filled in biographical information and done any necessary record keeping, the second reader's work is a bit less tedious. As a result, the second reader tends to more easily keep the whole picture in view as he or she assesses an application.

The regional admissions officer's comments from the initial reading generally end up in the back of an applicant's file, so each subsequent reader won't know the first reader's thoughts until after he or she has worked through the folder. This helps prevent bias and allows each reader to form his or her own insights and opinions. The second reader will then assign a score and send the folder along—either to a third reader or to the admissions committee.

Third Reader

Generally, the third person to read an application will be either the associate director of admissions or the director of admissions.

If both the first and second readers indicate an applicant should be rejected, the folder will be sent to the associate director for a decision. Typically, such applications are rejected, but sometimes the associate director disagrees with the first two readers and sends the folder to the admissions committee for further consideration.

On the other hand, if both the first and second readers indicate an applicant should be accepted, the director of admissions will receive the file and decide to either accept the applicant or send the folder on to committee.

Applications that are neither accepted nor rejected will end up going to the admissions committee for deliberation.

Again, this process varies from school to school, as does the way an application is scored and what codes and shorthand are used. But the general system is similar—and quite democratic. The various people involved in the process act as checks and balances.

So, while the director of admissions has quite a bit of authority, he or she rarely makes any decision in a vacuum. If the director disagrees with both the first and second reader, he or she is unlikely to make a decision contrary to their recommendations—instead, the application will likely be sent to committee for further consideration.

Admissions Committee

As we've discussed, at some top colleges, the strongest and weakest candidates' folders don't get sent to the admissions committee—they are simply accepted or rejected. But for those applications that go to committee, this is the final stop.

Like pretty much everything in this process, exactly how admissions committees are structured varies from one school to another. Some schools have a single committee comprised of admissions officers, the director of admissions, and possibly professors or trusted third parties. Other schools have multiple small committees made up of admissions officers and professors.

Typically, the admissions committee is told how many applications they have to consider and how many spots are available. Then, they have the unenviable task of working through a vast number of qualified applicants and deciding which ones to admit.

The committee process generally involves the regional admissions officer presenting an applicant and explaining why he or she should be admitted. The other members of the committee will review the information they have on the applicant, discuss his or her accomplishments and the value he or she would add to the school, and then make a decision.

How Do They Score Applications?

As an application goes through the reading process, it will be given an academic rating as well as a personal rating, which takes into consideration your child's extracurricular activities, recommendations, and admissions interview. The scoring varies from school to school. While some schools use larger ranges, for example, from 1 to 9, others use smaller ranges, such as from 1 to 4. For some schools, higher numbers in the range are better, and for others, lower numbers represent stronger applications.

Simply put, each institution has its own way of rating applications. Some even try to avoid numerical ratings and instead use descriptors to rank applicants.

When Does This Happen?

From start to finish, the reading process for regular decision applications takes roughly two months, possibly a week or two longer, and ends sometime in March.

For early decision, the application is typically submitted by November 1, and the reading process takes roughly a month. Generally, colleges send out letters by the middle of December informing applicants whether they have been accepted or rejected—or, in some cases, deferred for review under regular decision.

What Are They Looking For?

Admissions officers at top colleges are looking for applicants who truly stand out. Generally speaking, a student must have a profile that not only demonstrates strong academic achievement but also a commitment to an extracurricular pursuit and a track record of success. And personality matters. If a student isn't likeable, he or she is much less likely to be admitted.

Admissions officers are striving to develop an exceptional group of incoming students. With a massive pool of applicants to choose from, officers will select the lowest risk candidates—those whose grades, test scores, prior achievements, and personality all point to a student who will thrive at their school. In the end, of all the variables factored into admissions, the most important is value. Will this applicant add value to the college?

So, the more likely an applicant is to fail to bring value to the school, the lower his or her chances are of being admitted. And the higher an applicant's risk of failing to succeed at a top college and subsequent career—based primarily on past performance—the lower his or her chances of being admitted. Admissions success boils down to low risk and high value. That's what an admissions officer is looking for.

Low Risk

For an applicant to be seen as low risk, he or she must have outstanding academics. High GPA, class rank, and exam scores tell an admissions officer your child is likely ready for the rigors of a top-college education. Your child should aim for scores within the top 25% of the range of applicants the college admits.

Low risk applicants also demonstrate a history of success. The focal activities in which your child participates should be marked by various forms of recognition: awards, honors, acceptance into selective programs, grant funding, media coverage, third-party endorsement, etc. Prior success is a good predictor of future success, and so a strong display of success in whatever primary activities your child has pursued will tell an admissions officer your child has the drive, determination, and know-how to succeed at a top college.

Ultimately, an admissions officer risks the school's and his or her own credibility on the applicants he or she supports. As a result, an admissions officer won't support a student he or she doesn't believe will succeed.

High Value

Admissions officers are looking for more than just low-risk applicants who will likely succeed at their schools. They are looking for driven leaders who find creative solutions—students who will change the world for the better. To them, a strong applicant is an investment in the student that yields returns for the school and society in general. They are looking for students who will have interesting, successful, and meaningful lives, both during college and in their careers that follow.

Many top students read as one dimensional to admissions officers. They are excellent students, but they've demonstrated nothing significant aside from that. Sure, they participate in various sports, fine arts, or other activities, but they haven't shown determination to make a mark on the world. Their applications don't show how they'll add value to the brand of a top college.

An admissions officer is responsible for protecting the value of his or her school's brand—and so the value an applicant brings is paramount to his or her admissions success. Like any other form of investment, perceived value determines investability. The higher the return, the more willing the investor.

If by the time your child applies to a top college he or she has already begun to discover what matters to him or her and has invested considerable time, effort, and resources toward that pursuit, your child will have a much better chance of gaining admission. Again, prior success is what admissions officers are looking for.

So, when an admissions officer sees an application that has a compelling theme and unique narrative that clearly depict a low-risk, high-value student, the officer will work hard to see that student admitted.

Likeable Personality

One other factor bears mentioning here: personality. Even the most outstanding student with a track record of service and successful extracurricular pursuits may face rejection if he or she comes across as unlikeable and smug. Being self-aware is absolutely vital for developing a successful admissions profile—but sounding pretentious can ruin an application.

Artfully and modestly demonstrating one's achievements is a challenge, and so your child needs to take particular care when filling out applications and writing essays.

Chapter 6:
The College Application

Now that you have a bit of insight into how your child's application will be handled once it is received, let's look more closely at the application itself.

In this chapter, I'll outline some general strategy your child should keep in mind while filling out his or her college applications. Then, we'll walk through the common application one section at a time, offering strategic guidance along the way. After that, we'll discuss the supplemental application materials some colleges require.

General Strategy

The common application has several generic fields—elements like name, address, the name of your child's high school, etc.—that don't have any real strategic value. What your child writes in these fields should simply be the truth.

Other fields, however, require your child to make specific choices or write brief explanations. These are the elements of the application that require special focus. Your child has the opportunity to strengthen his or her theme and add to his or her unique narrative depending on how he or she treats these fields.

For example, the activities your child lists—and the order in which he or she lists them—can communicate a lot about what your child values.

As we examine the common application in detail below, we'll discuss specific strategic choices. But first, here are three general strategic considerations.

Carefully Proofread Everything

Your child should carefully examine his or her application for errors. He or she should look for spelling errors and typos, grammatical errors, factual errors, inconsistencies, unclear phrases, wordy phrases, etc. The document should be polished and pristine.

Admissions officers are likely to notice any mistakes—but a single mistake, depending on its nature, might not matter all that much. Particularly egregious or frequent errors, however, may have a significant adverse affect on your child's application.

Your child should have you or someone trustworthy with strong command of English proofread his or her application.

Provide Complete & Cohesive Responses

Your child's application should paint a complete picture of who your child is and what he or she is about. Each response should clearly point to your child's theme, and wherever possible, the application should help develop your child's unique narrative.

For example, this means selecting not only the most prestigious and noteworthy honors and awards—it means presenting each honor or award in such a way that it fits with everything else. Sometimes that cannot be done without explanation, and that's where your child's personal essay or additional information write up come into play.

Highlight Diversity

Anywhere your child can demonstrate diversity of any kind, he or she should. This means highlighting ethnic diversity, unique perspectives, rare opportunities, highly specialized abilities, and any other experiences or background that are likely to set your child apart from other applicants.

Admissions officers at top colleges place a high value on diversity—they want a well-rounded class formed not by well-rounded students, but by a wide variety students with diverse experiences.

Common Application

The common application has been in use since the mid-1970s and is accepted by a little more than 600 colleges. The goal of the common application is to help standardize the application process and make it easier for students to apply to multiple schools.

While not every college accepts the common application, most top-tier schools do. But many schools also require pre-applications or other supplemental application materials, which we'll discuss later in this chapter.

And even though the purpose of the common application is to standardize and streamline the application process, applicants seeking admission to the most selective schools should tailor the common application specifically to each school.

Below, we will examine each section of the common application and discuss specific strategic elements to keep in mind as your child develops his or her admissions profile.

Profile

The common application opens with a section with fields for personal data, such as legal name, birth date, address, etc. Obviously, this information needs to be filled in completely and honestly.

Your child should be careful about what email address he or she lists on his or her college application—avoiding anything that may come across as immature or inappropriate. If your child's email address clearly showcases his or her personality and ties in to his or her theme and narrative, this may stand out to an admissions officer. But it's always safe to use a simple, professional email address. First name period last name and a few numbers is always a safe approach, for example, Sam.Silverman561@gmail.com.

The next components of the Profile section are optional fields related to demographics: religion, ethnicity, birthplace, and language. Although optional, not including one's ethnicity might be perceived by an admissions officer as an attempt to hide information—and admissions officers value honesty and transparency. Besides, ethnicity tends to be somewhat obvious (though not assumed) based on an applicant's name.

Also, if your child is black, Hispanic, or Native American, he or she will be noted as an underrepresented minority (URM) applicant and will thus have an advantage in the admissions process. See Chapter 22 for more information about how being a URM applicant affects admissions.

Note that your child may mark all applicable ethnicities, and doing so helps give admissions officers a clearer picture of who your child is.

For example, an applicant may have one parent who belongs to a minority group—or both parents might belong to separate minority groups. Disclosing this information could provide an admissions advantage since that applicant is more likely to be classified as belonging to an underrepresented minority.

The optional language fields are also important to complete, if applicable, and so your child should list any languages he or she has studied in school and those he or she speaks at home. Foreign-language fluency is important to top colleges—and applicants that come from homes in which English is not the primary spoken language are more likely to bring a diverse perspective to the college. Also, if English is not your child's first language, an admissions officer may be a little more lenient toward a lower SAT Reading score or AP English exam score. Or, if these scores are excellent, your child might stand out a bit more to an admissions officer.

Family

The Family section of the common application is used to gather basic information about an applicant's family background, including what colleges his or her parents and/or siblings attended, if any. This information helps colleges get a picture of whether the applicant is from a privileged background or if he or she could qualify as a legacy applicant (see Chapter 19) to a particular institution based on where his or her parents attended college.

An applicant should indicate the highest level of education his or her parents have completed. For example, if an applicant's father attended college but never graduated, the applicant should not mark that he is college educated since the reader will assume this means he graduated.

For siblings who are or have attended college, an applicant should include completed education as well as current education.

Education

The next section of the common application is for basic information regarding your child's high school, such as its address and whether it is public, private, etc. The form also includes fields for any additional high schools your child has attended, including summer schools and programs, and any college courses your child has taken for credit.

Other information entered in this section include class rank, if any, GPA (and whether it is weighted), and a list of courses the applicant is taking in the current year. Here, the applicant should report every class he or she will take senior year, including any independent study, online courses, and dual enrollment courses. For AP courses, the full course name should be used, not an abbreviation. Your child will also have a place to list any college courses he or she has taken during high school.

The Education section also includes space for an applicant's top 5 awards or honors. Here, your child should list his or her most impressive honors. If the name itself does not adequately communicate what the award or honor is for, your child should provide a brief explanation. If an award or honor needs additional explanation in the application, your child might consider using the additional information component of the Writing section to elaborate.

Generally, your child should choose his or her most impressive honors. Top colleges want to see third-party validation that an applicant is exceptional, and so the more reputable, credible, or selective the third party, the better. For example, being admitted into MIT's Research Science Institute or placing in the Siemens Competition in Math, Science & Technology would be major accomplishments and would carry a lot of weight due to the selectivity of these programs.

Being a National Merit Scholarship Semifinalist or Finalist (top 1% of PSAT scores in the nation) is an honor that would help set an applicant apart, but even if your child received a commended letter (top 3% of PSAT scores in the nation), he or she should consider including it unless your child has something more prestigious to include.

The key consideration when listing honors is for your child to demonstrate that he or she stands out nationally or at the state or county level, not just at his or her high school—although such recognition and high regard from teachers is an important indicator of an applicant's strength.

The Education section also asks applicants to include his or her future plans, including possible career plans and the highest level of education the applicant expects to pursue. Marking "undecided" may not be best here since it won't help your child stand out. Your child should select the career interest most closely aligned with his or her personal narrative—not what your child thinks an admissions officer wants to see.

Testing

In this section, applicants include their SAT, SAT Subject Test, ACT, and AP exam scores as well as any planned test dates. In addition to reporting scores here, your child will also need to send official scores directly to the colleges to which he or she is applying.

Activities

The Activities section is optional, but your child should definitely fill it in. Up to 10 activities may be listed and should include the extracurricular pursuits, academic interests, research projects, community service, family responsibilities, work, cultural and religious activities, and hobbies your child is passionate about. Generally, your child should list these activities in order of importance.

With each activity, your child will need to include a brief explanation (no more than 150 characters, including spaces), the number of hours per weeks, and the number of weeks per year. Estimating the amount of time spent on an activity can be difficult, but your child should do his or her best to give an honest estimate. Remember, admissions officers know how many hours are in a day, and they'll be able to detect if an applicant is exaggerating.

Your child should select the most significant and impressive activities he or she participated in through high school. The best choices are those that demonstrate exceptional skill, knowledge, innovation, leadership, and commitment—and these activities should fit your child's theme and help build his or her narrative.

Your child should also strongly consider including any work experience in this list. For lower-income students, working a job, at least through the summer, is often just the reality they live in. For students in the middle to upper class, employment during high school may be unnecessary, but having some work experience is one way for such an applicant to help defend against any potential bias toward applicants from privileged backgrounds. Simply put, if your child is from a higher-income background, he or she must be careful not to come across the wrong way—and so the best jobs for your child are those typical of other high school students his or her age. Beyond this, if your child can pursue an opportunity that he or she finds genuinely interesting and that can be tied in to his or her theme and narrative, that's even better.

As we discussed in the previous chapter, admissions officers assess each application and assign it an academic rating as well as a personal rating that is, in part, based on extracurricular activities. The lower an applicant's academic rating, the more important this extracurricular rating becomes. So, this section is a vital part of the application, and your child should leverage it to help make his or her narrative as compelling as possible.

Top college admissions officers want to know what your child does outside of his or her studies—who your child is and what he or she is passionate about. Extracurricular activities help show an admissions officer what kind of contribution your child is likely to make on campus. Admissions officers are not looking for any activity in particular; instead, they are trying to understand who your child is. Your child should pursue what he or she is interested in and include those interests in this section.

If your child was just a participant in an activity, not a leader or major contributor, or if your child spent less than one hour on the activity each week, an admissions officer is likely to overlook it. So be sure your child spends adequate time considering what to include—not forgetting to carefully proofread each explanation.

Writing

The Writing section includes three primary elements: the personal essay, disciplinary history, and additional information.

We'll cover the personal essay in detail in Chapter 8, but basically, this is the primary essay your child will write, and it should tie together everything else in the application. This essay is the main vehicle through which your child will communicate his or her theme and unique narrative.

For disciplinary history, your child must indicate whether he or she has been in trouble at school (i.e., serious infractions involving the principal) or in trouble with the law (i.e., arrests and convictions).

Finally, your child will have 650 words to add any additional information. This part of the Writing section is an ideal place for your child to explain any situation he or she believes the college should know about. For example, if your child was ill for a prolonged period, or if there were illnesses or deaths in the family that had tangible effects on your child's education, this is the place to explain these circumstances. Your child might also use this additional space to further explain his or her most significant honor or add to his or her narrative in some other meaningful way.

Supplemental Application Materials

Your child may also need to send along several supplements. Some are required, as is typically the case with teacher and counselor recommendations, and sometimes peer recommendations (see Chapter 9); other materials, such art supplements, research paper abstracts, and music recordings, may simply help admissions officers get a better picture of who your child is (see Chapter 18). Each school's requirements are different, so your child will need to do a little research to find out what each college needs.

As mentioned earlier in the chapter, while most top schools accept the common application, they also often have school-specific application materials, either in the form of a pre-application, additional questions, or additional writing prompts.

For schools that require it, a pre-application is often the first admissions document an applicant sends to a college, and a student's application fee is typically due upon filing the pre-application. For most other schools, the common application will be the first document your child will need to send, along with his or her application fee.

Biographical Information

At some colleges, the pre-application is the first component of an applicant's file that an admissions officer sees. In such cases, the pre-application will typically include fields for biographical information, which is used by the admissions officer to create a new file for an applicant.

Prior Contact & Demonstrated Interest

In addition to requesting basic information, a college's pre-application or additional questions supplement might ask the applicant whether he or she has previously applied and to indicate how he or she learned about the school.

For some top colleges, demonstrated interest serves as an indicator that an applicant would seriously consider attending if given the opportunity. Contacting a college directly, visiting, attending an event—all of these can show demonstrated interest.

Again, not all colleges care about demonstrated interest. For many top colleges, including the eight Ivy League schools, Boston College, Stanford University, and University of Southern California, the act of applying is enough to demonstrate serious interest in the school. Other top colleges, such as Northwestern University, University of Chicago, and University of Notre Dame do consider demonstrated interest on some level.

Checking Whether Demonstrated Interest Matters

If you aren't sure whether a college considers the level of interest demonstrated by your child, you can check the school's website or call its admissions office. Alternatively, you can search online for the "common data set" for the particular college and navigate to the "First-Time, First-Year (Freshman) Admission" section (currently Section C). One of the tables in this section (currently C7) shows whether the "level of applicant's interest" is considered or not.

Typically, your child won't have to make too much of an effort to demonstrate interest if he or she is truly interested in a college. And being an exceptional admissions candidate is far more important to top colleges than a one-day visit during junior year.

Ethnicity Information

Pre-applications and other school-specific application materials often include an optional field for ethnicity. Again, although optional, your child should strongly consider filling out this information—if for no other reason, then for the sake of transparency and trust. And if your child is in a minority group, again, saying so will be beneficial since demonstrating diversity is so valued.

Description or Adjectives

Supplemental materials may also include a section that asks the applicant for adjectives that describe him or her. Your child should choose words that fit his or her theme and help contribute to his or her unique narrative. These adjectives should be dynamic, interesting, and representative of your child's personality.

Interests

Additionally, a college's pre-application or additional questions supplement typically has a section for the applicant to indicate his or her academic and/or extracurricular interests. Your child should not include fake interests that make him or her sound more interesting—or that he or she thinks an admissions officer will want to see. Again, honesty is vitally important.

Your child should select interests that fit his or her theme and narrative—but should also be sure to select the most interesting and unique of his or her interests. If, for example, the form asks for no more than three academic subjects, your child should include the three most interesting and uncommon.

Chapter 7:
Developing an Application Theme & Narrative

In this chapter, we'll examine two of the most important factors in making your child's profile stand out: theme and narrative.

The theme of your child's application is what unites the various components, and the narrative is the story your child's application tells about who your child is, what he or she is capable of, and what he or she has already accomplished. Every element of your child's application should be clearly tied together with a theme and presented in a way that furthers his or her narrative. The clearer the theme and more compelling the narrative, the more readable and memorable the application—and ultimately, the greater your child's chances of being accepted to a top college.

But it isn't enough to just have any theme or narrative—these are the vehicles through which your child must communicate how he or she will add value to the school.

Theme

Developing a cohesive theme that clearly demonstrates your child's potential value to a top college is one of the most effective ways to get the attention of admissions officers and help your child differentiate him or herself from the thousands of other applicants.

Admissions officers are looking for applicants who will contribute to the various programs of the college, add to its diversity, inspire other students to learn and innovate, and enrich campus life. Your child's admissions theme is the first step in effectively communicating value to an admissions officer.

Connect the dots betweens the classes your child took, the activities he or she participated in, and the college major he or she plans to pursue. If your child intends to pursue a business major, the other elements in his or her profile should support that choice. What business-related classes did your child take? What activities demonstrate an entrepreneurial spirit? What accomplishments indicate early business success? Linking these elements is vital to creating a compelling and logical theme that an admissions officer will more easily remember.

Basically, your child's theme brings everything into focus and allows his or her profile to be simplified into one or two words. Your child's theme might be his or her academic or extracurricular focus (e.g., tech entrepreneur, programmer and engineer, blog writer, microbiologist, etc.) or a specific project, as it was in my case. If an admissions officer can't figure out exactly what your child is interested in or focused on, the theme is not clear.

Narrative

While theme is the central idea every element of your child's profile ties into, narrative is how your child takes this theme and tells his or her unique story. Theme is about the *what* and the *how*. Narrative is about the *why*.

Your child's profile should present admissions officers with a sincere and interesting narrative that speaks more to who your child is rather than what he or she has done. The narrative should showcase your child's creativity and leadership, the motivation behind the *what* of his or her theme.

For example, in my own story, my theme was my literacy project, Childrens Books on Tape, and as a result, the *what* was creating listening libraries with recorded books on tape for children from underprivileged backgrounds. The *why* was beneath the surface—an early experience with elementary school children who were struggling to read English inspired me to help. But had I not told my story, the admissions officers reading my profile would have had no context for what I had done, and ultimately, the *what* of my profile would have been far less impactful.

By telling my story, I demonstrated who I was and the underlying motivation for my accomplishments. Showing the *why* took a theme that was not bad by itself but made it great by making it my own.

Your child's admissions profile should tell his or her story. It should present admissions officers with the *why* behind the *what*. The activities your child participates in; the hours, days, weeks, and years; all of the honors and accomplishments—these *what* elements will, in a lot of ways, look like the *what* of every other application. And as much as your child should work to have a unique *what*, he or she will be able to stand out the most through his or her unique *why*.

The *why* is what differentiates your child from other applicants. When an admissions officer sees your child's narrative, it will provide the necessary context for your child's theme, and everything will logically fit together. The admissions officer will have a much clearer sense of who your child is, what makes him or her unique, and why he or she belongs at the college.

Strategic Considerations for Developing Theme & Narrative

Start Early

The later in high school your child begins to focus on theme and narrative, the more difficulty he or she will have creating something compelling.

If your child doesn't begin to demonstrate any interest in a subject until his or her senior year, it will be more difficult—though not impossible—

to convince an admissions officer that your child is serious about that subject.

If, for example, during the summer before his or her senior year, your child decides to pursue business, it may be too late to do anything business-related before school starts up again. The fall classes he or she enrolled in may have nothing to do with business. As a result, demonstrating a passion for business may be quite challenging.

Rewind one year, though, and you'll see how much easier it becomes to develop a compelling theme. Instead of taking a fun but otherwise unhelpful history class, your child could enroll in an economics, management, or entrepreneurship class. If no such courses are available, your child may be able to take a summer college course or pursue dual enrollment. Or your child could pursue an internship at a local business.

Pursuing business even earlier, your child would be able to focus his or her course work through high school on business—not just one or two classes during senior year—and other educational opportunities will also be easier to pursue. Additionally, your child may have time to participate in an entrepreneurship competition, start and grow a small business of his or her own, or form a valuable relationship with a local businessperson who can act as a mentor.

We'll talk more about how early focus is strategically important in Chapter 24 and elsewhere throughout the book, but for now, the key takeaway is that the earlier your child begins to consider the theme of his or her admissions profile, the more compelling that theme will be— and the more easily your child will be able to craft an amazing narrative that will stand out to admissions officers.

This was true in my admissions story. My early focus on promoting literacy among ESL students in low-income schools—along with other complementary elements of my profile tied into this theme—made an impact on the admissions officers who read my profile.

So whatever your child's passion, he or she should pursue it earnestly and build a theme and narrative around that.

Demonstrate Value

Value is, perhaps, the most important single idea your child's admissions profile must communicate. Everything in the application should add to your child's perceived value and demonstrate how your child will contribute to the quality and overall success of the college and enrich the learning experience of fellow classmates and faculty alike. Top colleges are seeking applicants who show ample potential—not just for success at a top-tier school, but in their careers.

To create that kind of value, your child cannot do everything. Your child shouldn't try to take all of the hardest classes in every subject, be the star of multiple varsity teams, be engaged in student body politics and multiple clubs, and be an all-state musician. Being busy does not add value—being exceptional at something does.

So, your child should focus his or her time and energy on excelling in a limited number of activities, and these activities should be linked to your child's theme.

Your child does not necessarily need to take a dozen AP classes—he or she should focus on the AP classes that integrate best with his or her theme and help develop a compelling narrative. Instead of playing two sports fairly well, your child should consider playing one sport exceptionally well. If athletics are not part of your child's theme, he or she might consider playing no sport at all (unless required by the school)—or he or she might play simply for fun, knowing that this activity will not positively impact an admissions decision.

Deep, meaningful experiences help create a much stronger admissions profile than a broad array of shallow experiences. A few meaningful experiences can be used to shape an interesting, powerful narrative in a way that having a lot of shallow experiences never will.

Show Diversity

Showing diversity does not mean your child must be diversified—quality matters more than quantity. Colleges want a diverse *class*—not individual students that try to do everything.

Instead of trying to show a great deal of variety in his or her interests, your child should try to *be* the variety. And that doesn't mean being strange.

Your child should pursue opportunities that set him or her apart from the crowd of applicants. Programs with low acceptance rates, unique real-world experiences, and international exposure will all help your child develop a strong narrative. Such experiences communicate to admissions officers that your child has seen and done things that other students have not—that your child brings a unique perspective.

Present Evidence, not just "Passion"

Your child does not need to have discovered his or her lifelong passion by age 14, or even by age 18, to be a competitive applicant to a top college. But your child should be passionate.

If your child is passionate about a particular academic subject, extracurricular activity, social issue, etc., he or she should pursue that passion with focus and zeal. But passion for something is not enough— even if it results in a solid college application theme.

Passion must be accompanied by evidence.

Some of the ways in which your child can demonstrate passion are through leadership, skill, innovation, and accomplishment. Your child's admissions profile needs to include direct, measurable evidence of passion and success in his or her profile. This means numbers, details, specific awards and recognition. Without evidence, passion is just a buzz word.

Chapter 8:
The Personal Essay

Your child's personal essay is the ideal opportunity to take all the grades, scores, honors, activities, and other elements of his or her application and weave them together into a cohesive story—the narrative we discussed in the previous chapter.

While the other parts of the application are important, without proper context, they aren't relevant. Again, your child's grades and test scores may be excellent, but they don't tell an admissions officer who your child is, how he or she thinks, and what he or she is passionate about. The personal essay should be the centerpiece of your child's admissions profile, and all the other parts of the application—although important in their own ways—should point to the this brief snippet of prose.

Remember, the information in your child's application, the *what*, is obviously important—without the right *what*, your child will not be admitted. But the *why* makes the *what* interesting, and your child must effectively communicate his or her unique narrative through the personal essay. This essay is one of your child's key opportunities to really set him or herself apart from the thousands of other applicants.

I don't want to overemphasize the importance of the personal essay, however. It is only one of the many elements of your child's application, and it is not the sole determiner of your child's admissions success. A strong essay will not necessarily earn a weak applicant admission to a top college, nor will a weak essay ruin a strong applicant's chances of gaining admission.

For strong candidates, the essay by itself may not be as influential in a decision. The same is true of particularly weak applicants. The personal essay matters most for the applicants who are in the middle. But that doesn't mean a strong applicant should neglect his or her personal essay.

However strong you think your child's application is, he or she should strive to write a captivating personal essay that, if nothing else, takes a great application and makes it even better.

What the Personal Essay Must Communicate

The personal essay is a 650-word written component of the common application that currently offers seven diverse prompts. The short length of the essay and the narrow scope of each prompt means the essay must be a focused glimpse into who your child is and what makes him or her valuable to the college.

Most of the essays submitted to top colleges are average and don't attract much attention from the admissions staff. If your child's essay doesn't grab the admissions officer's attention, he or she might only spend a few minutes reading the essay.

So, what must your child's personal essay communicate to an admissions officer in order to be interesting, effective, and memorable?

Quality Writing

Your child's essay needs to indicate to an admissions officer that his or her writing meets a sufficient standard of quality and maturity. The essay should demonstrate that your child has a firm grasp on English grammar, diction, writing style, form, and logic. Since writing is a significant part of a college education, admissions officers will use your child's essay to gauge whether he or she will likely be up to the challenge of college-level writing.

Effective Narrative

Admissions officers are looking for prose that effectively communicates your child's narrative. If your child's essay is banal and uninteresting, an admissions officer reading it will likely be bored. Such an essay may not hurt your child's admissions chances, but it certainly won't help. Your child's essay needs to showcase his or her personality and unique perspective. Admissions officers don't want to read a description of your child, they want to understand who your child is through his or her unique story.

Conciseness

The online common application essay allows for no more than 650 words. While this may seem like too small a space for everything your child wants to communicate, it isn't. Admissions officers have piles of applications to go through, and so they consider brevity a virtue.

Narrow Focus

Being concise is not the same thing as having focus. It's possible to write a short but scatterbrained essay or one that is longer but laser focused. The key is for your child to keep the essay both concise and focused. Admissions officers get the broad picture of your child's high school education, extracurriculars, and other interests throughout the application. The essay is not about breadth, it's about depth. So, your child should focus in on a single experience and use that to communicate his or her overall narrative.

Individuality

Admissions officers don't want to see another clichéd applicant. They want to see a unique individual. The classes your child has taken, the grades he or she has earned, his or her test scores, and many activities are common among applicants to top colleges—even if extraordinary in your child's context.

Your child needs to focus in on his or her unique narrative. Whatever makes your child exceptional should come out in his or her essay. This means demonstrating authenticity, maturity, a unique perspective, and specialized knowledge or skills.

Admissions officers want to see an applicant's individuality shine through in his or her essay, but your child should be careful not to be so different and original that he or she comes across as silly or immature. The essay is an opportunity for your child to show an admissions officer his or her positive attributes—those that are valued by top colleges—like maturity, passion, determination, ingenuity, and intellect.

Value

As I've mentioned many times now, colleges are after the applicants who they believe will bring them the highest value. The personal essay is one more place to demonstrate to an admissions officer that your child will not only fit in on campus but will make the campus better. Your child should use the essay to show how his or her unique perspective, skills, and passions will inspire other students and enhance the college's learning experience.

Maturity

Top colleges often offer special opportunities—international study programs, recruitment to top firms, prestigious grants, etc. How students approach these opportunities directly reflects on the college, and so top schools want applicants who are mature enough not only to handle the rigors of a challenging academic environment, but also to take full advantage of these opportunities. The personal essay is one of the ways an admissions officer will gauge your child's level of maturity.

Passion & Ability

Admissions officers are looking for students who demonstrate a high level of passion and ability. Passionate students tend to lead and inspire others, and highly skilled students tend to contribute to the success of the college's programs. Your child's application will likely already reflect his or her passions and interest, but the essay is an opportunity to breathe life into the facts of the application.

Through the personal essay, your child can take the numbers of hours your child has poured into pursuing a passion or honing a skill and show that passion or ability in context. The essay is about showing why your child is so passionate and focused.

Essay Prompts

Admissions officers want to see how your child is unique—how experiences and challenges have shaped your child and why his or her background, identity, belief, interest, talent, or skill is fundamental to who he or she is. The common application essay prompts provide a subject or focus for your child to write about. What the essay says about the subject, however, is less important than what the essay says about your child.

Selecting the right prompt is foundational to creating a great essay. Note that these prompts change from time to time and were updated and expanded for the 2017–2018 application.

Following are the current seven prompts[7] from the common application and some specific strategies for each:

Prompt 1

Some students have a background, identity, interest, or talent that is so meaningful they believe their application would be incomplete without it. If this sounds like you, then please share your story.

Prompt 1 Strategy

If writing about his or her background, identity, interest, or talent, your child should be careful not to simply turn his or her résumé into prose. Your child should take some specific experience in his or her life and use that to demonstrate why his or her background or identity is important.

If showcasing a particular interest or talent, your child should be careful not to come off as arrogant about his or her knowledge or level of ability. Instead, your child should show why this aspect of his or her life is so meaningful. Your child's application will generally indicate to admissions officers aspects of his or her identity and ability—make sure this essay doesn't simply regurgitate these facts. Admissions officers want to see the *why*.

Prompt 2

The lessons we take from obstacles we encounter can be fundamental to later success. Recount a time when you faced a challenge, setback, or failure. How did it affect you, and what did you learn from the experience?

Prompt 2 Strategy

If your child chooses to write about some obstacle or challenge he or she has overcome, the focus should be on how this experience changed your child's perspective and led to his or her development as a person. Your child should take care not to be too melodramatic—the essay shouldn't be bleak or negative.

A strong focus on the positive that emerges from challenging experiences and a humble demonstration of how your child overcame the obstacle will help admissions officers see your child's ability to persevere. The challenge itself is less important than what your child did with it.

Prompt 3

> Reflect on a time when you questioned or challenged a belief or idea. What prompted your thinking? What was the outcome?

Prompt 3 Strategy

Questioning the status quo takes courage, and admissions officers want to see forward-thinking, pioneering attitudes. If your child writes about a time he or she questioned a belief or idea, the focus should be less about championing a cause and more about showing how the experience affected your child's worldview.

Your child shouldn't just say what he or she did, but should explain why he or she challenged the idea, what happened as a result, and how your child's actions affected his or her own thinking.

Prompt 4

> Describe a problem you've solved or a problem you'd like to solve. It can be an intellectual challenge, a research query, an ethical dilemma - anything that is of personal importance, no matter the scale. Explain its significance to you and what steps you took or could be taken to identify a solution.

Prompt 4 Strategy

If your child chooses to write about a problem he or she has solved or would like to solve, the focus of the essay should be on your child's passion and the significance of solving the problem. Your child should not focus on the *what* here—the problem isn't what is important. Instead, your child should focus on the *why*. Why does this problem matter to your child?

Using this prompt, your child can use his or her passion for solving a problem to demonstrate ingenuity, leadership, and entrepreneurism. The key is not what the passion is, it's that your child will bring passion to campus.

Prompt 5

> Discuss an accomplishment, event, or realization that sparked a period of personal growth and a new understanding of yourself or others.

Prompt 5 Strategy

When most people read the first few words of the prompt, "Discuss an accomplishment," they instantly interpret that to mean, "Discuss your greatest accomplishment." The problem with doing that, though, is that your child has already listed his or her top accomplishments in the application.

If your child selects this prompt, he or she should not write something that the admissions officer can read about elsewhere in your child's application. Writing about winning a particular award will not set your child apart—but that doesn't mean your child couldn't write about some narrow experience connected to that award. The key is that your child should take an experience—even if ordinary—to show personal growth. This prompt is less about the experience itself and more about what your child realized at that moment and how his or her perspective changed.

72

Prompt 6

Describe a topic, idea, or concept you find so engaging that it makes you lose all track of time. Why does it captivate you? What or who do you turn to when you want to learn more?

Prompt 6 Strategy

As with each of these prompts, Prompt 6 is not really about the *what*—it's about the *why*. Your child should use this prompt to demonstrate passion and focus. The second half of the prompt should be the focus. Your child should write about why this concept or topic is so captivating and how he or she learns more about it.

Again, the key is taking a specific event or experience and using it to showcase who your child is, how he or she thinks, and what he or she considers important. Instead of listing the people and ways he or she learns more about a subject, your child should focus on some meaningful experience with a mentor or peer and how that experience has shaped and continues to shape your child.

Prompt 7

Share an essay on any topic of your choice. It can be one you've already written, one that responds to a different prompt, or one of your own design.

Prompt 7 Strategy

If your child chooses to write an essay on a topic of his or her choice, the key is to keep the essay focused on an experience and how it affected your child—the *why* not the *what*—and to demonstrate the value your child will bring to the school.

Throughout the rest of this chapter, we'll walk through some general strategy for crafting a compelling essay—what your child should do, and what he or she should not do.

How to Develop a Compelling Personal Essay

Consider the Essay's Audience

Your child should keep in mind that the people who are going to read his or her essay are admissions officers at top colleges. This does not mean your child should write what he or she thinks admissions officers will want—that's actually a great way to accomplish the opposite.

Instead, your child should be authentic while keeping in mind the general elements admissions officers want to see in essays: quality writing, effective narrative, conciseness, narrow focus, individuality, value, maturity, passion, and ability.

These elements are foundational to a compelling essay.

Spend Time Drafting One Amazing Essay

If any of your child's college choices do not accept the common application, your child should try to draft a single essay that will work for all the colleges to which he or she plans to apply. This way, your child can focus his or her attention and draft one amazing essay.

Depending on your child's list of colleges, however, he or she may have additional essays to write. If that's the case, writing one essay won't be an option. But the same principle applies. Your child should choose prompts strategically so the least amount of time can be spent meeting the requirements of as many schools as possible.

Focus on a Specific Experience

Focusing on a single experience or specific chain of events does more for your child's essay than simply keep it concise and focused.

The best admissions essays are both personal and specific. Whatever prompt your child selects, he or she needs to focus on developing an essay that highlights a specific experience or series of events that offer a glimpse into your child's life and way of thinking. The more general the topic, the more likely it has been and will be done by many other applicants. On the other hand, if the essay's content is personal and shows insight into what your child learned from an experience, how it continues to affect his or her life, and what it means to your child—that's a unique narrative.

For example, a generalized essay might talk about the applicant's love for a sport and how he or she worked hard to lead the team to a championship victory. A personal essay, on the other hand, might focus on a specific practice during which the applicant learned something important about him or herself. That essay might not even talk about the big championship win.

By focusing in on an experience unique to the writer, an essay carries more authenticity and creates real human interest. Even if the topic itself has been done before—and it has—by telling his or her own story, the essay will stand out. Again, it isn't so much about the experience itself; it's why the experience is significant to your child.

Think of the personal essay as a single page in a book—it isn't a chapter, even. It's just a snippet of your child's life. The context of the previous and following pages aren't necessary—and there isn't room, anyway. The essay needs to be cohesive and understandable, but the admissions officer doesn't need to know all the background of an experience to appreciate the essay because the experience itself isn't what matters.

What matters is that your child effectively communicates his or her personality and perspective in an engaging essay using his or her own unique style. If he or she can do all that while clearly showing the personal significance of the experience, your child will have written a compelling essay.

Explain the Significance

As I've already said, the specific experience your child writes about in his or her essay is not as important as using the essay to explore the experience's significance. If by the end of an essay the admissions officer is wondering why the applicant wrote what he or she wrote, the essay was unsuccessful because it didn't convey any significance.

The significance of an experience relates to change—how the experience shaped your child into the person he or she has become and what he or she learned from it. An essay that demonstrates the significance of an experience is effective because it shows the admissions officer that the applicant is aware of how the events of his or her life have brought about change, growth, and learning. Self-awareness and a desire to learn and grow are seen as positive qualities in an applicant.

An essay that underscores the significance of an event also helps admissions officers get a better picture of the applicant's unique perspective. By writing with significance in mind, your child's essay is much more likely to show admissions officers the kind of person your child is—what he or she values and how he or she thinks.

Demonstrate Value

Whatever meaningful experience your child chooses to write about, he or she should use it as a vehicle to demonstrate value to a college—to showcase the character qualities that make him or her a compelling applicant and one that will add to the campus's diversity and quality.

An effective personal essay will in some way pivot to how the writer adds value to the college. Your child should connect the dots between his or her experience and how this experience makes him or her a stronger, more valuable candidate.

Some ways your child might make such a connection include pivoting to the plans he or she has to continue an activity in college, explaining the course of study he or she intends to pursue and why, or discussing the ways in which he or she hopes to bring an interest or passion to campus.

Create Human Interest

Creating a connection with the admissions officer is important, and this is, perhaps, the most important and most difficult aspect of writing the personal essay. The essay should be interesting and catch the admissions officer's attention, but more than that, it should forge some kind of emotional bond. Your child can accomplish this simply by giving the admissions officer a glimpse into his or her life.

Even if the experience your child writes about isn't overly emotional, a good essay makes your child's experience relatable—it causes the admissions officer to feel as if he or she knows your child, at least in some small but meaningful way.

Creating human interest does not, however, mean writing a sob story or going to some other extreme. Instead, your child should write in a carefully balanced but overall upbeat tone, keep his or her voice authentic, and avoid forcing any content (e.g., trying to inject humor where it doesn't naturally fit).

The most successful essays are memorable because of the human connection they create—they make the admissions officer look forward to meeting the applicant in person.

What Not to Write

Certain topics and themes are so common that they become cliché and trite. That's why it is important for your child to keep the essay personal. An essay about a community service experience—a common essay subject—can be original if your child effectively focuses on the *why* instead of the *what*. The motivation and reasoning behind your child's actions and the significance of the experience—the *why*—can take even a cliché and transform it into something unique.

So, I'm not going to list any general subjects about which your child should not write. If your child can create an essay that highlights his or her own unique story in a compelling, relatable way while demonstrating value to a top college, it doesn't really matter what the subject of the essay is.

Certain content, however, is generally inappropriate for a college admissions essay. And some content, for example, misrepresentations of the truth, are simply unacceptable.

Below are 10 types of content your child either should never include in his or her admissions essay or, at best, must approach with extreme caution. This is not an absolute or comprehensive list, and depending on your child's unique circumstances and ability to communicate sensitive material with maturity, it may be totally appropriate for him or her to write about subject matter that may, for other students, be inappropriate.

General Biographical Content

Since your child's application contains the biographical information needed by admissions officers, the essay should not be a regurgitation of your child's résumé. Obviously, the personal essay is about your child, and so some biographical elements will be present. Such data, however, should be presented in narrative form, not as a description of what your child has accomplished.

The more narrowly focused your child's essay is on a specific experience or series of events, the easier it will be to avoid writing generalized biographical content.

Research & Analysis

Although Prompt 7 invites applicants to submit formerly written content on a topic of the writer's choosing, your child should not submit a classroom assignment he or she is particularly proud of. If a research paper, literary analysis, or some other writing assignment fits your child's theme and narrative and is exceptional enough to warrant specific focus, it should be submitted as supplemental material to the appropriate college department.

Minor Health Problems

Health problems can represent major struggles that must be overcome—and if your child has faced a serious illness, he or she might draw on that experience in drafting the personal essay. But your child should be careful not to trivialize health problems by writing about overcoming some mild illness or condition.

Writing about such challenges is not in itself the problem. Exaggerating a minor illness into a life-altering experience may strike admissions officers as immature, naïve, and maybe even a bit odious. Your child should really only consider writing about a non-life-threatening illness if it is a key part of his or her narrative.

Complaints

Your child's personal essay should have an overall positive tone and should not at any point come across as complaining or whining. Admissions officers do not want to read about circumstances, events, people, objects, weather conditions, etc., that annoy your child.

This doesn't mean your child cannot write about problems, difficulties, or circumstances that he or she believes to be wrong or unjust. In fact, Prompts 2, 3, and 4 invite applicants to write about such subjects. But instead of complaining about unwanted circumstances, your child should address these issues with maturity and insight. Doing so requires proper focus, careful word choice, and the right tone.

Excuses & Blame Shifting

As with complaints, the personal essay is no place for making excuses or shifting blame. Your child should not use the essay to justify poor performance.

Admissions officers at top colleges are not interested in excuses—they are looking for applicants who own their mistakes and learn from them. They want students who are honest, self-reflective, and determined to succeed despite circumstances. And so writing about failures, mistakes, and shortcomings is okay—as long as your child accepts any responsibility and maintains an upbeat tone.

Lies & Misrepresentations

Your child's application, including everything in his or her essay, must be truthful. In the essay, however, this means more than just an accurate portrayal of facts and events. Your child's personal essay should be an honest reflection of who he or she is. Feigning interest, exaggerating ability, or hiding behind pretense is not only unethical, it's likely to be discovered—and when it is, your child's chances of being admitted will plummet. Your child should never misrepresent him or herself.

Disrespect & Bias

Top colleges value strong convictions and passion, but they don't tolerate disrespect, bias, intolerance, and bigotry. If writing about a firmly held belief, your child should take care to avoid coming across as inflexible and closed-minded—college is about learning from others, sharing insights, and broadening perspectives. Open-mindedness is a virtue.

Deeply ingrained biases have a way of working their way out in writing—even if unconsciously. Your child should carefully check his or her essay for racism, sexism, politically charged language, use of stereotypes, disrespectful statements, profanity, and vulgarity.

If your child's essay relates to community service, missions work, people from underserved or underprivileged backgrounds, or people from other cultures, he or she should be especially careful to write in a thoughtful and compassionate way.

Sexual Content

Your child should not write about his or her own or anyone else's love life or sexual encounters. But that doesn't mean all sexual content is inherently inappropriate. For example, an essay related to your child's work with a local service organization that helps victims of human trafficking or sexual abuse may be totally appropriate.

Drug & Alcohol Use

Your child should not reference any personal drug or alcohol experimentation, use, or abuse in his or her essay. Again, this does not mean your child cannot write an essay related to drugs or alcohol. If your child's background and narrative warrant writing such an essay, he or she might consider doing so.

Illegal Activity

Your child should not write an essay about any illegal activity in which he or she has been engaged. Writing about pranks or ethically questionable actions is also a poor choice. Depending on your child's narrative, however, an essay related to illegal activity may be totally appropriate. For example, if your child is applying to University of Pennsylvania specifically to pursue criminology, a compelling essay might focus on the experience that originally piqued your child's interest in criminology.

Supplemental Essays

Even if the colleges to which your child plans to apply use the common application, they may require supplemental essays. Prompts, word count limits, and other requirements of these essays vary from application to application, and so your child should carefully review what each college requires early in the application process.

Like the common application's personal essay, any supplemental essays should be taken as opportunities for your child to demonstrate value to the college and build his or her unique narrative.

Carefully Revise & Proofread

Once your child has a first draft of his or her essay, he or she should get some feedback. Early in the drafting process, your child should be less concerned about editing and refining the specific language of the essay and more concerned about whether his or her personality shines through in the content. Feedback early on will help your child determine whether the content and direction of his or her essay justifies committing the necessary time and energy to polishing the rough draft.

Transforming the initial essay into something compelling will require your child to go through several drafts. Along the way, your child will likely need to add content, remove content, replace generic descriptions with unique details, refine, cut, and condense. After making all of these content changes, your child will also need to carefully proofread the essay to ensure it is the best possible quality of writing he or she can deliver.

The key to your child revising and proofreading his or her personal essay is a focus on fixing real errors while leaving your child's tone, voice, and style intact. This does not mean, for example, that your child shouldn't replace less mature words with better diction. But too much editing—especially by adults who think the writing level should be more sophisticated and collegiate—can strip your child's essay of what makes it his or her own. Admissions officers don't expect applicants to write at the level of a college graduate. But they do expect clean, effective writing that offers a genuine glimpse into an applicant's personality.

Chapter 9:
Letters of Recommendation

At highly selective schools, letters of recommendation tend to play an important part in the admissions process. Admissions officers at top colleges use recommendation letters to get a better understanding of an applicant—his or her character, personality, intellect, determination, and other qualities.

In this way, recommendation letters allow college admissions officers to get a sense of the applicant beyond grades and scores and gauge what the applicant might be like as a person. Recommendations speak to how your child would contribute to the campus and the learning environment of the college. Even with a great transcript and excellent scores, your child might not gain admission based on poor teacher recommendations. If an applicant's teacher recommendations don't demonstrate how the student stands out from his or her peers, it might hurt the applicant's chance of gaining admission.

Typically, top colleges require letters of recommendation from the applicant's guidance counselor and two high school teachers. Some colleges require, request, or accept additional recommendations, and so your child will need to determine what he or she needs for each college on his or her list.

The key to a strong recommendation is standing out to the person who writes it. In other words, if your child doesn't stand out to a teacher, the recommendation will reflect that. If, on the other hand, a teacher considers your child one of the top students he or she has ever had, a recommendation from this teacher will likely help your child's chances of being admitted.

So, while there are some strategic choices to make regarding letters of recommendation, their effectiveness is largely rooted in what kind of student your child has shown him or herself to be. And that's why these recommendation letters are so valuable to selective colleges—they tend to highlight your child's character as a student in a tangible way beyond just grades and scores. Admissions officers read these letters carefully.

In this chapter, we'll walk through why the teacher and counselor recommendations are important and how they can affect your child's admissions profile. From that foundation, we'll build some specific strategies for getting the best letters of recommendation possible.

Teacher Recommendations

Admissions officers want teacher recommendations that give them an idea of an applicant's academic potential. Teacher recommendations are intended to provide a glimpse into an applicant's classroom participation, interest, ability, and achievement relative to what the teacher has seen over the course of his or her career.

Evaluation of Student Characteristics

When filling out the common application, your child will designate who his or her recommenders are and will include their contact information. Teachers will be sent an evaluation form to complete in addition to instructions for writing and submitting a letter of recommendation.

The teacher evaluation form is used to collect some background information regarding the teacher's knowledge of the student—how long the teacher has known the student and in what context, the courses in which the teacher has taught the student, etc. Additionally, the teacher evaluation asks teachers to rate the applicant using a list of characteristics, including elements related to intellectual promise, academic achievement, initiative, maturity, reaction to setbacks, integrity, leadership, concern for others, etc. These characteristics are rated from "below average" to "one of the top few I've encountered (top 1%)."

Using the evaluation and letter of recommendation, admissions officers are able to get a much clearer picture of the kind of student an applicant has been throughout high school and, in turn, what kind of student the applicant would likely be in college. The evaluation and letter helps demonstrate whether an applicant stands out, and if so, in what ways.

Insight into Classroom Engagement

Teacher recommendations tend to give admissions officers a behind-the-scenes look at a student's transcript. The transcript is certainly helpful, but it doesn't communicate whether a student has contributed in meaningful ways to classroom discussions, is intellectually curious, and is passionate or if he or she tends to simply do the minimum work necessary to get a good grade. Admissions officers also want to know whether an applicant actually challenges him or herself. Additionally, teacher evaluations and recommendations provide insight into an applicant's disposition, personality, and leadership ability.

Confirmation of Performance & Potential

One of the reasons teacher recommendations are so useful to admissions officers is that they have the ability to highlight students whose grades and tests may be great but whose attitude toward learning is not. For example, if a teacher's letter of recommendation indicates the applicant simply does not participate in class and seems to have little interest, good grades might actually be viewed negatively since the applicant didn't really apply him or herself. In this way, teacher recommendations provide a context for grades and test scores.

In combination with the other elements of your child's application, especially grades and test scores, admissions officers will use teacher recommendations to gauge your child's academic potential. Teacher recommendations can help confirm an applicant's academic record and point to potential success in key subject areas (i.e., those that align with the applicant's declared major or admissions theme).

Counselor Recommendations

In addition to two teacher recommendations, most top-tier colleges require a school report and letter of recommendation from an applicant's guidance counselor. While the teacher recommendations offer a deeper look at a student, counselor recommendations offer a broader picture.

Broader Context for Courses & Grades

The counselor report and recommendation offer admissions officers insight into an applicant's high school context, which helps admissions officers assess how demanding a particular course load is in light of school grading policies, expectations, limits, etc. The counselor recommendation will also shed light on how engaged a student is in the high school community and what role he or she has played on campus.

In particular, the information provided by an applicant's counselor helps admissions officers understand the applicant's transcript in context. Every high school offers a different number of honors, AP, and IB classes, and the normal course load also varies by the school. Thus, it is possible for your child to take challenging courses without really challenging him or herself—and it is also possible for your child to take what might look like a challenging course load that, given his or her high school context, may be the norm. These details tend to come out in the counselor recommendation and school report, which is why it is so important for your child to truly challenge him or herself.

Insight into Interests

In addition to providing some academic context, the counselor recommendation can serve to showcase what makes your child stand out at his or her high school. For example, your child's guidance counselor might detail some of your child's extracurricular activities, both on and off campus, which may offer some useful background information as the admissions officer works through your child's lists of activities and honors.

Your child does not typically get a choice regarding who will submit his or her school report and counselor recommendation letter. That's why it is important for your child to take time to interact with his or her counselor—the better your child's guidance counselor knows your child, the more detailed and personal the recommendation letter can be.

Additional Recommendations

Some colleges accept or require additional recommendations. Your child should carefully review the policies of each college on his or her list before pursuing additional recommendations. Some colleges consider such letters of recommendation helpful; others do not.

For those colleges that do find additional recommendations helpful, your child should select one person who knows your child well and can provide a unique perspective not already present in your child's application. Additional recommendations are often written by mentors, athletic coaches, private instructors, or clergy.

Dartmouth requires a peer recommendation, which is intended to provide another perspective on your child's personality, interests, and character qualities. Although peer recommendations aren't weighed heavily, your child should carefully determine who to ask. Peer recommendations typically serve to confirm your child's narrative.

The key for any additional recommendation is selecting a recommender who is likely to provide a depth of insight that contributes meaningfully to your child's narrative.

High School & College Guidelines

Your child's high school may have specific policies and procedures in place for requesting teacher recommendations. A policy could, for instance, indicate the earliest and latest dates a student may request a recommendation. Or a policy might dictate how many teachers a given student is allowed to ask for letters of recommendation. Your child will need to research what his or her high school's policies regarding recommendations are and abide by them.

Each college may also have its own set of policies governing teacher and counselor recommendations. Your child will need to research each college to which he or she intends to apply to determine the school's particular requirements, including the number and type of recommendations needed as well as submission deadlines.

Even if the common application indicates what a particular college requires, your child should check with each school to be certain of all requirements.

Family Educational Rights and Privacy Act (FERPA)

As its name suggests, FERPA is a federal law intended to protect students privacy. The law also grants students the right to access education records upon enrolling at a college.

During the application process, your child should consider waiving his or her FERPA rights to access counselor and teacher recommendations. By waiving his or her right to access these recommendations, your child signals to recommenders that they are free to honestly express themselves in their letters. Refusing to waive access to recommendations might create suspicion that your child's recommenders censored themselves to avoid any potential retaliation.

Strategies for Getting Great Recommendations

While you and your child have little control over his or her teacher evaluations, school report, and letters of recommendation, he or she does have control over which teachers to ask, when to ask them, and how.

And strong recommendation letters don't just happen. They are typically the result of a student's behavior, performance, and the overall impact he or she makes throughout high school. These are all factors over which your child has direct control.

Develop Strong Relationships

One of the ways your child can improve his or her chances of getting strong letters of recommendation is to develop strong relationships with select teachers and his or her guidance counselor. Your child should strive to keep his or her day-to-day interactions with teachers positive and productive. This does not mean engaging in flattery or putting on a front, but it does mean your child should show respect, appreciation, hard work, and dedication. Your child should participate in classroom discussions and help maintain a positive educational atmosphere—not clowning around, talking out of turn, messaging, or tuning out instruction.

Another way for your child to develop a stronger relationship with a particular teacher is to ask him or her to be the faculty sponsor or advisor for an on-campus student organization your child leads. If the teacher agrees, this creates additional opportunities for the teacher to really get to know your child—what your child is interested in and his or her accomplishments—and to see your child in a leadership role.

Although your child won't likely see his or her guidance counselor often, each interaction is an opportunity to make an impression. Your child should be respectful, thoughtful, and genuine.

Select Teachers Based on Your Child's Classroom Performance

Your child may not be able to select his or her counselor, but your child can select which teachers to ask for recommendations. The key is selecting the right teachers, and one important criteria is your child's performance in the teacher's classes. While certainly not the only consideration, your child should try to select teachers with whom your child excelled. The better your child's performance under a particular teacher, the higher the potential for a strong recommendation from that teacher.

But strong performance in easier classes won't likely impress admissions officers. So, your child should consider asking for recommendations from the teachers who taught his or her most challenging courses—granted your child did reasonably well in these classes. Teachers who have seen your child work hard and gain mastery of complex subject matter will be better equipped to write strong letters of recommendation and provide the kind of insights admissions officers are after.

Select Teachers Based on Familiarity

Another criteria your child should consider when choosing which teachers to ask for recommendations is how familiar that teacher is with your child and whether the teacher seems to like your child. Not only are teachers who have positive, friendly relationships with your child more likely to write recommendations, but these recommendations are more likely to be positive and compelling.

Your child should also keep in mind when he or she last had the teacher and how many of this teacher's classes your child has been in. For example, if a teacher has not taught your child prior to twelfth grade, that teacher's level of familiarity with your child is likely insufficient for a compelling recommendation. Similarly, if the teacher has not taught your child since ninth grade, that teacher's knowledge of your child is likely a poor reflection of your child's current level of maturity and academic achievement.

To put it simply, your child should ask for recommendations from teachers who can highlight his or her current level of ability, achievement, and maturity—who know your child's current interests and passions and who can speak to the kind of student your child is at his or her best.

Select Teachers Based on Your Child's Theme & Narrative

Your child should also think about his or her application theme and personal narrative when deciding which teachers to ask for recommendations. Letters of recommendation from teachers who teach the subject your child is most interested in can validate your child's academic strength in the subject and will be able to offer specific insight into the kind of value your child would add to that particular program at a college.

Ask for Recommendations at the Right Time

Asking for recommendations early is important, especially if your child is planning to apply early decision. Spring of junior year is generally a good time to ask for recommendations as long as this is permitted by your child's high school policy. Your child should ask teachers for letters of recommendation no later than September of senior year.

Not only is it considerate for your child to ask teachers for recommendations early in the process, doing so also gives your child time to ask other teachers for recommendations if one or both of your child's first choices fall through. Also, when asked early, teachers have time to reflect on their experiences with your child and may even be able to assess your child in the classroom, which might result in more detailed and personal letters of recommendation.

The teachers your child asks for letters of recommendation will likely have other students request recommendations as well. By asking early, your child not only has a higher likelihood of getting recommendations from the teachers he or she most prefers, but your child will also be more likely to receive higher quality recommendations since the teachers will have more time to write them.

Ask for Recommendations in the Right Way

Your child's teachers are not compensated for writing letters of recommendation. Doing so is not a requirement—and all of your child's teachers already have plenty of work to do. Teachers that willingly agree to write recommendations for your child are doing so as a favor—out of kindness and a generous spirit. Your child would do well to remember that when he or she asks for letters of recommendation.

Because of how important strong recommendations are for your child's admissions profile, he or she should ask teachers for recommendations in person. Your child should ask politely, careful to avoid manipulation or making the teacher feel guilty if he or she says no. If the teacher agrees to write the recommendation, your child should thank the teacher. If the teacher says no, your child should say something like, "I understand," and leave it at that—thanking the teacher for considering the request if appropriate.

If the teacher seems hesitant, your child might suggest asking another teacher instead—not in a condescending way, but to remove any pressure the teacher feels and give him or her an easy out. It's better for your child to get a recommendation from a teacher who is enthusiastic about writing one for him or her.

How Many Teachers Should Your Child Ask?

Even if your child's high school policy allows him or her to ask for extra teacher recommendations, your child should request no more recommendations than he or she needs. Requesting unnecessary recommendations places an additional burden on the staff and is inconsiderate of their time and effort.

Your child should carefully consider any specific college requirements to help ensure he or she can use each of the teacher recommendations for every school and to avoid needing to ask for extra recommendations.

Provide the Necessary Materials

Before even asking teachers for recommendations, your child should research whether his or her high school has information forms that he or she needs to complete and give to a teacher once the teacher agrees to write a letter of recommendation. Such a form might ask your child to list his or her interests, extracurricular activities, college plans, etc.

If your child's high school does not provide any such forms, he or she should create a brief document that includes the following basic information:

- The school or schools your child will be applying to, indicating which one is early decision (if applicable), all associated deadlines, and whether any of the schools do not require a recommendation

- The major your child plans to pursue and why that program interests him or her
- Your child's interests, passions, and extracurricular activities—including all relevant accomplishments
- Any additional information that would bolster your child's admissions profile or provide important context

Your child should also ask his or her counselor and each teacher what other information he or she would like. For instance, the counselor or teacher might want one or more of your child's best papers, his or her transcript, a copy of his or her personal essay, etc. The goal is to provide each recommender with whatever he or she needs to more easily and effectively write a strong letter of recommendation.

The more material the counselor or teacher has at his or her disposal, the easier it will be for him or her to write a compelling letter of recommendation. With basic information from your child, the recommender will be more likely to create a letter of recommendation that fits your child's theme and narrative because the background information helps provide direction. If your child provides the counselor or teacher with the list of activities that will be included in his or her application, the counselor or teacher will be more likely to draw upon those activities when writing the letter.

For example, if your child is planning to major in biology and asks his or her AP Biology teacher for a letter of recommendation, that teacher is already likely to add meaningful information to your child's narrative by virtue of the subject he or she teaches. But if your child includes information that reminds the teacher of past accomplishments related to science in general and biology in particular—such as a national competition your child placed at—this might guide the teacher to write a paragraph about that experience from his or her own perspective.

If any of the colleges to which your child is applying do not accept online letters of recommendation, your child should also provide each recommender with addressed envelopes, postage included, using the high school's return address.

For each teacher, your child should include a note explaining in a sentence or two why your child selected the teacher and thanking him or her for being willing to give up time to write the recommendation. Your child should also mention the other teacher who will be providing a recommendation.

Because of the broader role your child's counselor plays in the admissions process, your child may need to provide additional information to his or her counselor. Specifically, if your child has experienced extenuating circumstances that adversely affected his or her academic record in some way, or if he or she has a record of misconduct, your child needs to proactively discuss these circumstances with his or her counselor to ensure the counselor fully understands these situations.

Follow Up with Each Recommender

Your child should keep his or her counselor and the teachers writing letters of recommendation informed of any changes to his or her plans— including changes to his or her college list, the major he or she intends to pursue, etc.—and any significant accomplishments or achievements.

About one week prior to recommendation due dates, your child should politely check with each teacher and his or her counselor to ensure the recommendations have been submitted. This is particularly important for early decision recommendations since they are due much sooner and recommenders may be more prone to forget this early deadline.

Two to three weeks after applications are due, your child should consider asking each college whether or not it has received all the necessary letters of recommendation. If a college has not, your child should graciously double check with the recommender to ensure that the letter has indeed been sent. If the letter has been submitted, your child should just check periodically to ensure it's received.

Upon receiving acceptance letters, your child should follow up one last time to let the teachers and his or her counselor know which college he or she will be attending. Once again, your child should express appreciation for the time and energy they spent writing his or her recommendations.

Chapter 10:
Admissions Interview

The college admissions interview will not, in most cases, significantly change an applicant's admissions chances. Instead, the interview serves as an opportunity for an applicant to confirm what the admissions officers see in his or her application. A strong interview will not necessarily result in admission, nor will a weak interview necessarily result in denial. The interview is a single indicator among many, and it is considered in the context of an applicant's entire admissions profile.

The interview is optional, and because not all applicants are able to do interviews, it is not as significant as other components. That doesn't mean the interview is pointless—even if only marginally beneficial, every advantage, no matter how small, is valuable.

In this chapter, we'll discuss why the interview may be worthwhile for your child, some basics about the interview, and strategies for success.

Why Admissions Interviews Matter

If your child chooses to do an alumni or on-campus interview, he or she should not stress over it. Rather than viewing the interview as a vital component of the admissions process, your child should approach it as one more way to showcase accomplishments and demonstrate value— one more opportunity to stand out.

So, when the interviewer asks your child to talk about him or herself, your child has an opportunity to begin talking about the most significant aspect of his or her narrative—what makes your child most unique and compelling as a candidate.

Your child could also use an interview to demonstrate accomplishments physically or visibly—a product your child developed, a book he or she wrote, a website your child designed, an informational video about your child's community project or nonprofit organization, etc. Your child's goal is to make an impact and demonstrate how he or she stands out, and visuals can be great tools when used to generate meaningful, substantive conversation about who your child is, what he or she has done, and why.

One of the reasons the admissions interview is helpful to admissions officers—and a reason your child should consider scheduling an interview—is that it provides a unique perspective on your child. Unlike teacher and counselor recommendations, the admissions interview is conducted by someone who does not know your child. The interviewer has a fresh, unbiased perspective. The only image the interviewer will have of your child is the one your child presents during the interview itself.

The fresh perspective of the interviewer is largely what gives the interview its value. Many of the things your child will talk about in the interview will be present in his or her application. It's about making a good impression—and if your child can do that, it may nudge his or her application in the right direction, even if only slightly.

How much the interview affects the decision will largely depend on how strong your child's application is to begin with. Really strong admissions profiles will be largely unaffected by interviews, even if they go badly. Likewise, especially weak applications will not likely be salvaged even by an exceptional interview.

The applicants most affected by interviews are those with middle-of-the-road profiles. If your child's application is scored somewhere in the middle of the rating scale by an admissions officers, a strong interview might be incredibly helpful in gaining your child admission—and a really poor interview might sink a mid-range application.

Even if your child's interview does nothing to impact his or her admissions profile, the admissions interview is a great way to demonstrate interest in a school—which is important for your child to do if applying to a school that considers level of interest in admissions decisions (see the section "Prior Contact & Demonstrated Interest" in Chapter 6).

But the interview isn't just about moving your child's application closer to the acceptance pile—it is just as much an opportunity for your child to ask questions and get a better sense of what a particular college is like and whether he or she would fit in there.

Who Conducts Admissions Interviews?

If an applicant chooses to do an interview, typically, the options are to do an alumni interview, an on-campus interview (if available), or both.

Interviews by Alumni

Alumni interviews represent the most common type of admissions interview. For an alumni interview, the interviewer is an alumnus or alumna with limited training, and so the quality and effectiveness of these interviews varies greatly.

The value of alumni interviews from the college's perspective is keeping alumni engaged with their alma mater—there is a definite financial motivation. These interviews also serve as opportunities for the applicant to ask questions of the alumnus or alumna and get a better sense of what a college is like from the perspective of someone who attended. Granted, the interviewer may have graduated recently or decades ago, and so his or her experience may be more or less relevant.

In terms of admissions value, some alumni will be able to articulate why an applicant should be admitted while others won't. Even if the alumni interview report is compelling, it will likely be used only in the rare event that all other application components are equal.

Interviews by Admissions Officers

For the top colleges that offer on-campus interviews, spaces are limited, and not all applicants will be able to get on the schedule. Early planning is particularly important, so your child should research each college on his or her list to determine the college's specific policies. For example, some colleges will only conduct on-campus interviews with high school seniors.

If your child is able to secure an on-campus interview, he or she will likely be interviewed by a member of the admissions staff. Although many colleges indicate that in-person interviews with admissions staff have no effect on an applicant's chances of being admitted, such interviews can help your child make a real connection with the interviewer.

By making personal contact with the admissions officer, your child has an opportunity to become more than just a name, some numbers, and an essay. Your child can establish a human connection with the admissions officer and affirm what makes him or her a unique applicant. While the other components of your child's application are certainly much more important, a good interview might help cast these other elements in a more positive light. If the admissions officer was impressed by your child's interview, he or she may evaluate your child's application with a more positive disposition.

What Your Child's Interview Should Communicate

Generally speaking, how your child presents him or herself does matter. But admissions interviews are about substance, not social polish. The substance of your child's interview must be focused on his or her academics and the value he or she would add to a top college campus.

Academic Interests

Because your child's academic record is so important to an admissions decision at a selective college, one of the most important things your child ought to communicate during an admissions interview is his or her academic achievement, intellectual curiosity, and ability to handle the rigors of an education at a top-tier school.

Your child also needs to effectively communicate his or her passion for learning, especially as it relates to his or her core academic interests. Your child should speak in concrete terms using specific examples of which subjects, classes, books, etc., he or she enjoys most and why.

Preparation is important, and your child should plan which interests to talk about and how to transition from one interest to the next.

Value & Contribution

While academic topics should take up a significant portion of your child's interview, that isn't all your child's interview should communicate. At some point, the interview should segue into how your child will contribute and add value to the college.

Predominantly, your child's discussion of his or her value to the college should be driven by the previous discussion about his or her academic interests. For example, during an on-campus interview at Yale, your child could transition from talking about his or her love for advanced math and computer science to how excited he or she is to get involved with the Yale Computer Society. Your child could also talk about the

103

computer science courses he or she is most interested in taking and how previous programming and development projects have generated interest in specific areas, such as artificial intelligence and machine learning algorithms.

The key is that your child discusses the specific ways in which he or she plans to get plugged in to the college's academic programs and student organizations. This level of detail and planning requires research, but it helps demonstrate genuine interest, passion, and excitement.

While your child should focus largely on his or her academic interests, skills, and unique experiences, some of the interview should be spent discussing extracurricular activities, leadership opportunities, and accomplishments.

Whether being interviewed by an admissions officer or an alumni volunteer, your child should artfully highlight his or her strengths and accomplishments in such a way that the interviewer wants to advocate for your child's admission to the college. Your child should be careful not to brag, but the interview is his or her opportunity to showcase his or her intellectual depth, love of learning, and overall potential value to the college.

Common Interview Questions

While your child can, to some extent, control the direction of an interview, he or she cannot control the questions the interviewer will ask. Questions will vary from one interviewer to the next, and so there is limited value in listing potential questions and memorizing answers. Rather than preparing for specific questions, then, your child should consider the themes and topics that will likely be addressed during an interview and prepare to discuss them with specific details and examples.

That may seem much more challenging than simply memorizing answers to specific questions—but if your child focuses on what he or she is actually interested in and is well rehearsed in those areas, responses to questions should come somewhat naturally. The key is being genuine and thoughtful.

Why should your child prepare, then? To avoid being caught off guard and to polish his or her delivery. The goal is to make a great impression, and if your child is asked a question he or she didn't anticipate, the response might be stilted, vague, or rambling. And one unanticipated question has the potential to throw your child off, raise his or her level of anxiety, and may even adversely affect the remainder of the interview.

Preparing for questions, then, is important. Following are several of the themes and topics likely to be addressed in an admissions interview:

Family

The interviewer may ask about family. This is an opportunity for your child to highlight any interesting and unique background that helps flesh out his or her narrative. For example, your child might talk about how a family tragedy inspired him or her to start a nonprofit, how growing up in a blended family offered multiple cultural perspectives, or how a meaningful experience with an older sibling led to a passion for a particular activity. Your child should focus on details and narrative—not just talking about the *what*, but dwelling on the *why*.

Intellectual Curiosity

Much of the interview will be spent answering questions about your child's academic interests—both in and out of the classroom. The interviewer will likely ask about the kinds of academic subjects your child is interested in, and your child should do more than simply list the subjects. He or she should talk about what he or she finds particularly exciting about a subject, what piqued his or her interest in it, and what your child hopes to learn and accomplish in the future.

The interviewer may also ask about the kinds of literature your child likes, who his or her favorite author is, and the books he or she has read the past year. Again, your child should offer more than lists, providing specific insights into why he or she likes a genre so much and how an author or work has influenced your child's thinking.

High School

Since admissions interviews tend to focus heavily on intellectual curiosity and academics, your child will almost certainly be asked about his or her high school experience. The interviewer may ask questions about your child's high school itself—its size, strengths, weaknesses, etc. These aren't really important questions, so your child shouldn't dwell on them.

The more substantive questions will relate to the courses your child took—which ones he or she found most interesting, which he or she enjoyed least, which ones were most challenging, etc. Your child should feel free to elaborate here, drawing on specific experiences to illustrate his or her reasoning.

Your child may also be asked questions that require some reflection about his or her experiences in high school. For example, your child might be asked to share his or her biggest regret, disappointment, or failure; or the interviewer might ask your child what he or she would change about the school. Your child is also likely to be asked to talk about his or her favorite teacher—or the one who has had the greatest impact on your child's life.

College

An admissions interviewer is also likely to ask your child questions about his or her college plans—why he or she is interested in the college, what your child plans to study, and why the college should accept his or her application. These questions require careful research and a fresh memory; the last thing your child wants to do is speak at length about the major he or she is excited to pursue only to be informed the college doesn't actually have that major.

When asked about the college, your child should strive to frame his or her response in terms of the value he or she will bring to the college, pointing to past achievements as reasons for future plans, describing how specific experiences prompted his or her interest in the school, etc.

How to Respond if an Interviewer Asks About Other Schools

The admissions interviewer should not ask your child which other schools he or she has applied to or which school is his or her top choice. If, however, the question comes up, your child should respond carefully—especially if the school is not your child's first choice.

The key is making the admissions interviewer believe your child wants to attend his or her college more than others. The stronger that belief, the better.

To communicate this effectively, your child should indicate that the college is one of his or her top choices and might mention a couple of other schools from his or her list—though your child should select only those colleges from his or her list that are less selective or equivalent—but not more selective. If your child were to indicate he or she is considering a more selective college, the interviewer would likely assume your child would prefer to attend the more selective college, which introduces the risk that your child might not enroll if admitted. For the same reason, your child should not indicate whether he or she applied early decision or early action to another school.

Extracurricular Activities & Interests

The interviewer may ask questions about your child's extracurricular activities, hobbies, interests, talents, employment experience, summer activities, and the ways he or she spends free time.

While your child should generally avoid talking too much about his or her basic extracurricular activities and interests—apart from those that fit into an academic category or can be used to showcase intellectual curiosity—your child should take time to discuss any activity that represents his or her primary focus. For example, if your child is passionate about a particular issue and started a nonprofit, he or she should spend time talking about the importance of the organization, what it is accomplishing, why it was started, etc.

Current Events

Some interviewers ask about current events—especially if your child indicates an interest in politics, government, journalism, or philosophy. If your child has no interest in current events, he or she should actively avoid leading the interview in that direction. If the subject comes up anyway, your child should be prepared to answer based on his or her primary area of interest. For example, if your child is into computers more than politics, a current story about advancements in technology might be an appropriate direction to take.

The interviewer may ask your child what he or she perceives to be the biggest problem facing the U.S. or world today. Again, while some applicants thrive on these types of questions, if yours does not, he or she should prepare for such a question in a way that ties in to his or her narrative.

Alternatively, your child could acknowledge that the nation or world faces many problems but pivot to an issue closer to home as a case in point of one of the problems facing the nation or world. For example, if your child has helped serve local veterans struggling to transition to civilian life, he or she could use personal experience to outline a national problem and offer some solutions. This keeps the discussion personal and relevant to your child—and allows your child to talk from his or her knowledge and experience.

Personality & Character

The admissions interview might include questions that focus less on what your child has done and more about who your child is—his or her character qualities and how he or she thinks. The interviewer may ask your child to describe strengths or weaknesses, to talk about times your child showed leadership, or to share his or her dreams and aspirations.

Other common prompts might ask your child to describe how he or she would use a completely free day or who your child would have a conversation with if he or she could pick anyone, living or dead.

Questions like these may be difficult to prepare for, so your child should just be genuine—and it's okay to pause for a few moments to think before responding.

Accomplishments

If your child is asked about his or her accomplishments, he or she should try to avoid sounding braggadocious but should certainly elaborate on his or her major accomplishments. Your child should be specific, indicating how selective or prestigious a program or award was. After explaining the accomplishment itself—the *what*—your child should focus on the *why*. He or she should describe the underlying motivation that led him or her to pursue a particular accomplishment.

What to Say & Do

The admissions interview is about making a positive impression, and so your child should be careful to conduct him or herself in an engaging, professional way. Following are several things your child should say and do throughout an admissions interview.

Be Engaged

From beginning to end, your child needs to be engaged in the admissions interview. This means making eye contact, politely greeting the interviewer with a firm handshake, listening carefully, and avoiding distraction. Also, your child should consider bringing his or her résumé (with a copy for the interviewer) and possibly some notes to help keep him or her focused. If your child's interviewer doesn't want to use the résumé, that's fine, but many interviewers use the résumé as a guide.

Be Professional

Your child needs to present him or herself to the interviewer as a mature, professional applicant. This means being polite, showing respect, speaking clearly, and giving the interviewer undivided attention—your child must not be distracted by anything, including other people in the room or out the window, art on the wall, his or her résumé, and certainly not his or her phone. Your child should avoid interrupting the interviewer and should not appear in a hurry to end the interview.

Be Independent

Your child should go to the interview alone—no parents. If you are dropping your child off, drop him or her off and return when he or she lets you know the interview is finished.

Dress Appropriately

How your child dresses for his or her admissions interview is important. While some colleges may have a specified dress code for interviews, others may not. If no dress code is given, your child should dress business casual. For interviews that take place in public places like coffee shops or libraries, the interviewer might indicate the interview is casual and your child should wear jeans. If this is the case, your child should choose nice jeans—no rips or heavy distressing. Casual does not mean anything goes, and so your child should wear nice, clean, wrinkle-free clothes that communicate maturity and professionalism, even if his or her clothing is casual.

Business Casual

For male applicants, business casual attire generally consists of the following clothing types:
- Khakis or slacks
- Button-down shirt and jacket (optional)
- Sweater
- Dark socks
- Dress shoes
- Tie (optional)

For female applicants, the following articles of clothing and accessories constitute basic business casual attire:

- Khaki, corduroy, or patterned slacks
- Skirts (knee-length or below)
- Nice cotton top (covers back, chest, cleavage, midriff)
- Sweater or cardigan
- Tights (optional)
- Boots, pumps, or sandals (no flip flops)
- Jewelry, scarves, etc. (less is more)

Think Before Speaking

When your child is asked a question, he or she should pause to think before responding. Your child ought to be developing his or her narrative through the interview, and so he or she should listen to the questions and answer in a way that naturally pulls in his or her story. Instead of saying whatever comes to mind first, your child should filter his or her thoughts and say what is most relevant. This doesn't mean being disingenuous, but it does mean selectively sharing information.

For example, if your child is asked what his or her favorite class junior year, and his or her favorite was an art class—but art has nothing to do with your child's admissions profile—it would probably be best for your child to say something like, "One of my favorite classes was," and then speak about a more relevant course than art. Alternatively, your child could say that art was his or her favorite class even though he or she is an amateur because it provided a creative outlet, but might then pivot to another favorite class more relevant to his or her narrative.

If your child simply blurted the first thing that came to mind, which in this case is the art class, without thinking through how to get from art to a more relevant course, he or she won't likely pivot and would lose an opportunity to further develop his or her narrative.

Explain the Why

One of the most important things for your child to do in an admissions interview is explain the *why* behind his or her *what*. All of the topics discussed in the interview—the courses, interests, activities, college plans—lose their significance if your child fails to tell his or her story. Just as he or she ought to do through the personal essay, your child must show how he or she is different from all the other students whose favorite course is AP United States History, and that is accomplished by explaining the *why*.

But your child should go beyond just the *why* of his or her past activities and accomplishments. He or she should also explain the *why* behind his or her interest in the interviewer's school—why the college is vital to his or future activities and accomplishments. Not only does this demonstrate the college's place in your child's narrative, it helps illustrate your child's potential value to the college.

Express Interest in the College

Even if the college for which your child is interviewing is not his or her first pick, your child should at some point indicate to the interviewer that if admitted, he or she is highly likely to attend. This might raise questions about whether your child is planning to apply early decision—or if past the application deadline, why your child did not apply early decision or early action. Your child should prepare to answer in an honest way—for example, saying that his or her application wasn't ready by the deadline—but must be careful not to suggest he or she applied early decision or early action elsewhere.

During the interview, your child must also be careful not to confuse the college for which he or she is interviewing with any other schools—this means your child needs to refresh his or her memory about which majors, courses, extracurricular activities, student organizations, etc., are available at the college. Your child wants to express interest in what the college actually offers—not what other selective colleges offer.

Demonstrate Substance

Your child should be well prepared and present him or herself in a polished manner—but not at the expense of actual substance. Admissions interviewers see through shallow applicants, regardless of their confidence, charisma, or communication skills. The reverse is also true—interviewers are typically able to see the substance of an applicant regardless of how soft spoken or reserved he or she might be.

What is important is that your child is natural and authentic—not putting on a front or trying to say what he or she thinks the interviewer wants to hear, but, instead, talking about his or her passions, accomplishments, and the *why* behind it all. Your child should focus on details and concrete examples, demonstrating depth and establishing a human connection with the interviewer.

Save Questions for the End

As much as possible, your child should save his or her questions for the end of the interview. Unlike job interviews, the admissions interview is an opportunity for your child to take a single-sentence question and provide a deep, expansive answer. Instead of breaking the flow of his or her narrative, your child should stay focused on demonstrating him or herself to be a compelling applicant.

When it comes time to ask questions, your child needs to have at least four or five—having none tends to be viewed poorly. But having just any question isn't a good plan either. Your child should do some preliminary research and prepare specific questions about the college that cannot be easily answered by checking the college's website.

For example, your child might want to ask about the faculty at the college—their strengths, availability, and personalities. Or your child could investigate what the social life is like on campus. Your child could ask about favorite courses, interesting campus events, unique opportunities—anything that won't readily be found online but that will give your child a taste of what the college has to offer.

For alumni interviewers, your child should ask about the interviewer's experience at the college. Doing so will help give your child an idea of what the college is like from the perspective of someone who attended, and may even lead to new ideas or plans. In addition to providing your child with insights, engaging the interviewer helps create a connection that can lead to a more detailed and positive interview report.

Section Three:

Academics & Tests

Chapter 11:
Academic Record

In this chapter, we'll examine what makes a winning academic record. We'll consider why the transcript is so important, what it needs to communicate to admissions officers, and strategies for developing a competitive transcript.

Why Is the Transcript Important?

Your child's transcript is an incredibly important part of his or her admissions profile. While a high school transcript is not, by itself, enough to get your child into a top college, it is enough, by itself, to keep your child from being admitted. Your child's course load and grades must meet the high minimum standard of a top college—otherwise, admissions will be incredibly unlikely.

The high school transcript shows an admissions officers what kind of academic performance an applicant has demonstrated over the course of his or her high school education. It shows whether the student has embraced a demanding course load and met that challenge, and in that way, it is an excellent predictor of a student's college readiness.

According to the National Center for Education Statistics,[8] about 3.5 million students were expected to graduate from high school in the 2016–2017 school year. Of those, approximately 68.4% were expected to enroll in college in the fall of the same year. This means about 2.4 million students are competing for admissions.

So, even if your child's transcript places him or her in the top 1% of all applicants, he or she is still in a pool of 24,000 candidates. This should demonstrate how important it is to have an exceptional transcript—the most selective colleges receive applications from so many phenomenal students, and if your child doesn't have a strong transcript, the chances of his or her being admitted to a top school diminishes significantly.

As a result, the first step toward gaining admission to a top-tier college is a strong high school transcript. That's why your child's transcript is important. Poor grades or anything less than a challenging course load, or both, can quickly sink an application.

The courses your child takes and the grades he or she earns are one of the ways your child will communicate to admissions officers he or she is ready for college. In addition to demonstrating college readiness, course selection plays an important role in building a compelling narrative.

So, now that you know why the transcript is so important, let's look at what the transcript needs to communicate to admissions officers.

What Does a Transcript Need to Communicate?

Admissions offices at top colleges receive tens of thousands of applications and can accept only a small fraction of them. As we've already discussed, the transcript is a useful tool for admissions officers to identify which applicants have competitive grades and those that do not.

Admissions officers at top colleges are trying to determine whether or not an applicant is ready for the challenging courses offered by the school. This assessment goes beyond simply determining whether the applicant took the necessary courses for the required number of years. Admissions officers want to know whether the applicant challenged him or herself. They are interested in applicants who took the most demanding course load offered at their school and excelled—those who show determination, hard work, and intellectual curiosity.
This means taking honors, AP, and IB courses and doing well in them. You and your child will need to carefully plan his or her courses from

freshman through senior year to develop a transcript that demonstrates a challenging course load and academic excellence.

In the following two sections, we'll discuss each of these in turn.

Challenging Course Load

Some students mistakenly believe that high test scores will be enough to get them into a top college. Admissions officers will recognize the intellectual ability of such students, but if an applicant's coursework does not reflect a willingness to work hard and be challenged, admissions officers won't be impressed.

If your child does not take a challenging course load, it doesn't really matter what test scores he or she achieves. And apart from a challenging course load, it doesn't really matter what grades your child earns.

Top colleges admit students who choose not to take the easy road and instead pursue the most challenging, rigorous courses they can handle. Good grades are important, but academic excellence begins with intellectual challenge.

Regional admissions officers generally know what classes are offered at the high schools in their purview, and so they have a good idea based on the transcript whether an applicant took the school's most demanding classes. Your child will not be a competitive applicant to a top college without successfully taking on challenging coursework.

Focused or Well Rounded?

Back in Chapter 3, I mentioned that in order to stand out, your child needs to be academically diverse. While this does not mean your child has to be outstanding in every academic subject, it does mean he or she has to be strong in every subject. Strategic focus is important in academics, and your child can be disproportionately strong in one area, but if his or her grades in other areas dip too low, his or her chances of admissions may decrease.

So, your child does need to be well rounded, but only as well rounded as necessary to remain eligible for admission to a top college. This means your child should take diverse courses and do well at them but should otherwise focus his or her energy on one area and be as exceptional as possible in that subject or activity.

Selecting Core Courses

Your child's high school will have specific requirements that generally include four years of English and three to four years of foreign language, math, science, and social studies.

The graduation requirements of your child's high school may not, however, match the expectations of selective colleges. For example, some top colleges prefer four years of English, two or more years of a single foreign language, and four years of math (including calculus depending on the applicant's intended major). The key is to take the most challenging courses available and, once your child has an idea of the schools to which he or she will apply, check the school's specific requirements and preferences.

Selecting Electives

Early in high school, electives are your child's opportunity to explore new academic subjects, fine arts, or some other discipline. As your child develops a particular focus and narrative, however, electives serve as opportunities for him or her to develop a deeper knowledge of a subject, hone a particular set of skills, or pursue his or her primary interests.

While electives can be fun and a great way to counterbalance more challenging coursework, your child should not throw away time on electives that add no value to his or her admissions profile. Electives should augment your child's academic record, add to his or her narrative, and create opportunities for distinction.

And before signing up for electives, your child should always make sure the electives don't interfere with any core requirements, advanced classes, or prerequisites for advanced classes.

Foreign Language Proficiency

While most top colleges require or strongly prefer a certain number of years of a single foreign language—and most high schools have similar requirements—your child should consider going beyond the minimum requirement. Selective colleges are looking for global leaders, and foreign language proficiency is highly valued. Since top-tier schools generally expect graduates to gain foreign language proficiency during the course of their college education, gaining proficiency in one or more foreign languages before applying can help your child demonstrate value to admissions officers.

Selecting Advanced Courses

Admissions officers at top colleges want to see advanced courses on your child's transcript because such courses better prepare students for college. Success in advanced courses signals to admissions officers that your child is ready to succeed at a top college.

Each high school has different opportunities for advanced coursework, and their policies regarding course enrollment vary as well. Check with your child's high school to determine what prerequisites exist, if teacher recommendations are required, etc. Think strategically and plan ahead.

Following are the most common types of advanced courses:

Honors – Generally, honors courses are the lowest tier of advanced courses, but admissions officers will consider honors courses in context. For example, sometimes a high school's honors course is more challenging than an equivalent AP course. Or, on the other hand, honors courses may be the most rigorous academics offered at a particular high school. In either case, regional admissions officers generally understand these school-specific dynamics and consider them while reviewing an applicant's academic record.

Advanced Placement (AP)[9] – AP classes are some of the most demanding classes offered and are a decent gauge of college preparedness. One advantage to AP classes is that they can result in college credit depending on end-of-year exam scores. Another advantage is that the AP scores provide colleges with another standardized indicator with which to evaluate and compare applicants. And while these courses are not as difficult as their equivalent courses at top colleges, they do offer challenging coursework and help develop many skills vital to college success such as time management, critical reading, critical listening, and critical thinking. As such, this program is incredibly valuable for students who wish to attend a top-tier college, not only because of the potential to earn college credit and the positive impact such classes have on admissions, but because of how these classes will help your child grow and mature.

Dual Enrollment – In some ways similar to the AP program, dual enrollment programs give qualified high school students the opportunity to enroll in specific classes at local community colleges, granting both high school and college credit. Dual enrollment classes are particularly useful if your child's high school lacks equivalent honors or AP courses, but they can also be a way for your child to take classes that aren't offered at his or her school.

Summer College Courses – In addition to dual enrollment programs, your child may be able to earn college credit and take more challenging courses in a subject area of interest during the summer. The common application has a place for listing any college courses your child has taken, and so this is an opportunity for your child to set him or herself apart from other applicants and demonstrate a higher degree of college readiness.

Online Opportunities – Online education offers an additional way for your child to pursue specific academic interests at a more advanced level and with greater focus. Numerous programs exist, and your child should do considerable research on a program before enrolling—checking to ensure the program is credible, whether it is associated with a major college or university, whether it offers college credit or some other certification, etc.

International Baccalaureate (IB)[10] – This two-year diploma program offers an international perspective and rigorous course of study. The program includes six subject groups and a core curriculum focused on theory of knowledge, creativity, activity, and service. The program also requires students to complete an extended research essay. Students do not have to be enrolled in the IB diploma program to take IB courses.

Every college has its own policy regarding AP, dual enrollment, and IB credit. Some accept college credit based on AP exam scores, for example, while others base college credit on AP grades. Some colleges don't award credit for advanced coursework in high school but do allow students to skip college prerequisite courses such as a first-semester English class. To find out how a specific college handles advanced courses, visit the college's website.

How Many AP & Advanced Courses?

The number of AP and other advanced courses a student should take depends on several factors. We've already discussed how your child should take the most challenging course load he or she can handle—and that's really the primary consideration.

But you and your child may want to consider other factors as well. College admissions officers will gauge your child's academic performance against the rigor of his or her course load, but the course load will also be gauged against the typical course load of top students at your child's high school. In other words, if your child takes several honors and two AP courses during junior year but the typical top students at his or her school takes four or five AP courses, your child will not appear to be as academically competitive.

The school report submitted by your child's guidance counselor will notify admissions officers of how many honors, AP, and IB courses are offered at your child's school. From this report, admissions officers will also know whether your child's school has any policies that limit the number of advanced courses a student may take each year. Your child's guidance counselor will also rank your child's course load on a scale from "below average" to "most demanding."
Obviously, you want your child to receive a "most demanding" rating for his or her course selection.

Instead of taking every AP course offered, your child should focus first on those that bring the most value—the courses that would be required to effectively develop your child's unique narrative. After that, your child should focus on advanced courses that fit his or her interests and strengths. If the "most demanding" course load means taking a total of eight AP classes, your child should strive to do so in the most strategic way possible.

Lack of Opportunity

Admissions officers consider a student's admissions profile in context. They are sensitive to applicants who have fewer available opportunities—they'll know, for example, if your child's high school offers only a three AP courses and provide few other opportunities for academic challenge. This doesn't mean that students with fewer opportunities at their high schools should be content with what opportunities they have—as much as admissions officers are sensitive to an applicant's background, they also want to see a desire to learn that results in finding other opportunities.

So, if your child's high school does not offer a challenging enough curriculum, this does not mean your child cannot be academically competitive. In such cases, being competitive will likely require your child to pursue opportunities like dual enrollment, evening courses at a local community college, challenging summer academic programs, independent research projects, etc.

Academic Excellence

Besides having a transcript filled with advanced courses, your child will need great grades to get into a top-tier school. The most selective schools admit from about 5% to 15% of applicants, and so they have their choice of top students. At such colleges, perfect high school grades are the norm.

Remember, however, that perfect grades won't get your child into a top college because they don't help your child stand out. But with anything less than excellent grades, your child will stand out for the wrong reasons.

Your child doesn't need perfect grades to get admitted to a top college—I was admitted to Yale with a 3.95 GPA—but without straight As, your child will have to stand out even more in some other significant way.

Grades are important to admissions officers because when combined with a challenging course of study, academic excellence demonstrates a higher degree of college preparedness and a higher likelihood of success. In Chapter 5, we talked about how admissions officers at top colleges are unlikely to take risks on applicants. The lower an applicant's academic performance, the higher the risk. Admissions officers at top schools look for students whose transcripts show strong grades from freshman through senior year despite increasingly demanding courses.

Lower grades early on may not have much of an adverse effect on your child's chances of being admitted to a top school as long as the grades have an upward trend throughout your child's high school education. If your child's grades have a downward trend, this will be a major red flag to an admissions officer at a competitive school. Declining grades suggest an inability to keep up with the increasing demands of advanced courses.

Again, for admissions officers, the primary concerns are whether your child has taken on a challenging load and demonstrated academic excellence. A single B may not be an issue, but a trend of Bs would be.

What If Your Child Gets Some Poor Grades?

If your child gets one or more anomalous low grades, he or she should address the situation proactively. One of the most important steps is to ensure that his or her counselor understands the extenuating circumstances that led to the poor grades. If your counselor understands, he or she may include an explanation in your child's recommendation.

In addition to talking about the situation with his or her guidance counselor, your child should also inform the admissions office of each school to which he or she submits an application. If the application does not offer sufficient space or is not the best format for such an explanation, your child should consider sending a separate letter to address the lower grade(s).

In such circumstances, your child must not assign blame or make excuses. Instead, he or she should simply explain what happened, how it affected his or her grades, and what he or she learned from the whole situation. Your child has the opportunity to demonstrate perseverance and a positive outlook despite circumstances—qualities that are valued by top colleges.

Grading Policies

High schools around the country calculate and report grades in a variety of ways. At some high schools, the GPA is based on a 4-point scale that correlates to the letter grade assigned in class—and this is probably what most people think of when they think of high school grades.

But many high schools use variations of this system, and some use a different system altogether. As your child enters high school, you should take time to understand the school's grading policy. Knowing how a school grades will help you and your child develop proper expectations.

For example, if your child's high school uses a tough grading scale, a strong grade might be in the high 80s or low 90s. You and your child's expectations should match what is normal at your child's high school. Admissions officers are aware of schools with tougher grading scales, and so your child's transcript will be viewed in that light. The opposite is also true: if the grading scale is particularly easy, your child should, respectively, have stronger grades.

In addition to affecting you and your child's expectations, the grading policies of your child's high school might also affect your child's strategy.

For example, some schools report letter grades with pluses and minuses on transcripts while others don't. If your child's high school reports only the letter grade without pluses and minuses, an A- is as good as an A. In such cases, if the effort to get an A in one class would result in a B+ in another, it would be better to get an A- in both.

Your child should perform well within his or her high school's grading context, whatever it may be. Admissions officers are aware of how schools differ in their grading policies, and they take steps to mitigate these differences.

One way they do this is by recalculating applicants' GPAs based on their own standards. For example, they might not consider certain courses in calculating GPAs, or they might only include grades from sophomore through senior year. They'll also consider whether grades are weighted and might recalculate GPAs using students' actual grades.

Admissions officers may use other metrics, such as grade distribution, range, and median, to help create a clearer picture of how grades from one school stack up to those from another.

Challenging Courses versus Good Grades

One of the dilemmas your child will face as he or she tries to develop a challenging course load is not knowing whether the coursework will be too difficult to handle—both for each individual class and taken as a group. For example, an A in AP Calculus BC may be attainable, but if taken with other courses that also require a lot of focus, your child might not be able to get an A in every class.

The key to solving this dilemma is self-awareness, timing, and careful strategy.

You and your child need to focus on his or her strengths, and wherever possible, play to those strengths. Your child should not select advanced classes simply because they are available. Instead, he or she should select the advanced classes that fit his or her narrative and that he or she finds interesting—those in which your child can excel.

Also, do some research to learn which advanced courses are generally easier than others at your child's high school. You and your child could talk to his or her counselor about which advanced classes would fit best and make for a doable course load. Talk to other parents. Have your child talk to other students. Discover which advanced classes will be best suited to your child and easiest to earn As in. Place these easier courses strategically to counterbalance more challenging courses.

When your child must take a course that is likely to prove incredibly challenging, timing and strategy are vital. If your child knows he or she is not great at math, Calculus may be a struggle. If possible, your child should consider taking an honors Pre-Calculus class before taking AP

Calculus AB. Or if your child struggles with science, carefully planning when your child takes which course could be the difference between an A and a B.

Additionally, too many advanced courses at one time can result in poorer performance and may not even be necessary. As we've already discussed, the key is that you and your child need to have an idea of what he or she can handle and plan accordingly.

If your child needs help, the best thing for him or her to do is to get it. For example, your child may be able to meet with a teacher after school for extra guidance. Or, if more help than that is needed, a private tutor may be a good option. There is nothing wrong with getting additional support—part of being self-aware is knowing one's weaknesses. Better for your child to take the class, get whatever help is needed, and do well than to avoid the class or struggle through it and earn a poor grade.

Chapter 12:
Tests

Top colleges require applicants to take the ACT or SAT and, typically, at least two SAT Subject Tests. As we've already discussed, applicants' scores have a significant impact on the admissions process, but your child does not need perfect test scores to get into a top-tier college. Top colleges do, however, use test scores to help filter applicants—just as they do with grades. Grades and scores do not get applicants admitted, but they can keep applicants out. That's why test scores remain important.

In this chapter, we'll examine the ACT, SAT, and SAT Subject Tests and then walk through some strategies to help your child prepare for these entrance exams.

Entrance Exam Overview

The ACT and SAT are aptitude tests that are intended to assess the test taker's ability to analyze and problem solve. The organizations that design and administer these tests claim they offer many benefits—particularly that the tests measure high school learning to demonstrate whether the test taker is prepared for the academic rigors of college.

These tests have strict time limits and produce a range of scores that help differentiate students. Opinions vary concerning the effectiveness of such exams to accurately assess aptitude, but the reality is admissions officers at top colleges use standardized testing as they consider whether an applicant is a strong enough candidate for admission.

Some of the primary differences between the ACT and SAT are how the tests are structured, how many questions are asked, and how much time is provided for each exam.

The ACT has four sections: English, Math, Reading, and Science. The SAT is composed of two sections that include three tests: Reading, Writing, and Mathematics. Both tests offer an optional Writing or Essay section.

ACT		
Section	Questions	Time (min)
English	75	45
Math	60	60
Reading	40	35
Science	40	35
Writing	1 prompt	40

SAT		
Section	Questions	Time (min)
Reading	52	65
Writing	44	35
Math	58	80
Essay	1 essay	50

The total time allowed for the ACT, with the optional Writing section, is 3 hours and 35 minutes. The total time for the SAT, with the optional Essay, is 3 hours and 50 minutes.

How Test Scores Affect Admissions

ACT and SAT scores are just numbers. They measure the test performance of an applicant at a specific moment. Although scores are somewhat impersonal, they do provide admissions officers one additional metric by which to gauge an applicant's academic readiness for college-level work.

Like his or her transcript, your child's test scores will be used to compare your child to all the other applicants. This adds a level of competitiveness to the ACT and SAT and is why your child needs to do well.

At top colleges, many applicants have phenomenal test scores. The most selective schools could even require perfect ACT or SAT scores and still have plenty of qualified applicants. While perfect scores are not required, statistically speaking, your child needs strong test scores in order to be a competitive applicant.

Generally, the higher your child's test scores, the better his or her chances. But again, this doesn't mean your child needs a perfect score.

Consider the ranges of test scores from a small sampling of top colleges below. Note that scores in the "25th Percentile" column indicate that 75% of admitted students scored at or above the listed level; scores in the "75th Percentile" column indicate that 25% of admitted students scored at or above the listed level.

ACT Composite			
School	Admission Rate	25th Percentile	75th Percentile
Harvard	5%	32	35
Yale	7%	31	35
Duke	9%	31	34
Cornell	13%	30	34
Notre Dame	18%	32	34
Emory	21%	29	33
New York U.	28%	28	32
Boston College	32%	30	33

SAT Composite			
School	Admission Rate	25th Percentile	75th Percentile
Harvard	5%	1470	1600
Yale	7%	1490	1600
Duke	9%	1480	1600
Cornell	13%	1410	1570
Notre Dame	18%	1410	1550
Emory	21%	1350	1520
New York U.	28%	1320	1500
Boston College	32%	1350	1510

As you consider these score ranges, don't be fooled into thinking that just because students are admitted with SAT scores in the low 1400s that your child will be too. Unless your student is an athletic recruit, underrepresented minority, legacy, or has some other hook, the chances of being admitted with a score on the low end of a college's range are slim.

Also, notice the overall correlation between the selectivity of the school (given in the "Admission Rate" column) and the scores. This may seem obvious, but the more selective the school, the higher the scores your child will need to gain admission.

The standard is high, and so your child needs strong scores to remain competitive. So many students who apply to top colleges have perfect or near perfect scores—if your child doesn't, the rest of his or her application will have to make up for it.

But even if your child does achieve perfect scores, these scores alone will not significantly differentiate your child, and they certainly won't result in guaranteed admission. At the most selective schools, perfect scores will place your child at only the 75th percentile. So, test scores are not the only factor in earning admission to top colleges. But they do matter: the lower your child's scores, the lower the likelihood he or she will be admitted.

The ACT[11]

The forerunner to the modern ACT was first used as a college entrance exam in 1959, and since then, this test has become one of the most popular college admissions exams in the U.S. Instead of focusing on cognitive reasoning, the ACT seeks to assess college readiness. The questions presented in the ACT are intended to reflect what students are taught in middle school and high school curricula.

Test Dates

While specific dates change from year to year, the ACT is currently administered seven times annually on Saturdays in February, April, June, July, September, October, and December. The registration deadline for each date typically falls on the Friday five weeks before the test date, though late registration (with a late fee) is permitted for an additional two weeks.

Location & Format

The ACT is administered in a proctored environment to ensure secure testing, but in addition to the traditional physical test, the ACT can be taken online using approved, site-ready laptops.

Services & Fees

While they may change from time to time, the current ACT fees are as follows:

ACT (no writing)	$46.00
ACT (with writing)	$62.50
Late registration	$29.50
Date change	$25.00
Test center change	$26.00
Extra score reports	$13.00 each

ACT offers additional services related to the ACT assessment as well as services beyond the assessment. For a complete list of available services, up-to-date fees, and information on fee waivers, visit www.act.org.

Subjects Tested

The ACT contains multiple-choice questions in four test areas—English, mathematics, reading, and science—and an optional writing test.

- English – assesses your child's understanding of English language, grammar, and writing
- Mathematics – assesses your child's knowledge of basic arithmetic and math skills typically acquired by the end of junior year, including algebra, geometry, and trigonometry
- Reading – assesses your child's comprehension at a first-year-college level
- Science – assesses your child's evaluation, analysis, reasoning, interpretation, and problem solving skills related to biology, chemistry, earth science, astronomy, and physics
- Writing (optional) – measures your child's writing skills relative to entry-level college composition

Scoring

Each section of the ACT is scored from 1 to 36, and the composite score of all sections also ranges from 1 to 36. The writing test section does not affect the composite score.

When to First Take the ACT

Your child should consider taking the ACT as early as sophomore year.

The SAT[12]

The precursor to the modern SAT was developed from a U.S. Army intelligence test and was first administered in 1926.[13] The test's name and scoring have gone through several iterations, but the SAT remains one of the foremost aptitude tests used in the college admissions process. The

College Board, who owns and administers the SAT, recently redesigned the exam to better reflect what students learn in high school.

Test Dates

The SAT is currently administered seven times each year on Saturdays in March, May, June, August, October, November, and December. The registration deadline for each date is four to five weeks prior to the test date, though late registration (with a late fee) is possible for as many as three additional weeks if done online or by phone. Registering late, however, is not recommended since test center spaces fill up quickly.

Location & Format

Like the ACT, the SAT is administered only at specified test centers to ensure testing integrity. The SAT is offered in paper form with an accommodation for the use of a computer word processor for essays and short answers. Use of a computer is limited and must be approved. Students who are approved to use a computer on the SAT must take the exam at their own school rather than one of the designated test centers.

Services & Fees

The current SAT fees (subject to change) are listed below:

SAT (no essay)	$45.00
SAT (with essay)	$57.00
Late registration	$28.00
Date change	$28.00
Test center change	$28.00
Extra score reports	$12.00 each

The College Board offers other registration and score reporting services. For a complete list of available services, up-to-date fees, and information on fee waivers, visit www.collegeboard.org.

Subjects Tested

The SAT is comprised of two sections—Evidence-Based Reading & Writing and Mathematics. The first section is divided into two tests, Reading and Writing. An optional essay is also available.

- Reading – assesses your child's English comprehension and analysis skills, knowledge of English vocabulary and usage in context, and his or her command of evidence
- Writing – assesses your child's understanding of standard English conventions (e.g., grammar and vocabulary) and the expression of ideas
- Mathematics – assesses your child's problem-solving and data analysis skills as well as his or her knowledge of algebra and advanced math
- Essay – assesses your child's ability to analyze a source and write an evidence-based essay from that analysis

Scoring

Both sections of the SAT are given scores ranging from 200 to 800, and the total composite score is the sum of both section scores, yielding a range of 400 to 1600. The essay is given three separate scores of between 2 and 8 for reading, analysis, and writing, and these essay scores do not affect the total composite score of the two main SAT sections.

Note that the recent change to the SAT also changed the test's structure from three sections to two, which resulted in a new score range of 400–1600 rather than 600–2400.

When to First Take the SAT

Your child should take the SAT during junior year, preferably after taking the PSAT since this practice test gives him or her one extra opportunity to prepare in a real testing environment.

SAT Subject Tests[14]

In addition to the SAT, the College Board offers twenty SAT Subject Tests. These tests are 60 minutes long and assess student knowledge of specific subject matter, including math, biology, chemistry, physics, U.S. history, world history, and language. The complete list is available at www.collegeboard.org.

Number of Subject Tests to Take

Many of the nation's top colleges and universities require applicants to submit scores for at least two SAT Subject Tests. Generally speaking, the more selective the school, the more important the SAT Subject Tests are. And even if a college does not require but recommends that applicants submit SAT Subject Test scores, your child should do so.

Although most colleges that request SAT Subject Test scores ask for results from only two tests, your child should consider taking at least three.

Which Subject Tests to Take

Some colleges or programs have specific SAT Subject Test requirements that relate to the specific program; however, others want to see scores from different subjects. Your child will need to consider the specific requirements of each school to which he or she plans to attend when deciding which SAT Subject Tests to take.

Also, if your child has an idea of what major he or she might declare on his or her college application, he or she should be sure to take the relevant SAT Subject Tests. For example, if your child plans to study biology in college, he or she should take one or both biology Subject Tests and possibly the chemistry Subject Test as well.

Your child has likely studied a foreign language all through high school, and if so, he or she should take the SAT Subject Test for that language. The value of taking the SAT Subject Test in a language is that your child may be able to test out of entry-level language courses in college.

The nine language Subject Tests offered are Spanish, French, Chinese, Italian, German, Modern Hebrew, Latin, Japanese, and Korean. Some of these tests offer a standard reading-only version of the test as well as a listening version. Others offer only the standard version or listening version, but not both.

The standard language test is comprised of three categories—vocabulary and structure, paragraph completion, and reading comprehension—each of which takes up about one third of the test.

For the listening versions of the tests, the audio component is 20 minutes long, asks 40 questions, and represents 40% of the test's score. The listening portion of the test focuses on identifying sentences that describe photographs, determining which sentence is most likely to continue a short conversation, and answering comprehension questions. The reading portion of the listening test is structured the same way as the standard language test—roughly equal parts vocabulary and structure, paragraph completion, and reading comprehension. The language tests with listening require the test taker to bring an acceptable CD player with headphones

Your child should carefully consider whether to take the reading-only language test or the test with listening, if available. The test with listening component may be preferred, but it will also likely be more of a challenge since many of the audio elements are spoken only once. Some students are better at speech comprehension while others are better at reading comprehension. It may be best for your child to take both the standard version of the test as well as the listening version, selecting the best score of the two.

Registration, Services, & Fees

The current SAT Subject Test fees are listed below:

Registration Fee	$26.00
Subject Test	$20.00 per test
Language Test (Listening)	$26.00 per test
Late registration	$28.00
Date change	$28.00
Test center change	$28.00
Extra score reports	$12.00 each

Additional registration and score services are available, and fees tend to change from time to time, so be sure to check www.collegeboard.org for a complete list of services, up-to-date test fees, and information about fee waivers.

While your child must register in advance to take Subject Tests, he or she can switch which Subject Tests to take given the particular test is offered on that date, it is not a language test with listening, and your child does not require a special format (e.g., Braille) or any school-based accommodations. Your child can also choose to take fewer tests than originally planned or more (up to three; fees for additional tests apply).

Scoring

Like the SAT, SAT Subject Test scores are given as a range from 200 to 800.

Some colleges want to see the scores from all the Subject Tests your child takes. For those that don't, your child can select which scores to send by using Score Choice through his or her College Board account, otherwise, all his or her Subject Test scores will be automatically transmitted to the selected colleges.

Scores for tests on a given test date can also be canceled within a few days of the test. This might be a good option if your child determines he or she was not adequately prepared for a test. But canceling scores cannot be done selectively—so canceling one test means canceling all the tests taken on a single date except for cases of equipment failure.

Colleges that require SAT Subject Tests will use your child's best scores, so your child should focus on taking tests in his or her strongest subjects and those most relevant to his or her narrative. Unless a particular subject test is required or highly recommended, your child should simply avoid taking tests in his or her weaker subjects.

When to Take Subject Tests

SAT Subject Tests are generally offered on the same dates as the SAT, but not all tests are offered on each test date. The World History test, for example, is offered only in December and June. Some of the language tests are offered only in June, and the language tests with listening are only offered in November. Your child needs to plan ahead and be sure he or she knows when tests are offered to avoid missing opportunities.

Students may take only three Subject Tests on the same test date and cannot take any Subject Tests on the same day as the SAT.

Scores need to be submitted to colleges by December of senior year for regular decision applications, earlier for early decision and early action applications.

Beyond navigating these scheduling constraints and deadlines, your child will want to consider the optimal timing for taking specific Subject Tests.

Typically, the best time for your child to take an SAT Subject Test is at the end of the academic year in which your child takes the most advanced course he or she will take on that subject. For example, if your child takes AP Biology as a junior, he or she should consider taking one or both biology Subject Tests in May and/or June of that year.

Your child should be adequately prepared for an SAT Subject Test upon completing the honors, AP, or IB class for the subject. Even so, doing additional test preparation is prudent.

The same principle applies to the language Subject Tests. Your child should take the language test at the end of junior year if he or she does not plan to take that language during senior year. If taking the language course during senior year, however, your child should consider waiting to test until fall of senior year.

Essentially, your child should wait to take SAT Subject Tests until he or she is as prepared as possible—but no longer. He or she should take the tests while content knowledge is fresh and skills are sharp.

PreACT[15] & PSAT[16]

Before getting into more general test preparation strategies, I want to discuss the various preliminary or preparatory tests, such as the PreACT and PSAT. Familiarity with test format, pacing, etc., is one of the most important elements of successful test taking, and so you and your child should consider these pretests as part of his or her test prep strategy.

PreACT

The ACT offers a pretest, known as the PreACT, which is intended to help 10th-grade students prepare for the ACT through a multiple-choice assessment patterned after the ACT. The PreACT uses the same format and types of questions, and the test results range from 1 to 36, just as they do for the ACT. Additionally, the PreACT provides a predicted ACT score. The fee for the PreACT is currently $12.

The PreACT helps students engage in strategically focused preparation with no real admissions risk and a low cost.

ACT Aspire[17]

Another product offered by ACT for college readiness is ACT Aspire, a longitudinal assessment system anchored by the ACT. This system uses benchmarks to help identify weaknesses early in an effort to correct any academic deficiencies. ACT Aspire uses periodic and summative assessments to test students in English, Math, Reading, Science, and Writing—much like the ACT—but it's scope is much broader than admissions and the format is different from the ACT.

As a result, the ACT Aspire could be a useful tool in gauging a student's trajectory, but a practice test will better inform your child of whether he or she is ready for the ACT itself.

PSAT

The PSAT is slightly shorter and easier than the SAT, but it assesses students using the same content and format, providing valuable experience and a baseline for estimating potential SAT scores. More than that, the PSAT is also used as the National Merit Scholarship Qualifying Test (NMSQT), which is why you may see the test referred to as the PSAT/NMSQT.

High school juniors should take the PSAT in the fall since test results are used by the National Merit Scholarship Program to determine eligibility for scholarships and recognition (see the section "Standardized Testing" in Chapter 27 for more about the National Merit Scholarship Program).

One of the advantages of taking the PSAT is that your child's scores will not be reported to colleges. Fees are also low, currently only $16 (though subject to change), and fee waivers are available for low-income students in 11th grade. Since the PSAT is inexpensive and risk-free from an admissions standpoint, this practice test is an ideal way to gauge where your child stands with regard to the SAT. Your child will be able to identify his or her strengths and weaknesses, which allows for focused preparation.

Test Preparation Strategies

Getting a high score on the ACT or SAT requires hard work and smart preparation. Your child will likely need to take advanced courses and be well read to develop the necessary knowledge and critical thinking skills to do well on these entrance exams.

As mentioned in the last section, familiarity with the tests themselves is important, but your child should consider a broader strategy than just familiarizing him or herself with the ACT and SAT. Following are several strategies for effective test preparation.

Start Test Prep Early

Because of their importance in the admissions process, the ACT and SAT may be intimidating to your child. And if your child waits until junior year to prepare for the tests, they *should* seem a bit daunting. But early planning and preparation can significantly reduce the stress associated with these entrance exams and at the same time greatly increase your child's chances of success.

Your child should start preparing for the ACT and SAT as a sophomore, at least by taking the PreACT and PSAT.

Sufficiently preparing for the ACT and SAT will likely require a significant investment of time and effort, and so the earlier your child begins to prepare, the more he or she will be able to spread the test prep out. The summer before junior year, for example, is a prime opportunity to invest time in test prep since your child will be able to do so without having to balance his or her time between homework, extracurricular activities, test prep, and any other responsibilities.

Preparing for the SAT the summer before junior year is also vital since the 11th grade PSAT score determines National Merit Scholarship Program eligibility. Early preparation could mean markedly better performance on the junior-year PSAT/NMSQT, which in turn could have a strong influence on your child's admissions chances as well as his or her financial aid.

Another key advantage to beginning test prep early is that more time means more opportunities to take tests. For example, your child can take the ACT a total of 12 times—not that he or she should—but early preparation means additional time to bring scores up.

Early preparation also makes it possible to take more SAT Subject Tests. As we've already discussed, these tests are only offered a limited number of times throughout the year, and only three tests can be taken on a given day. The earlier your child is ready to take these tests, the more he or she will be able to take before scores must be submitted—and the fewer he or she will have to take at one time.

Because course load and grades are also important to your child's admissions success, test preparation cannot get in the way of your child's academics. By starting to prepare for the ACT and SAT early on, your child is less likely to be forced to choose between good grades and good test scores—he or she will have time to achieve both.

Spreading test prep out over a longer span of time also allows you and your child to evaluate his or her strengths and weaknesses, try different strategies, and, if necessary, get help.

Be Familiar with Test Format & Instructions

By getting to know the ACT and SAT before taking these tests, your child will be able to more efficiently use his or her time while testing. Instead of having to become familiar with particular instructions on test day, if your child carefully reviews the instructions in advance, he or she will already know what to do in each section.

Take Advanced Classes to Learn Content

The best way for your child to prepare for entrance exams—and college in general—is by taking the most advanced course load he or she can handle. Gaining mastery of subject matter will certainly help your child do well on these tests, but that isn't all there is to test taking. By taking more advanced courses, your child will not only learn the subject matter being assessed, he or she will also develop the critical thinking skills necessary for strong ACT and SAT scores.

Taking advanced courses is most important for the SAT Subject Tests, since these tests assess your child's content knowledge more than his or her ability to reason.

Develop Test-Taking Skills

Effective test taking requires a strategic approach. Your child needs to spend time learning basic test-taking skills:

- Manage time carefully (use an approved watch)
- Use process of elimination to make informed guesses
- Answer easy questions first
- Follow instincts (first responses are often correct)
- Pay attention to key words and qualifiers (e.g., "usually," "none," "all but the following," "the best," etc.)
- Anticipate answers before looking at choices

Not all techniques work for all students, and so your child will simply need to spend adequate time developing the skills and strategies that make him or her most effective at test taking.

Top Score Watch

Time management is one of the most important skills in taking the ACT, PSAT, SAT, and SAT Subject Tests. But most exam rooms have no clock, and without a watch, the only indication of how much time remains on a section of a test is the five-minute warning from the proctor.

Top Score Watch is a timer that meets the strict requirements of the College Board and ACT, Inc., and allows test takers to easily see how much time is left on each section of an exam.

Top Score Watch can be used with the ACT, PSAT, SAT, and SAT Subject Tests and is updated to account for any changes to test format, including the recent March 2016 redesign of the SAT and 2015 change to the ACT Writing Section.

For more information, visit www.TopScoreWatch.com.

Focus on Weak Subjects Based on PSAT & PreACT Scores

If possible, your child should take both the PreACT and PSAT to determine the subject areas in which he or she needs the greatest investment of time and study. These pretests provide valuable feedback that can help your child more effectively prepare—and they can also help your child determine which test he or she prefers and is better at.

Take Practice Tests

Not only does taking practice tests help your child become familiar with test format and instructions, it helps your child develop test taking skills and determine which subjects and question types need the most attention.

Your child should practice with actual ACT or SAT test materials. Both ACT and the College Board offer official practice tests on their websites for free. Test prep books are also available that include practice tests, but you should be careful to ensure the test materials are both up to date and actual ACT or SAT content.

Practicing for the ACT or SAT is most effective if it closely simulates actual testing conditions. This means sitting at a desk or table, using #2 pencils, observing strict time limits, etc.

And when your child takes the ACT or SAT, he or she should take advantage of the ACT Test Information Release or SAT Question and Answer services. These services provide detailed insight into your child's scores on these tests and can help you and your child further refine his or her test preparations.

Plan Ahead

While no one-size-fits-all timetable or plan exists, your child will generally want to first take the ACT as a sophomore and the SAT during the winter of his or her junior year. When to take these tests will be largely affected by what classes your child has completed. For example, if your child hasn't yet learned the necessary algebra or advanced math skills, it is likely too early to take the ACT or SAT.

Because of the limits to test dates for the ACT, SAT, and SAT Subject Tests, your child will need to carefully plan when he or she will take which tests to ensure adequate space between tests for additional study.

Spend Free Time Reading

In addition to taking advanced courses, one of the best ways for your child to prepare for the ACT and SAT, college, and a career is to read voraciously. Your child should read from a wide range of authors, styles, genres, and eras—Greek mythology, news articles, the classics, biographies, current bestselling novels, historical accounts, etc.

Several books have been written specifically about testing strategies, and your child should consider reading one or more of these books. Be sure your child gets only up-to-date content since these tests are subject to change—sometimes in significant ways, as is the case with the recent SAT redesign.

Get Help

One of the best ways to help ensure your child is adequately prepared for the ACT, SAT, and SAT Subject Tests is for him or her to get plugged in to an independent test prep program, enroll in a group class, or engage a professional service like Ivy League Prep. The more individualized the attention, the more effective it will be.

Chapter 13:
The Academic Index

The eight Ivy League schools use a numerical ranking system known as the Academic Index (AI)[18,19,20] to rank students. The Ivy League originally developed the AI to ensure athletic recruits met a minimum academic standard that was relatively uniform across the eight schools.

In this chapter, we'll briefly discuss the AI—what it is, and why it matters.

What Is the Academic Index?

Essentially, the AI is a score from 60 to 240 derived from an applicant's GPA or class rank and his or her SAT scores. The AI is then used to determine a recruited athletes eligibility for admission. The minimum score changes from year to year, and exceptions can be made, but the current minimum for athletic recruits is thought to be in the upper 170s. The majority of Ivy League athletic recruits, however, have scores above 200.

The primary function of the AI is maintaining a high academic standard for recruited athletes at Ivy League schools. The average AI of any given team must be no more than one standard deviation below the average AI of the entire student body.

Modern computing has made calculating an applicant's AI relatively simple. So, while the AI was created to compare recruited athletes within the Ivy League, for several of the eight schools, the AI is also used to determine the academic rank of all applicants. Not all of the Ivy League schools determine applicants' academic rank directly from the AI, however, and some don't even calculate the AI of every applicant.

Does the Academic Index Matter?

For athletic recruits at Ivy League schools, the AI is an important metric since it is used to determine whether the recruit is eligible to play on a team.

Again, no team at an Ivy League school may have an average AI more than one standard deviation below the average AI of all students at the college. The average U.S. college athlete has a significantly lower AI than those of Ivy League athletes, and so this policy effectively limits Ivy League schools to recruiting only exceptional student athletes whose academics are strong enough for the rigors of a top-tier college education. Other schools are not limited in this way and may recruit athletes with lower academic performance.

While the team average has to fall within one standard deviation of the school's average AI, this does not mean every athlete has that high of a score. Some student athletes have AIs two or more standard deviations lower than the school average. Such students are recruited for their athletic abilities, and teammates with higher AIs bring the average up to where it needs to be. In some cases, students are recruited to Ivy League teams specifically because they have higher AIs, and they may never actually play. While this doesn't happen at all the Ivies, it does happen.

If your child is seeking to be an athletic recruit, the main reason he or she should be aware of the AI is that being an exceptional athlete is not enough to get in to an Ivy League school—and many other top schools, even if they don't use the AI. Your child must be academically competitive.

If your child is not planning to pursue Ivy League sports as an athletic recruit, his or her AI still matters, but not as much. In either case, your child should focus on getting the best grades possible while taking the most demanding courses he or she can handle, scoring well on the ACT or SAT, and creating a compelling narrative to tie everything in his or her admissions profile together.

One final note: the AI is not a reliable predictor of admissions success. Your child's academic record does matter, but other factors can influence his or her chances of being admitted a lot more—such as strong teacher recommendations that recognize your child as truly exceptional, significant achievements in extracurricular activities, and prestigious third-party recognition.

Section Four:

Interests, Innovation, Community

Chapter 14:
Extracurricular Activities

As we've already discussed, extracurriculars and third-party recognition represent the most important elements of your child's admissions profile. In this chapter, we'll consider the bigger picture of how your child's extracurricular activities affect his or her application as well as how your child can leverage extracurriculars to enhance his or her profile.

The activities your child invests time into are the perfect place to highlight his or her primary interests, demonstrate innovation, and display community-mindedness.

Authenticity, Passion, & Excellence

If you've been told your child should be well-rounded in his or her pursuit of extracurricular activities, you and your child need to forget that notion—it's wrong. Your child needs to be highly focused. The extracurriculars your child pursues should enhance his or her profile, tie into his or her theme, and help develop a unique, compelling narrative.

In my case, my theme centered around Children's Books on Tape—so I took a childhood psychology and learning course and volunteered as a teacher in a summer reading program for 4th graders.

Your child should consider the theme of his or her application and pursue related opportunities. He or she might get involved in a service organization, participate in a summer program, or pursue an internship—the key is focusing extracurricular activities on building a cohesive theme and strong narrative.

While there is no perfect combination of extracurriculars that will guarantee admission, following three basic rules will help your child stand out as he or she decides what to do: your child needs to be authentic, pursue what he or she loves, and be innovative.

Admissions officers will see through any attempts your child may make to pad his or her profile. They will be able to distinguish between your child's actual interests and the activities he or she pursued thinking that the activities were what a college admissions officer would want to see.

So, your child should not do something because he or she has been told it looks good on an application or because he or she think it's what top colleges want to see. Your child should be authentic and pursue what truly interests him or her.

The extracurricular activities your child pursues help admissions officers understand who he or she is—what your child cares about, his or her values, and your child's personality. The clubs, sports, and musical ensembles your child participates in, the jobs he or she holds, and the organizations your child volunteers at all speak to who he or she is as a person. What your child does reveals his or her qualities: compassion, work ethic, knowledge, skill, talent, leadership, innovation, and perspective.

Top colleges view extracurriculars as strong indicators of the ways in which an applicant will contribute to the school. Being passionate about a specific activity and accomplishing something in that area of interest demonstrates not only that an applicant is truly interested in the activity, but that he or she is already achieving success—and there is no better predictor of future success than past success.

So, the key is for your child to take an activity or issue he or she is passionate about and to invest time into it—channeling passion into accomplishment and creative innovation that will improve the status quo. What your child accomplishes through extracurricular activities will help distinguish him or her from the myriad other applicants.

Think of it this way: the courses your child takes, the grades he or she earns, the test scores he or she achieves—these will not likely be too different from any other applicant. How your child synthesizes what he or she learns in school into the real world through extracurricular activities—that's what will stand out to admissions officers.

Top colleges understand that the major driver of economic development in the coming decades will be creativity and innovation. As technology improves, global competitiveness will rely more on ingenuity and out-of-the-box thinking. That kind of thinking is what colleges are looking for in applicants, and those who demonstrate innovation through their extracurriculars show admissions officers that they will add value to the college and to society, making them more desirable than those applicants who were simply busy.

So, your child should be sure his or her extracurricular pursuits aren't merely activities to participate in and enjoy. A basic rule of thumb is that if anyone can show up and get "credit" for an activity, then your child should avoid it because it will not be something that will distinguish him or her as an applicant. Instead, your child should choose activities he or she can enjoy that will result in some kind of tangible accomplishments or provide a platform for your child to demonstrate leadership and creativity.

Strategic Focus

The value of your child's extracurricular activities is not determined by how many activities he or she participates in—it's all about focus. Spreading time across numerous, unrelated activities will actually work against your child.

Again, your child must focus his or her attention on what he or she is truly passionate about and can excel at. Remember that passion and excellence often go hand in hand. The more passionate your child is about an issue or activity, the more likely he or she is to excel at it.

Your child should carefully weigh the activities he or she is most interested in against one another, considering which will create the most opportunities for your child to grow as an individual and, at the same time, showcase your child's strengths.

Increasing your child's chances of being admitted to a top college is all about strategic thinking—so your child must think strategically about the extracurricular activities he or she will pursue and focus on only the most valuable.

So, how can your child know which activities deserve his or her focus? Your child should ask the following questions:
- Am I passionate about the activity?
- Does the activity fit my theme and narrative?
- Does the activity provide opportunities to excel and demonstrate my leadership ability?
- Does the activity provide opportunities to gain third-party recognition or other evidence of success?
- Does the activity reflect the future impact I'll make at college?
- Does the activity provide valuable, real-world experience?

We'll examine each of these questions in more detail below.

Is Your Child Passionate about the Activity?

Passion means different things to different people. According to Merriam-Webster's dictionary[21], passion can be defined as "a strong feeling of enthusiasm or excitement for something or about doing something."
Passion does not have to mean some kind of deep, esoteric connection to an activity. And being passionate about an activity doesn't necessarily

mean your child has to excel at it—though as we've already discussed, there is a nexus between passion and excellence.

Admissions officers want to see that your child isn't simply going through the motions—participating in an activity he or she cares nothing about. They want to be convinced your child genuinely cares about, is committed to, and is excited by the activities he or she pursues outside the classroom.

So what demonstrates passion? Passion tends to be impossible to hide. But generally, passion is revealed through interest, commitment, and excitement. The higher your child's interest, the stronger his or her commitment, and the greater your child's excitement, the more passionate he or she is about the activity.

Passion tends to be the most reliable indicator of authenticity. So, your child should not be afraid to pursue his or her passions and integrate them into his or her admissions profile—they show admissions officers who your child is and how dedicated he or she can be.

By itself, however, passion is not sufficient. For admissions success, your child will need to take what he or she is passionate about and tie it to his or her theme and narrative, demonstrate achievement, and show how he or she will add value to the college.

Does the Activity Fit Your Child's Theme & Narrative?

Keeping a highly focused profile means choosing extracurricular activities that fit together and all tie in to a single cohesive theme and compelling narrative.

Your child has a vast array of opportunities, and even after filtering his or her options by the activities he or she is most passionate about, your child is likely to have a list of potential extracurriculars that is simply too long. Your child will need to filter that list further by selecting only those activities that fit his or her theme and narrative.

The goal is to create a list of activities that fit together in such a way that an admissions officer can quickly identify your child's theme and follow it throughout the various written components of his or her application. A focused list of extracurricular activities that ties in to your child's personal essay and additional information—and that is also reflected in your child's recommendation letters—will be powerful and will clearly convey your child's theme to the admissions committee.

Also, your child should consider how different activities harmonize with one another to offer a complete picture of his or her character, personality, and ability. Your child should choose extracurriculars that will stretch him or her in different ways, developing leadership and other skills that will not only set him or her apart for college admissions but will also be useful as your child pursues his or her career.

For example, if your child's passion is web design, he or she should pursue a variety of related activities that fit together but highlight different aspects or abilities. Your child could take an online SEO course to expand his or her knowledge and demonstrate self-determination and academic competence. He or she might design a website to demonstrate technical know-how and innovation. Your child could start a web design club at his or her school to demonstrate leadership. He or she could offer free web design services for local non-profits that do not have the budget but need websites—or could create YouTube channels or blogs for them—to show an awareness of and interest in community.
After your child weeds out activities he or she has no interest in, and after filtering his or her list further by removing activities that don't fit the admissions theme and narrative, your child can focus on the activities that provide him or her the best opportunities to accomplish something of value. What your child accomplishes throughout high

school will serve as a predictor of the impact he or she will have at college.

Does the Activity Create Opportunities to Excel & Lead?

Strategic focus means quality, not quantity. A handful of activities through which your child can gain meaningful experience and actually accomplish something of value is far better from an admissions standpoint than having a long list of activities to participate in.

Admissions officers want to see tangible accomplishments. As your child refines his or her list of potential extracurriculars, your child should consider what he or she might achieve when committing time to any given activity.

Activities that give your child the opportunity to lead are also important simply because colleges want to see that your child is a leader. While your child is unlikely to start out as a leader, four years of just participating in a given activity is nominally valuable. Your child should pursue an upward trajectory, taking on more and more leadership responsibility over time.

As your child goes through high school, he or she will want to keep track of these activities: how much time he or she spends on each activity and any related accomplishments. As we discussed in Chapter 6, your child will list his or her extracurricular activities on the common application—including how much time he or she spent on each—and your child will want to use this as an opportunity to highlight the accomplishments he or she has made along the way.

Your child should list the awards, rankings, and any other recognition he or she receives and should be sure to use numbers to emphasize the accomplishment (e.g., "3% acceptance rate" or "1 of 11 Award Recipients from pool of 9,700 applicants").

Does the Activity Provide Opportunities to Gain Third-Party Recognition or Other Evidence of Success?

Remember, third-party recognition is one of the key factors admissions officers from top colleges are looking for, so any such recognition is incredibly valuable. This should always be considered when deciding between different activities and different areas in which to spend a significant amount of time—the key question to ask is, How will I get third-party recognition for this activity? The recognition could be in the form of a letter from a supervisor, a newspaper article at a local or student paper, an award for innovation or service, or placing at a national competition.

Not all accomplishments, however, need third-party recognition. If your child helps lead a fundraising effort for a local charitable organization, he or she could highlight how much money was raised. If your child runs a blog, he or she could include how many unique visitors the site gets each day. If your child has started a business, he or she should emphasize his or her business accomplishments.

Does the Activity Reflect the Impact Your Child Will Make at College?

Extracurricular activities are such a valuable indicator of the strength of an application because they tend to show the potential impact the applicant will have at a college.

The more your child accomplishes outside the classroom and the greater his or her level of skill or specialization, the higher the likelihood he or she will make a positive contribution to the college. Admissions officers at top colleges are weighing the value your child brings to the school versus the value other applicants bring. By strategically focusing extracurriculars to create a high level of value, your child will increase his or her chances of admissions success.

Following are several types of extracurricular activities and some general discussion of each:

Specializations & Advanced Skills – Extracurricular activities built around a specialized field of study or advanced skill set can add significant value to your child's admissions profile because specialized college programs depend on student participation. Foreign language fluency, specific science and engineering knowledge (e.g., aeronautics, geology, astronomy, etc.), and other niche pursuits tend to stand out.

Volunteering & Community Involvement – While your child shouldn't volunteer or engage in community service activities solely for the sake of his or her college admissions profile, such involvement is valued by admissions officers. One of the most important factors to officers, however, is that your child demonstrate genuine interest in the service opportunities he or she pursues and that he or she can demonstrate a level of participation and impact beyond just adding volunteer hours to his or her application. Admissions officers will see through any attempts by your child to simply bolster his or her application through volunteer work, and so it's better for your child not to pursue community service activities than to do so under false pretenses. If, however, there's an issue your child genuinely cares about or a situation that inspires him or her to help in some way, your child should find a way to tie it into his or her admissions profile. We'll discuss volunteering and community more in Chapter 16.

Athletics – If your child is passionate about and skilled at a particular sport, he or she should pursue it. Top colleges are always recruiting new athletes to replace outgoing seniors. We'll discuss athletics more in Chapter 17.

Performing Arts – Like college athletics, college bands, orchestras, choirs, drama teams, etc., are always recruiting new members to replace graduating seniors. If your child loves to sing, play an instrument, or act and is committed to developing that skill, he or she should do so. If your child is able to demonstrate exceptional musical or performing arts ability, he or she will add value to his or her admissions profile and increase his or her chances of admissions success.

Research – Academic research experience gained through internships or independent study can add value to your child's profile because of the potential impact he or she will have on a college's research program.

Does the Activity Provide Valuable, Real-World Experience?

Top colleges want successful alumni, and demonstrating a capacity for success during high school through real-world experience is highly valuable.

In particular, internships and international exposure that build upon your child's application theme and narrative will give your child opportunities to demonstrate real-world success. Relevant pre-college summer programs are another way to gain valuable experience and create stronger ties to a college.

Internships

One great way for your child to get real-world experience and demonstrate value to college admissions officers is to participate in summer internship opportunities.

Again, focus is the key. Your child shouldn't pursue just any internship—the role should bolster his or her personal narrative.

If no such internship program is available, you should encourage your child to work with an appropriate organization to develop one. If your child is persistent and can clearly demonstrate how he or she will add value to the organization, the organization will be more willing to commit the time and resources necessary toward creating an internship opportunity for your child.

The primary purpose of a summer internship program is to give your child additional exposure to his or her interests and to provide him or her with real-world experience in that field. Such experience adds value to an admissions profile and is the perfect opportunity to showcase skills, knowledge, and accomplishments.

Obviously, an internship doesn't mean taking on a leading role in an organization, but that doesn't mean the experience has little value or isn't something to be proud of. Students that contribute to an organization, research project, etc., through an internship will demonstrate value to top colleges.

If your child has a pretty good idea of which colleges he or she is interested in attending, another option is to consider summer programs at one of these schools.

Many top colleges offer pre-college summer programs intended to help introduce high school students to the college—and sometimes offer high school credit.

While such programs may be expensive, they are helpful in two primary ways. First, attending a summer program at a college will help give your child a better understanding of what that college is like and may make all the difference in choosing which college to attend. Second, attending such a program may help form a stronger bond between your child and the college, creating one more connection to the college and, in turn, potentially improving admissions success—particularly for colleges that consider demonstrated interest in their admissions decisions.

So, if your child is fairly confident about where he or she would like to attend and that college offers a pre-college summer program that fits your budget, you might consider the program for your child. If, however, your child has a conflicting opportunity that fits his or her admissions profile better, that is what you should pursue. And as with all extracurriculars, a summer program shouldn't interfere with any necessary academics or test prep.

International Exposure

Like internships, experiences abroad can be valuable additions to your child's admissions profile. Colleges value international exposure because they are seeking to shape their students into world citizens and to create a global alumni network. While most top colleges have some kind of foreign language requirement, combining foreign language proficiency with international exposure can help your child stand out.

Studying abroad or pursuing an international internship could help your child grow in ways few experiences in the U.S. make possible, and such exposure to another culture will likely change your child's perspective of the world. Taken together, the language immersion and experiences gained overseas will make a student much more desirable to top colleges—so you should strongly consider any opportunity your child has to travel overseas through an exchange program or summer internship.

Participating in a service mission or similar community-minded program in a developing country is another way to gain international exposure, demonstrate compassion, and either learn a new or strengthen an existing foreign language skill.

Chapter 15:
Social Entrepreneurism

One of the foremost characteristics college admissions officers are looking for in applicants is an ability to innovate. Top colleges want students who know how to identify problems or opportunities and formulate solutions.

Entrepreneurism

Being entrepreneurial is a powerful way to demonstrate value to colleges because it brings together a number of desirable traits, such as leadership, innovation, determination, and commitment.

Top-tier colleges want students who are the future leaders in their respective fields, and in today's competitive marketplace of products, services, and ideas, being a leader means investing time and resources into something, taking risks, failing—then getting back up—and learning from every experience.

Whether or not your child is naturally entrepreneurial, taking the seed of an idea and growing it into a project, business, or organization requires a great deal of drive, effort, and perseverance. Playing it safe is easy—any student can participate in a club or group—and even contribute in great ways. But that isn't really what top colleges are after.

If anyone can fill a role, that role won't make your child stand out. Top colleges want applicants who are indispensable. So, as your child considers his or her extracurriculars, look for activities that help your child stand out.

Social Entrepreneurism

Exhibiting an entrepreneurial spirit is good and will certainly set your child apart from many other applicants. But being a social entrepreneur—someone who seeks to use entrepreneurial means to develop solutions to social issues—this adds an additional layer to your child as an applicant that can take a great admissions profile and make it truly exemplary.

Top colleges are community minded, and they want a student body that cares about the issues facing our world. Graduates that solve social problems reflect well on a college. As with every other aspect of your child's application, past demonstration of social entrepreneurism is the best indicator of future engagement.

Your child should consider his or her interests and passions and draw inspiration from that to make something bigger happen. For example, if your child has a passion for helping erase the stigma associated with autism, he or she might start out by advocating for this cause, but anyone can do that. Subsequently, your child might consider starting a community project in partnership with a local organization—and maybe even ultimately founding an organization of his or her own to meet a particular unmet need.

I started Children's Books on Tape as a community project to help meet a need in my community. The project started somewhat small, but eventually grew into a non-profit organization that is still making an impact today. I didn't just advocate for better ESL programs—I did something to help.

Colleges want doers—people who take action and don't just talk. Don't get me wrong, using your voice *can* be an effective means of taking action. Starting a blog, contributing to a local newspaper, writing a book, and speaking publicly at events can be incredibly effective at raising awareness and inspiring change.

The key is that your child accomplishes something through what he or she says and does. Your child should strive not only to make a difference, but he or she should try to make a measurable difference. If your child cannot tie an activity to some measurable effect, the admissions impact is diminished. That doesn't mean the activity wasn't important or meaningful. But from an admissions standpoint, your child should try to communicate the tangible results of his or her efforts. How many people does your child's blog reach? How much money was raised? How many people were served? What did the petition accomplish?

So, how does being a social entrepreneur fit into the rest of your child's application? What's the strategy here?

Being community-minded is valued among top colleges, and entrepreneurship helps demonstrate leadership, innovation, and determination. All of these are highly desirable qualities in applicants.

But the experiences gained pursuing an entrepreneurial endeavor also provide ample material for shaping a unique theme and narrative that has the potential to captivate and even inspire an admissions committee. Your child's unique journey will help him or her stand out and be memorable against a backdrop of white-noise applicants.

Is It too Late to Start?

If your child is close to applying to college, you might be thinking it is too late for him or her to start pursuing some kind of entrepreneurial activity. Every student is different, however, and admissions officers understand that people begin to discover their passions at different times in life. Ingenuity often requires some kind of catalyst, and any experience can awaken the entrepreneurial spirit within your child.

If your child is passionate about something, a nudge may be all it takes to start transforming that passion into a project, business, or nonprofit. Even if the project is small—a small start is a start, nonetheless. And the experience your child would gain pursuing a social project or starting a business will likely prove invaluable.

The key is keeping your child's theme and narrative sharply in focus. Your child should not start a business because he or she thinks that will help him or her get into a top college. Whatever the logical next step toward becoming a social entrepreneur is, that is what your child should do.

Chapter 16:
Volunteering

Many parents and their students believe volunteering is necessary in order for an applicant to get into a top college—but this is not true. In fact, if your child volunteers just to add the experience to his or her application, chances are the hours spent will actually add no significant value to his or her admissions profile.

In this chapter, we'll briefly examine some of the core strategic considerations for incorporating volunteering and community service into your child's admissions profile.

Be Authentic

Admissions officers value honesty and transparency, and so any volunteer work your child does needs to come from an authentic desire to serve. Whether it's working with underprivileged children, singing at a nursing home, serving homeless people at a soup kitchen—if your child has a genuine heart for people, that will show. And if your child does not, that will show, too.

Demonstrate Commitment

As far as how much volunteering will strengthen your child's admissions profile, several factors are involved. One of those factors is commitment. A single mission trip to a third-world country will not result in your child gaining immediate admission to a top college. Many high schools require community services, and the vast majority of college applicants indicate they engaged in some form of community service. As a result, volunteering does not, in itself, set your child apart. But being committed to a particular work or organization for a number of years—taking on increasing levels of responsibility—that can strengthen your child's profile.

Be Indispensible

Another factor in determining how volunteering will affect your child's admissions profile is the nature of his or her involvement. As we discussed in the last chapter, filling a role that anyone else could fill does not generally help your child stand out. If volunteering at a local service organization is what your child loves, that's great—but if this service is going to stand out on a college application, your child should not just be another volunteer—even if he or she is a frequent volunteer.

Instead, your child should become a valuable, integral member of the service organization. As with any other activity, the key is showing deep commitment, initiative, and passion—truly making a difference in the community and revealing the character qualities that college admissions committees want to see.

This kind of dedication to service tends to be easily integrated into an applicant's profile. In his or her application, your child will obviously list the names of any organizations he or she has served in along with the years and number of hours—but beyond this, your child might consider writing about his or her commitment to the service organization in the personal essay or additional information section of the common application. Your child should also refer to any recognition he or she has received for his or her service, and if a teacher is familiar with your child's service to the community, that teacher may be a good choice for one of the teacher letters of recommendation.

Chapter 17:
Athletics

One of the most obvious interests that can result in college admissions is athletics. If your child is a skilled athlete, you and your child will want to consider pursuing recruitment because once recruited, your child is admitted. Being an exceptional athlete, however, does not mean your child can neglect academics—top colleges still have fairly stringent academic requirements for their athletes.

For Ivy League schools in particular, the Academic Index (AI) is used to determine an athlete's eligibility for recruitment. The AI was created to prevent Ivy League schools from recruiting phenomenal athletes with low academic achievement.

As we discussed in Chapter 13, while the specific number varies from year to year, the AI cutoff is consistent across all Ivy League schools, and so students with lower AIs (in the mid 100s) will not be eligible for recruitment at these select schools. A candidate with a lower-than-the-minimum AI may, however, be presented at an all-Ivy meeting for special consideration. In such cases, an explanation for the low AI must be given and the applicant would have to be approved by the deans of admission.

But we won't rehash the AI in this chapter. Instead, we'll focus on how top colleges recruit athletes and what factors influence recruitment—with some strategic pointers along the way.

Athletic Recruiting Process

From an admissions perspective, the athletic recruiting process involves two basic phases: (1) coaches travel the country and conduct extensive research in an attempt to find the premier high school athletes that meet necessary academic requirements, and (2) admissions officers review coach recruitment lists and make admissions determinations. We'll discuss each phase of the recruiting process below.

First, coaches travel extensively, review local news columns, and conduct other research in order to find potential recruits. Coaches look for distinguished players (e.g., all-Americans, state and national champions, etc.) and then consider whether such players meet the academic standards of their specific college. For Ivy League schools in particular, this means meeting the minimum AI. Coaches may encourage potential recruits who haven't yet taken the necessary standardized tests to do so.

After finding potential recruits, a coach must painstakingly compile his or her list of high school athletes who will contribute not only to the athletic program of the college, but who will also meet all the other eligibility requirements of the school. Regardless of their athletic ability, students with low academic achievement (or low AIs) are not going to be admitted into top colleges. So if your child is an athlete and wants to attend a top college, academic success must also be a priority.

Once compiled, a coach's list will be used by his or her athletic liaison in the admissions department in the admissions process. Each time a liaison is given a list, he or she will examine the applicants, consider the strength of their profiles, and offer the coach preliminary feedback. The coach will then use this feedback to modify his or her list and resubmit it to the liaison.

Each of a college's teams has a specific target for how many students will be admitted as athletes, which varies by college and sport. While the specific number of desired recruits is kept secret, generally speaking, sports with more players, like football, have higher target numbers than sports with fewer players, like squash.

Also, some sports are given a higher priority than others. The priority of a particular sport at a college is typically affected by two factors: money and history. Sports such as football and basketball, which sell tickets for admission to their games and generate significant funds through alumni donations, are of greater value to colleges.

The history of a sport at a college also factors into the priority given to recruitment for that sport. Most colleges have one or more specific teams with track records of success that make recruitment for those teams a higher priority.

Ultimately, admissions officers review their coaches' potential recruits and mark their folders with some form of code, indicating they are athletes.

But how much does being an athletic recruit influence an admissions decision? That all depends on where the applicant ranks on the coach's list, how many spots are open, what position your child plays, and whether or not the admissions officer thinks the recruit will be a good fit for the school.

Again, the key is not that your child is an exceptional athlete—granted, top colleges do want great athletes. The primary factor affecting an admissions decision is whether your child is perceived as someone who will add value to the school as a whole and be able to keep up academically.

Factors that Affect Athletic Recruiting

Often, admissions officers view the applications of athletes through a different lens. They tend not to ask what impact the student would have—as an athlete, the student would have a direct impact on the school's athletics program. Instead, admissions officers are concerned with whether the athlete will be able to succeed academically. Admissions officers are looking for signs of academic strength.

The best thing your child can do is make it obvious that he or she is a serious student athlete who will succeed at a top college.

As with admissions in general, however, it is impossible to give a definitive formula for how to get your child recruited—every college is different, every class distinct, and every student unique. But you and your child can make educated decisions about what courses he or she should take, how much time to dedicate to his or her sport, and how to fit athletics into his or her admissions profile.

Grades & Course Load

As with all applicants, when considering potential athletic recruits, top colleges consider more than just what grades a student gets—they look at the classes that student took while getting those grades.

Many athletes achieve what seem like relatively high academic marks (or high AIs), but their course loads may not be rigorous. However, athletes who maintain strong grades while taking more demanding courses demonstrate a greater level of preparedness for the challenging academics offered by top-tier schools. Your child will have the best chance of being recruited if he or she takes a demanding course load that demonstrates academic strength, determination, and commitment.

Grades & Accomplishment

Throughout this book, we've discussed what makes a great admissions profile in general, and that the key consideration is ensuring not only that your child is strong enough academically, but that he or she stands out in some other significant way. In general, the more your child stands out, the more leeway he or she will have—and this is perhaps no more true than in the area of athletic recruiting.

If athletics is your child's way of really standing out—if he or she has poured countless hours into a sport and is truly exceptional—it's understandable if your child isn't quite as strong in other areas. Most top-tier athletes accomplish what they do by a great deal of hard work, and so many of the best high school athletes don't have much free time for studying and preparing for college entrance exams.

But remember, top schools do have high academic standards, and so even the most amazing athlete with a weak academic record will have trouble gaining admission to a top-tier school. If, however, your child can pursue a rigorous course load, get strong grades, and develop exceptional athletic ability, he or she will have much higher chances of being admitted.

Very few athletes at top colleges are admitted based solely on their athletic ability.

Grades & Student Background

Generally speaking, the athletes at top colleges who, on average, have the weakest academics (lowest AIs) play football and hockey—though there are such students across all sports. These students tend to be from middle-class backgrounds due largely to bias against applicants from privileged backgrounds.

Athletes who attend private or college preparatory schools, maintain average grades, don't work, and do nothing else to stand out are much more unlikely to be admitted—regardless of their ability—than students from low-income schools with lower grades.

That isn't to say athletes with affluent parents can't be admitted—or even that they'll have a harder time being admitted. It's all about strategy.

Don't Rely on Recruitment Alone

Even if your child is a skilled athlete, he or she should still focus on creating a compelling admissions profile that makes him or her a stand-out candidate. This is particularly important because your child will not likely know whether or not he or she is going to be recruited until later in high school. If your child doesn't end up getting recruited, athletic ability alone will not earn your child's admission.

Communicating with Coaches

Technically, coaches are not supposed to make promises to potential athletic recruits—but sometimes they do. A coach is not authorized to make final decisions about which athletes are recruited, and any number of the athletes on a coach's list may be rejected by the admissions department.

All a coach really knows is where he or she has placed a given athlete on the list—and that list changes as the athletic liaison provides feedback and the coach makes contact with other athletes. So if a coach tells your child his or her position on the list, bear in mind that this position might change.

When it comes to communicating with coaches, one of the most important considerations is that your child be truthful. If your child is undecided or otherwise not committed to a particular school, it is best to be honest if a coach asks so he or she can make informed decisions.

Also, coaches from different schools communicate with one another—so your child should not tell a coach that a college is his or her top choice unless that's true. If your child is duplicitous, he or she will likely be caught in the lie.

Scholarships

While many of the top colleges can and do award athletic scholarships, none of the eight Ivy League schools do—and so this is something to keep in mind as you and your child consider your options. Ivy League financial aid is based entirely on a student's need, but other top colleges are not restricted in this way and often award athletic scholarships to the best athletes.

As a result of this policy, many outstanding athletes who would otherwise matriculate at an Ivy League school instead choose to attend other, often less selective universities that offer scholarships. But this doesn't mean Ivy League schools aren't competitive in sports. On the contrary, these eight colleges are often well ranked among Division I colleges across the nation, many of which incentivize athletic recruitment through scholarships.

The top colleges outside the Ivy League are free to offer scholarships to athletes, but remember that athletic scholarships are typically performance based. So, if your child is admitted as an athlete on scholarship, his or her continued participation in the athletic program and success at the sport will be necessary to maintain that scholarship.

On the other hand, because Ivy League schools do not award athletic scholarships, a student's financial aid is not tied to athletic participation or performance. As a result, the temptation may be to use athletic accomplishments as a hook to gain admission to an Ivy League school without ever having any real intention to play. If your child doesn't plan to participate in his or her sport at an Ivy League school, don't pursue athletic recruitment. This is unfair to the school, the coach, and other potential recruits.

The "Squeeze Play"

For many competitive high school athletes being pursued by both Ivy League schools and other top colleges, a situation can arise in which one of the schools offers the student a scholarship and definite acceptance if he or she will commit in writing to attend.

This situation does not generally apply to the majority of athletes recruited by Ivy League schools, who are accepted through early decision or early action programs.

Recruited athletes applying through regular decision, however, are often faced with this decision early in the year—months before Ivy League schools send out acceptance letters. A single offer this early creates a tension between the certainty of a student being admitted to a particular school and the uncertainty of whether he or she will be admitted to any of the others.

The "squeeze play" is what results.

Basically, an athlete in such a scenario has the opportunity to learn whether he or she is likely to be admitted to the Ivy League schools in question and what their financial aid packages might be.

On one hand, the squeeze play prevents the student from losing the scholarship offer if none of the Ivy League schools end up accepting his or her application. On the other hand, the squeeze play allows the student to avoid passing up the opportunity to attend an Ivy League school based on the certainty of acceptance elsewhere.

If your child is being recruited by multiple top colleges and finds him or herself in this scenario, immediately contact the coaches at the Ivy League schools. Generally, you'll need to fax the initial offer and any financial aid or scholarship information to the Ivy League coaches.

Your child's admissions file will then be evaluated by the athletic liaison and possibly the regional reviewer. The financial aid department will also put together a potential financial aid package (again, at Ivy League schools, this is based on your child's need, not athletic ability).

Within one or two days, your child will be told whether he or she will be accepted and what financial aid is likely to be offered. At this point, your child will know what his or her options are and will be able to choose between them. Once your child makes his or her choice, he or she will need to notify the other schools of that decision.

Chapter 18:
Talent

Another way in which your child might distinguish him or herself to a top college is by building his or her admissions profile around a particular talent or ability, such as art, photography, music, or another performing art.

Supplemental Materials

Generally speaking, your child should not send example material such as artwork or a recording of his or her music unless he or she is exceptionally skilled and planning to use that skill to contribute to the school. College performing and fine arts departments are inundated with materials from applicants seeking recommendations, so, if your child is a hobbyist, don't send additional materials. Also, if your child has no intention of participating in the college's fine arts program, he or she should not include example work.

Since the admissions office is not generally qualified to assess artistic ability, any additional materials your child submits will be forwarded to the appropriate department. Once reviewed, that department will send admissions a ranking of your child's skill level.

Depending on whether the college allows it, your child might consider sending materials directly to the relevant department—but your child should be sure to indicate that he or she is an admissions applicant seeking a recommendation letter.

Professors who take the time to review your child's example work and write a recommendation assume that your child is serious about pursuing that skill in college—so again, it would be discourteous for your child to submit example work and seek a recommendation if he or she has no intention of continuing to develop this skill at the college level.

Strategy for Incorporating Talent in a Profile

Remember, your child's admissions profile should demonstrate how he or she will add value to the college. As we've discussed throughout the book (see Chapters 7 & 14 in particular), your child's profile should be unified by a theme, so unless his or her talent or ability is clearly linked to that theme, it may be better as a footnote rather than a major focus. On the other hand, if your child is particularly gifted and can demonstrate his or her high level of ability through third-party recognition and accomplishment, he or she should consider highlighting this talent even if it is not the primary focus of his or her admissions profile.

Even then, it is typically sufficient to simply list your child's talent in his or her application under the Activities section and mention any awards, honors, distinctions, etc., under the "Honors" heading of the Education section. Such accomplishments speak for themselves and tend to give a fairly good indication of your child's skill level.

Consider Making a Talent or Ability Central to the Theme & Narrative

If your child is exceptionally gifted or has a natural ability that he or she has highly developed through practice and training, your child should consider making this gift or ability the focus of his or her theme and narrative. For example, if your child loves acting, wants to pursue it professionally, and has the ability to do so, perhaps he or she should build his or her admissions profile around acting. The key here is having third-party recognition that affirms not only your child's passion for acting but his or her ability as well.

Find Ways to Merge Exceptional Talent with Theme & Narrative

Your child's talent or unique ability might not be his or her primary passion and focus, but if there is a way to somehow integrate that talent into his or her narrative in a natural way, your child should consider doing so.

For example, if your child is particularly gifted in one or more musical discipline, he or she might integrate music into his or her passion. Whatever your child's passion is—mechanical engineering, medical research, biology, computer science, psychology—he or she could draw upon his or her skill and love for music to lead a unique community project, develop a mobile application, or study the effects of music on the mind.

Don't Focus on Talent or Ability at the Expense of Academics

Your child's talent or ability may help him or her stand out, but by itself, exceptional skill will not result in admission. Solid academic performance is still an absolute must for admission to a top college, so your child should not develop any skill to the detriment of his or her academic discipline.

Section Five:

Other Hooks

Chapter 19:
Family Legacy

A legacy applicant is the son or daughter of an alumnus or alumna. At top colleges, the definition tends to be fairly narrow. Typically, the parent must have graduated from the undergraduate college. Some of the schools consider an applicant a legacy if his or her parent attended an undergraduate college's graduate school. But being the sibling, grandchild, or great-grandchild of a graduate does not make one a legacy applicant.

Why Being a Legacy Matters

Your child has no control over whether he or she is a legacy, but if you or your spouse attended a top college and your child applies there, his or her chances of being admitted are significantly higher—about twice the rate of other applicants, on average.

While a 20 to 40 percent chance of being admitted is far better than a 10 to 20 percent chance, this obviously means not all legacy applicants are admitted. Since roughly two-thirds of legacy applicants are rejected, being a legacy is clearly not enough by itself to guarantee admission. But that doesn't make being a legacy applicant trivial.

Why Legacy Students Matter to Colleges

Admitting legacy students at a higher rate than others may seem unfair—and it may actually be unfair—but it isn't done without what top colleges consider acceptable reasons.

First, top-tier schools see legacy admission as a recognition of the special relationship between a school and its alumni—a connection between past students and future students. The preference for legacies is not really concerned with fairness, and none of the top colleges try to hide their preferential treatment of legacy applicants.

And while a commitment to alumni takes priority, each year, many alumni are disappointed that their children's applications have been rejected.

Second, as much as prioritizing legacy admission is about community, it is likewise about economics.

Many of a school's most generous donors are alumni. And while regular donations won't affect your child's chances of admission (unless those donations are in the hundreds of thousands of dollars, in which case your child might be considered as a development applicant; see Chapter 20), the combined effect of loyal alumni donating funds to the school makes a major impact. In many cases, legacy admits provide a short-term economic benefit in the form of full-paying students, but top colleges are more concerned with the long-term, cumulative benefits of developing a loyal network of successful alumni.

Strategy for Legacy Applicants

If your child is a legacy applicant, he or she should certainly leverage that status in his or her application to increase the likelihood of being admitted. But being a legacy is no substitute for being a strong applicant.

Legacy applicants with mid-range academic ratings have better chances of being admitted than other applicants of comparable academic rank, but the pool of applicants to any given highly selective college is incredibly competitive. Only the best legacy applicants will be admitted.

If your child is applying as a legacy, he or she should not rely on that status and should instead build a compelling profile that stands on its own merits. Being a legacy should serve only to augment an already excellent application.

Chapter 20:
Development/VIP

If you plan to purchase your child's admission, it takes more than an annual thousand-dollar donation. Such donations, while certainly appreciated by colleges, have no real bearing on an applicant's admissions success.

But money, influence, and celebrity status can buy admission.

Development applicants are those admitted by virtue of their parents donating vast sums of money—hundreds of thousands of dollars, if not millions—to the college.

VIP cases, on the other hand, relate to applicants who are either themselves celebrities or who are the children of celebrities. This category would include child stars seeking to enroll in college as well as the children of actors, actresses, and high profile political figures (e.g., U.S. presidents and vice presidents).

The Case for Development & VIP Applicants

For schools that pride themselves in being highly selective, it may seem particularly inconsistent and perhaps a bit unfair to allow the financial means or celebrity status of an applicant's family determine his or her admissions success. And just as with legacy applicants, it may well be inconsistent and unfair to admit students for financial reasons. But colleges would likely argue that such cases are relatively rare and tend to have a net positive effect, which makes admitting development and VIP applicants not just a tolerable practice but a sensible one.

While every school's policy regarding development and VIP cases is different, generally speaking, the number of applicants that fit into this category is low—and the number of such applicants admitted by top colleges is even lower. Smaller yet is the number of development and VIP applicants who gain admission based solely on that single consideration. Despite any pressure from the offices of development or alumni affairs, a college's admissions director remains autonomous and will reject any candidate he or she deems unsuitable, whether for academic or other reasons.

Not all development and VIP applicants have weak academic records, and even those that do must meet the minimum academic requirements of the schools they attend. The tension here lies in the fact that the admission of a development or VIP applicant probably means the rejection of an otherwise more qualified applicant. Again, this seems inherently unfair at face value.

The rarity of development and VIP cases, however, coupled with the positive impact they bring to a college makes admitting such students a reasonable practice. Why? Because that one weaker student may mean better facilities that improve the quality of the education for the thousands of other students who are currently enrolled and all those that come after.

Strategy for Development & VIP Applicants

If you have the wherewithal and the will—or if you or your child is a celebrity—contact the development office of your child's top pick and have a conversation about how you might contribute to the college's development. If you are an alumnus or alumna of the college, contact the alumni affairs office instead.

Development and VIP applicant files are specially marked, but this does not guarantee admission. While the admissions policies vary from school to school, top colleges rarely admit applicants who fall below their minimum academic threshold. So, if you plan to pursue a development-

or VIP-based admissions strategy, your child must still be a viable candidate for admissions.

If your child has a strong admissions profile without being marked as development or VIP, his or her profile will be that much stronger with it.

Chapter 21:
Faculty & Trustee Recommendations

Faculty and trustee recommendations are fairly uncommon, and the value they add to an applicant's profile depends largely on the reason for and strength of the recommendation.

The Danger of Faculty & Trustee Recommendations

Few students are admitted to top colleges simply by virtue of a recommendation from a faculty or board member. And if your child is not already a strong candidate, he or she is unlikely to be given a faculty or trustee recommendation since the reputation and credibility of that faculty or board member is on the line.

But pursuing a faculty or trustee recommendation may adversely affect your child's profile for several reasons. First, admissions officers often bristle at the idea of a trustee or member of the faculty trying to influence the admissions process for a friend. Second, such letters are often short with little substance and may make your child appear to lack confidence in the merits of his or her admissions profile.

Effectively Incorporating Recommendations

While recommendations based solely on relationship (e.g., from a professor or trustee who is a family friend or business partner) are unlikely to carry much weight and may actually hurt your child's chances of admission, that doesn't mean your child should never consider asking a faculty member or trustee for a letter of recommendation. A recommendation from the right person for the right reasons will augment your child's profile and set it apart from other applications.

If, for example, your child attended a summer course at the college and impressed a professor through strong participation and exceptional work, a recommendation from that professor demonstrating the kind of student your child is might add significant value to your child's profile. Or perhaps a member of the college's board of trustees is a partner at the firm your child interned at over the summer. If that trustee worked with your child and can write a letter offering insight into the kind of character qualities, skills, and potential your child has, such a letter could serve to strengthen your child's admissions file.

As with all other hooks, the key is to not rely solely on that hook for your child's admissions success. With recommendations in particular, your child is unlikely to benefit unless he or she is already a strong candidate. And if your child's application is weak, faculty or trustee support won't likely help and may even hurt his or her chances.

Chapter 22:
Underrepresented Minority (URM)

At top colleges, the term underrepresented minority (URM) is used narrowly to refer to black, Native American, and Hispanic applicants since admissions rates among these groups has been historically low.

Top colleges strive to create racially, ethnically, and socioeconomically diverse classes, and so URM applicants tend to have improved chances of being admitted since the pool of qualified URM applicants is relatively low.

Of course, the pursuit of diversity affects more than just URM applicants. Top-tier colleges give special consideration to serious applicants from rural, low-income backgrounds as well as to all first-generation college applicants—regardless of race—since such applicants tend to have less access to educational resources. Admissions officers tend to weigh these applicants' test scores and academic records against the resources, support, and opportunities they had.

These are all factors outside a student's control but are nonetheless important to consider when compiling an admissions profile. Even if your child is a nonminority applicant, the principle of diversity applies. By emphasizing what sets your child apart from the norm, you improve his or her chances of admission—and this is perhaps most especially true for URM applicants.

Therefore, if your child is black, Native American, or Hispanic, his or her chances of admission to a select college will be higher, but in no way is his or her admission guaranteed. The best thing your child can do if he or she is a URM applicant is to develop the strongest possible admissions profile that stands out on its own. The more ways in which your child adds to campus diversity, the stronger his or her profile will be.

In this chapter, we'll examine how the term "underrepresented minority" departs significantly from the term "minority"—and why this is important to understand—as well as what priorities a college has when it comes to the admission of URM applicants. We'll also walk through the admissions process for URM applicants and discuss some related strategic considerations.

"Underrepresented Minority" versus "Minority"

Perhaps one of the reasons the admission of minority students to top colleges tends to be so misunderstood is the conflation of the terms "minority" and "underrepresented minority." The former term is well understood by most people, while the latter requires some context.

Not all traditional U.S. minorities are in view when referring to underrepresented minorities in the college admissions context. The URM designation refers specifically to black, Hispanic, and Native American applicants—often including Alaskan Natives, Hawaiian Natives, and Pacific Islanders. And so, for example, Asian Americans, while a U.S. minority, are not considered URMs since their enrollment at top colleges is relatively high.

Also, African Americans are a U.S. minority, but black international students from Africa are not. And while colleges should classify students from Africa as international—not minority—this isn't always the case. The same issues arise when considering Hispanic students—Central and South American international students may be presented as minority students to make the college appear to have a higher minority count.

Note that such international students would not be viewed as URM applicants during admissions—positioning them as minority students after they've been admitted is about optics. Top colleges generally want to have as high a level of diversity as possible.

The reason it is important to understand the distinction between URM applicants and applicants who identify with U.S. minority groups is that unless your child is a URM applicant, minority status likely has little impact on his or her admissions chances. On the other hand, being a URM applicant can significantly increase your child's odds of being admitted.

Diversity, Equal Opportunity, & Affirmative Action

The key factors driving URM admissions on top college campuses is a desire for diversity and equal opportunity coupled with affirmative action policies.

We've already discussed how colleges value diversity on campus. But top colleges seek to balance diversity with an admissions process built around principles of equal opportunity and merit.

On the one hand, colleges strive to carefully shape each class into a diverse group of premier students. On the other hand, colleges strive to promote an admissions environment of equal opportunity. These two goals, along with the special priority given to legacy applicants, are often in conflict. Selecting students based on how they'll make the college more diverse tends to result in stronger consideration going to one applicant over another equivalent choice. And prioritizing legacy applicants both affects a class's diversity and demonstrates a lack of equal opportunity.

To confound the situation further, affirmative action also plays a role in admissions. Affirmative action policies favor neither diversity nor equal opportunity—affirmative action seeks to remedy past and current discrimination, particularly against African Americans.

The result of these conflicting priorities is a somewhat messy, relatively subjective system, and admissions officers cannot typically provide substantive rationale for why some students are admitted over others.

Minority Recruitment & Admission

Top colleges are concerned with keeping a high enough level of URM students, and so they actively recruit black, Hispanic, and Native American high school seniors. Recruitment efforts involve paying for qualified URM applicants to visit the college and maintaining admissions staff specifically for recruiting URM students.

The admissions process for URM applicants is the same as the process for all other students, but like athletes, legacies, and other applicants with hooks, URM applicants are evaluated using different standards. This doesn't mean URM applicants have a lower standard or are not otherwise qualified to attend a top college, but it does mean that the diversity these applicants bring to the college is counted as an asset that gets weighed in the overall admissions decision.

Strategic Considerations for URM Applicants

Like the other hooks in this section of the book, an applicant cannot control whether he or she is part of an underrepresented minority group. But applicants can choose how to use that in their admissions profile.

The key strategy for URM applicants is the same strategy for all applicants: develop the strongest possible academic record by taking advantage of every possible opportunity for rigorous course work, score well on entrance exams, and create a compelling personal narrative. Beyond this, URM applicants can emphasize aspects of their lives that add to the diversity of top college campuses.

And if your child identifies as part of an underrepresented minority group, he or she should indicate his or her ethnic background on the college application.

Chapter 23:
Geography

Top colleges don't generally release statistics about how many students apply from each state or how many of those applicants are admitted. As a result, it's difficult to say precisely how much of a difference it makes to apply from an underrepresented geography—but it can make a difference.

In this chapter, we'll briefly examine how geography fits into the admissions process and examine some related strategies.

Why Geographic Diversity Matters

Top colleges strive to build a diverse incoming class, and that includes geographic diversity. At the end of the admissions process, every school wants to be able to claim it has students from all 50 states.

Geography matters to top-tier schools for various reasons. While admitting students from every state is a matter of pride, it is also about brand and image—being seen as ubiquitous and diverse.

If a student from an underrepresented geography is admitted to one of the most selective colleges in the nation, other students—those in his or her peer group, those who attend the same church, those who look up to him or her, the student's siblings and cousins, etc.—are more likely to consider applying to that college. By admitting a single student, a college can gain influence in an entire community.

The Admissions Impact of Geographic Diversity

As with any single element of an admissions profile, being from an underrepresented state will not get your child into the most selective colleges. While top schools won't admit unqualified students, every state is likely to produce at least one qualified applicant—even if only barely qualified. And admissions officers are looking for at least one qualified applicant from each state so they can maintain the college's "freshmen from all 50 states" status. For many top colleges, leaving a single state unrepresented would be seen as failure.

Generally speaking, though, top colleges receive a geographically diverse pool of applicants, and so filling the incoming class with students from every state tends to work itself out.

But where an applicant is from can be a deciding factor between two equally qualified students—and can even result in favorable decisions for less qualified applicants. Among qualified applicants from a single state, the lower the number of applicants, the higher the chances of being admitted to a top college. On the other hand, states with vast numbers of applicants—like New York and California—are much more competitive. A less qualified applicant from an underrepresented state has a higher chance of being admitted than a more qualified student from a highly represented state.

But being from an underrepresented state does not guarantee a higher likelihood of being admitted. The quality of an applicant's admissions profile does matter, and in the rare event that no qualified applicants apply from a given state, a top college might admit no one from that state. But if an applicant is the only one qualified from his or her state—even if the college had thousands of more qualified applicants to choose from—the likelihood of that one student being admitted is fairly high.

Strategic Considerations for Geographic Diversity

If your child lives in an underrepresented geographic region like Alaska, Idaho, Nebraska, Montana, North Dakota, South Dakota, or Wyoming, he or she stands a better chance of being admitted if his or her academic record meets the minimum threshold for the school in question. And while your child doesn't likely have significant control over where your family lives, he or she does have control over how his or her location is used in the college admissions process.

If from an Underrepresented State, Use It

Just being from an underrepresented state gives your child at least a slight admissions advantage—but the more your child can demonstrate how where he or she lives sets him or her apart from other applicants, the better. Your child should consider what environmental factors and experiences give him or her a unique perspective and draw from those—not overtly pointing to where he or she lives, but subtly injecting these distinct elements into the narrative.

An applicant from Wyoming, for instance, might include details in his or her personal essay that hint at the unique perspective he or she has gained from living in that state. Such a student could flavor his or her essay with words and phrases describing the small, conservative ranching community where he or she lives, the distance between his or her house and the nearest grocery store, an economy built on natural resources, or the activities that are normal for most residents (e.g., hunting, fishing, backpacking, rock climbing, etc.). These details do not need to be the central focus of his or her essay, but can instead be used to create the atmosphere for the narrative.

Consider Colleges in Other Regions

The closer your child lives to a particular college, the more competitive the applicant pool will be. As a result, your child should consider applying to colleges outside of the region in which he or she lives. If on the East Coast, your child should consider keeping Stanford, University of California (Las Angeles and/or Berkeley), University of Southern California, Northwestern University, and University of Chicago on his or her list. This doesn't mean excluding top colleges on the East Coast, but including colleges from varying regions can help improve your child's chances of being admitted to one of these schools.

Section Six:

Timetable

Chapter 24:
Before High School

When should you start preparing your child for admission to a top college? Is it ever too early?

While some parents start preparing their children for college admissions before they are even school age and then on through their elementary years—hiring tutors, visiting colleges, and practicing for college entrance exams—such tactics are not necessary.

At an early age, the most important thing you can do to help your child succeed academically is create an environment in which he or she loves to read and learn. Everything else will follow.

Early Years

What can you do to help set your young child on the right track for a top college? While many have obsessed over getting their children into the best nursery, preschool, and kindergarten programs, nothing indicates that such programs produce any greater intellectual curiosity, love of learning, and overall development than the right attention and encouragement at home.

All children are different, and some seem to have a greater bent toward reading, for example, or math. But young children who are read to and read at home can learn just as much as if they were attending a great preschool program.

Children that are read to and who develop a love of reading at a young age tend to perform well on the SAT Reading section regardless of how rigorous their education through high school. So, if you want to equip your child for academic success, do your best to instill in him or her a love for reading. Read to your child while he or she is little, and help him or her develop the ability to read.

Reading and writing skills are foundational to learning, and so if your child learns to read and write early on, other academic skills will follow. For your child to gain admission to a top college, he or she will likely have to be a strong reader and writer.

So, instead of focusing on nursery, preschool, and kindergarten options, focus on creating a home environment that stimulates learning and encourages a love of reading. Children do not tend to develop a love of learning at school—this passion for discovery tends to originate in the home. It's never too early to start encouraging your child to love learning and reading.

Middle School & Junior High

While you don't want your child to start preparing for college too late, elementary school is too early to begin. But that doesn't mean you can't guide your child with college in mind or take steps early on. Encourage your child to explore different subjects and activities to discover what they enjoy.

As your child enters middle school and junior high, one of the most important things for you to keep in mind is what academic track your child is on. Your child should pursue as many honors courses as he or she can handle. Determining which honors classes your child should or should not take will require some honest and careful assessment from you, your child, and his or her teachers.

As mentioned in Chapter 11, one of the most important factors in a successful academic record is a rigorous course load. Getting on the right academic track is important because the courses your child takes in middle school and junior high will directly affect what courses he or she will be able to take in high school.

Academic track tends to be even more important for students who will attend high schools that assign higher grade-point value to taking honors and AP courses. The key is for your child to remain academically competitive given the specific details of his or her high school.

Therefore, while your child is in middle school and junior high, you should begin to assess what classes need to be taken to be on track in high school. It is much easier to course correct early but not so easy once your child is in high school.

Chapter 25:
Freshman Year

Starting freshman year, your child should begin to begin to take his or her first real steps toward college preparation. These steps are more about awareness and early strategic planning—a foundation—not an end in themselves.

You and your child should schedule a meeting with his or her high school guidance counselor so your child and the counselor can meet each other and begin what will hopefully be a positive, productive relationship. In this meeting, your child should discuss his or her favorite subjects and interests, strengths, and weaknesses. Also, your child should ask about any special opportunities that may be available, such as afterschool programs, classes, tutoring sessions, practices, etc., that your child might be able to attend—and even get credit for. Knowing what your child's options are allows you and your child to make informed decisions and long-term, strategic plans.

Academic Planning

One of the primary reasons your child should meet with his or her counselor is to determine what track he or she needs to be on to pursue a competitive course of study. You and your child should familiarize yourselves with high school graduation and college admissions requirements. Take time to review which courses your child must take over the next four years, and consider mapping these out in some way.

The courses your child takes his or her freshman year will largely determine his or her entire high school track, particularly for math, science, and language courses. Higher level and advanced placement courses are bound to have certain prerequisites, and you and your child should think strategically about which advanced courses to aim for.

Generally, your child should choose the most rigorous classes offered, including as many advanced or honors classes as are available. Early on in high school, your child may not know what subject he or she really enjoys and wants to focus on. So, while we've discussed how specialization and focus are good, as a freshman, your child will largely be taking prerequisites for other classes and should focus on being academically strong across the board.

While selecting courses for freshman year, however, your child should select a fun elective that matches his or her interests—doing so will provide a bit of a reprieve during the school day and a little less homework at night and over the weekends.

As your child enters high school, the goal is to create a challenging but achievable list of classes. Your child should primarily focus on participating in class, contributing to and leading discussions, and just doing his or her best—studying diligently and completing the work for each class. Grades do matter, though, and your child should strive to do well. But if your child loves to learn and is committed to working hard, the grades generally follow.

One way your child can help prevent him or herself from falling behind in homework or study is to create a study schedule and to stick with it. If your child hasn't already developed good study habits, freshman year is the time to do so—good study habits will be an essential part of succeeding both at high school and college.

Keep in mind that even now, your child's narrative is being formed. If your child struggles with a particular subject, has a learning disability, or faces some other challenge that affects his or her grades, these circumstances—and how your child worked to overcome them—contribute to your child's unique narrative.

The opposite is also true, however. Your child's academic success and overall narrative will be adversely affected by poor choices—even during freshman year. So while your child's peers are tempted to just get by, your child must be determined to excel. Poor performance during your child's freshman year will adversely impact his or her overall academic rank by the time your child graduates.

Your child should also consider gaining some exposure to entrance exams by reading a test prep book and taking a practice test sometime during the spring of his or her freshman year.

Extracurricular Activities

During your child's freshman year, he or she should continue to explore subjects and activities in order to discover his or her interests, passions, and natural abilities. Your child shouldn't take on activities just to fill empty time or pad his or her résumé. Instead, he or she should pursue what seems interesting.

After considering all of the extracurriculars that are available, your child should get plugged in to those that he or she thinks will be the most enjoyable. Top colleges tend to view consistency and long-term commitment favorably, so your child should try to find a few activities in which he or she can become more deeply involved for three or, better yet, four years. The more activities listed on your child's application with "9-12" as the years of participation, the better.

Freshman year is also the time for your child to start recording what extracurricular activities he or she is involved with along with any accomplishments, awards, or other recognition.

Working toward gaining admission to a top college does not mean your child should have no downtime. Freshman year especially, your child should take time to just have fun, to spend time with family and friends, and to read for enjoyment. Doing these things is as much a part of your child discovering who he or she is as any academic or extracurricular pursuit.

Summer Activities

Winter break is a great time for your child to begin contemplating his or her summer and investigating programs that sound interesting. Your child should try to find a short summer program—two to four weeks long—at a college or summer school. The summer after freshman year is a great time for your child to pursue a subject that interests him or her or perhaps one that he or she didn't have a chance to explore during the school year.

But your child's summer shouldn't be filled with only academics—he or she should take time to relax and enjoy family and friends, to have experiences, and to read.

In fact, reading should be one of your child's foremost pastimes. He or she should read novels, magazines, blogs, news, scientific journals, historical accounts, cultural documents—pretty much anything and everything. By reading a wide array of styles, genres, and authors, your child will gain new insights and perspective, an expanded vocabulary, and better reading comprehension. These factors are all important for strong ACT and SAT reading scores.

Chapter 26:
Sophomore Year

By sophomore year, your child should be starting to develop a clearer idea of what subjects and activities he or she really enjoys and does well at. If not, don't panic—but your child should certainly take some time to seriously consider how to focus his or her time on a handful of strategic activities that tie in to a clear theme that fits his or her unique narrative.

The longer your child waits to begin focusing his or her theme, the more disjointed and watered down his or her admissions profile might be. Beyond that, the closer your child gets to junior year, the more responsibilities pile up—studying for AP courses, maintaining strong grades, preparing for standardized tests, and narrowing down the list of dream colleges. Your child will have a hard time doing all of those things while at the same time exploring various activities and trying to discover where he or she fits.

So, during sophomore year, encourage your child to narrow his or her interests and focus on the activities he or she likes most and is best at.

Academic Planning

At most high schools, the sophomore year is when students are allowed to start taking AP, IB, and other honors courses. If this is the case for your child's high school, your child will want to strongly consider which advanced courses he or she should pursue.

AP and IB courses are challenging and can be stressful, but they are worth it in the long run. Not only will they have an impact on your child's college admissions success, such classes have a way of shaping your child into a stronger, more mature person. They'll stretch your child—not only expanding his or her understanding of the subject matter but forcing him or her to think critically, balance a demanding work load, and cope with stress.

While AP classes and IB programs are not as challenging as courses at top-tier colleges that cover the same material, these courses will give your child a taste of what college is like.

We've already discussed some strategies related to AP and IB courses (see Chapter 11), and so we won't rehash that here. In any case, the more intensive and demanding the course load your child tackles sophomore year, the better.

While the grades your child achieved freshman year are important, grades during sophomore year are even more so. Therefore, your child should work hard and stay on top of homework. If your child is having trouble keeping a particular grade up, he or she should consider talking to the teacher to determine what actions your child might take to do better in class. However, your child should take care not to come across as begging for a better grade—instead, he or she should focus on mastery of the subject matter and demonstrate concern over not meeting his or her own high standard.

Achieving As is important for your child's admissions success, but some Bs won't result in outright rejection. As we discussed in Chapter 11, grades are an important factor in being admitted to a top college, but the key is standing out. If your child has a lower GPA, he or she will have to stand out in other ways—through extracurricular activities, academic pursuits outside the classroom, athletic or intellectual accomplishments, social entrepreneurism, etc.

A demanding course load will leave little time for other activities—which will likely be filled by a handful of extracurricular commitments. But when your child has free time, he or she should try to spend some of it reading. As mentioned in the previous chapter, your child should read a variety of styles and genres.

Standardized Testing

Like the courses your child takes through high school and the grades he or she achieves, the ACT or SAT is an important element of your child's admissions profile. The greater your child's familiarity with these exams before taking them, the better his or her chances of scoring well.

Your child should take the PSAT as a sophomore. Colleges only see SAT scores, and so your child can take the PSAT each time it is offered without penalty. Taking the PSAT will give your child an idea of what score he or she would likely get on the SAT, allowing for informed decisions regarding where your child should focus his or her energy.

In early spring, your child should determine which SAT Subject Tests to take in June and get signed up. Generally, your child should try to plan which SAT Subject Tests to take based on his or her academic course schedule—generally speaking, honors, AP, and IB courses tend to match up well with SAT Subject Tests (see Chapter 12 for more information on SAT Subject Tests). Throughout May, your child will need to spend a little time every day studying for the tests he or she has selected. Your child will want to use strong review materials, such as those from Princeton Review or Barron's Educational Series. The more your child prepares, the better he or she will do.

Your child should also take the ACT and/or SAT as a sophomore. Students are allowed to take the ACT up to 12 times, and so your child will certainly have time to take the test again. There is no limit for the SAT. Furthermore, your child will be able to select his or her best combination score by section to create what's known as a "super score."

Top colleges typically want applicants to send all ACT and SAT scores, however, so your child would do well to limit the number of times he or she takes each test. Too many attempts with little growth can reflect poorly on your child.

Extracurricular Activities

The sophomore year is a good time for your child to assess his or her extracurriculars and determine whether or not to pursue different activities. Sophomore year is an ideal time to make any such changes because it leaves time for three years of commitment.

Summer Activities

Winter break is a good time for your child to begin looking into summer opportunities related to his or her focus. For example, your child might consider studying abroad over the summer, which would give your child the opportunity to focus on an academic subject of interest while at the same time giving him or her international exposure and the opportunity for language immersion.

Alternatively, your child might consider an internship at a business or organization related to his or her field of interest—such as a law firm or local nonprofit. An internship would provide your child with valuable learning, real-world experience, and an expanded network—and it may even open doors to future opportunities.

Your child should also consider finding a job and working through the summer. Not only does this provide some real-world experience, it demonstrates responsibility—something top colleges want to see. Your child should try to find a job that aligns with his or her interests and skills. For example, if your child is interested in animal biology or zoology, he or she might consider working at an animal shelter. If your child is interested in marketing, a local print shop may be a good fit.

Myriad summer opportunities are possible, so encourage your child to pursue something that fits his or her theme and will contribute to your child's narrative.

As your child has the time, he or she should continue to prepare for the ACT and/or SAT. The summer after sophomore year is the best time for your child to take practice tests and invest time in preparing for the these exams, which should each be taken for the first time no later than junior year.

Early in the summer, your child should take some time to look at colleges online. By now, your child may have a fairly good idea of which top colleges appeal to him or her most. If your child is fairly certain about where he or she wants to attend and you have the availability, consider visiting one or more colleges in June and July while the campuses are a bit less busy. See Chapter 31 for more information on college visits.

Chapter 27:
Junior Year

Your child's junior year will be challenging. In addition to the heavy course load necessary for developing a strong academic record, your child will have to prepare for and take college entrance exams and keep up his or her extracurricular commitments. Demonstrating leadership and innovation should also be high priorities during junior year.

And if all that weren't enough, your child may want to visit one or more colleges and might begin working on his or her college applications and essays.

Academic Planning

Academically, your child's junior year is critical—and as such, it will likely be the most challenging. Gaining admission to a top-tier college will require your child to pursue a full complement of AP, IB, and other honors courses.

Grades couldn't be more important, and so your child will need to focus on doing well in every class. But getting As, while vital, shouldn't be an end in itself. Your child needs to be driven to excel—to pursue subjects of interest beyond what is required in the classroom, and even beyond the classroom.

As your child completes academic projects or research papers, he or she should be sure to save that work for potential use in the admissions process. Once your child has narrowed his or her list of colleges, for example, he or she might consider sending a copy of the work to appropriate department heads (see the section "Supplemental Materials" in Chapter 18 for related discussion).

While spring break may seem like the perfect time to do some college visits—and many students do just that—your child should focus instead on preparing for his or her AP exams. The extra time for study will not only help your child perform better on the exams, it will also help prevent any unnecessary stress.

Standardized Testing

While junior year is the year in which your child will be most focused on college entrance exams, if he or she has already taken the PSAT once or twice, one or more SAT Subject Tests, and the ACT, this year will be a lot less stressful—and your child will have more scores to choose from.

Starting in August, your child should focus on preparing for the PSAT, which is taken in October. The PSAT taken during junior year is used by the National Merit Scholarship Program to select approximately 50,000 high school juniors for recognition. About two thirds of the recognized students receive Letters of Commendation, and the top third are National Merit Scholarship Semifinalists. Most of these go on to be finalists. Commended students represent the top 3% of test takers, and semifinalists/finalists represent the top 1%—such recognition would certainly help set your child apart from other applicants.

Your child should definitely plan to take the PSAT during his or her junior year since these scores are not reported to colleges.

In addition to the PSAT in the fall, your child will need to carefully plan out his or her other exam dates.

Your child should take the ACT in October or December and compare that score to his or her latest PSAT score, which is very similar to the SAT. If the equivalent ACT score is significantly higher than the PSAT score and makes your child competitive at top colleges, your child has no need to take the SAT—though he or she should still take two or more SAT Subject tests since these are required by most selective colleges.

If your child is not pleased with his or her current ACT score, he or she should weigh whether to simply retake the ACT or to take the SAT. In either case, your child will have additional opportunities to improve his or her scores.

In the spring, your child should take at least one more SAT Subject Test.

If your child doesn't have high scores on his or her SAT, two or three SAT Subject Tests, and the ACT, he or she will want to retake the appropriate tests in the fall of his or her senior year.

As your child approaches each exam, he or she will need to spend adequate time preparing for these tests since these scores will have tremendous impact on admission to a top college.

Extracurricular Activities

While your child's main focus junior year is certainly maintaining grades and scoring well on tests, he or she must also continue pursuing his or her core interests. Junior year is the time for your child to really let his or her leadership and innovation shine through.

Building on what he or she has done in the previous two years, your child should seek to outdo him or herself. Thinking in literary terms, your child's freshman and sophomore years are all about rising action leading to junior year and the climax of your child's story so far.

Extracurricular Activities Story Arc

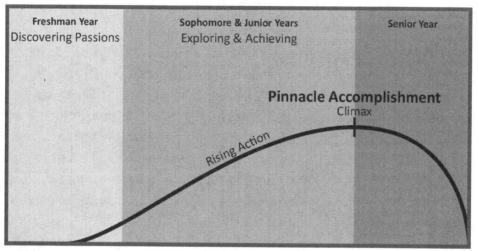

Like any good narrative, your child's story needs to swell to a high point. If possible, that high point should happen around the end of junior year or during the summer before senior year. As a result, junior year is the right time for your child to start and lead an innovative community project, take an idea and develop it into a business, enter a major competition, or engage in some other creative leadership activity. The goal is for your child to build his or her narrative toward a pinnacle accomplishment.

At this point in high school, many students are tempted to add new extracurriculars to their lists of activities due to a perception that they haven't done enough or aren't well rounded. This is just résumé stuffing, and admissions officers at top colleges won't likely be impressed.

Remember, your child does not need to be well rounded. The key is being strategically focused.

If your child is pursuing certain subjects, like math, science, and engineering, he or she may feel pressure to win awards to demonstrate excellence in his or her field of study. If he or she hasn't achieved any major science fair victories or earned other recognition, that's okay. Your child should try to set him or herself apart in a different way.

An alternative strategy would be for your child to combine his or her interest with a community outreach project or entrepreneurial pursuit. Your child can use his or her inside knowledge of a field to make a meaningful contribution outside of the competition environment. For example, your child could spearhead a project to inspire elementary and middle school children to explore STEM, organize a local event, or use his or her skills to help solve some problem in a local community (see Chapters 14–16 for more about extracurriculars, social entrepreneurism, and volunteering).

Summer Activities

Like the summer before junior year, the summer that follows is full of possibilities—the only difference is that the summer after junior year is even more important.

This summer, your child should strongly consider pursuing an excellent academic program in the U.S. or abroad that fits his or her narrative. But he or she need not focus on academics. Instead, your child might finish a major writing, art, research, or community outreach project started earlier in the year. The primary goal is to do something meaningful and interesting that tightly fits your child's theme and augments his or her narrative in a significant way.

Depending on how your child chooses to spend his or her summer, a part-time job or short-term internship may also be worth considering.

College Visits & Applications

Sometime in the spring, you'll want to work with your child to develop a list of potential college choices and discuss finances, including the potential need for scholarships and grants. Once you've created a list of schools, you and your child should meet with your child's counselor to talk about his or her top choices. (See Chapter 30 for more about creating an initial college list.)

Generally, your child should wait to do any college visits until summer—this gives your child time to develop his or her list of potential colleges and helps prevent your child from missing class and getting behind in homework.

Spring of junior year is also a good time for your child to ask for teacher recommendations. Your child should ask for recommendations from two of his or her favorite teachers and should give them his or her résumé—with key points highlighted—to provide some extra context and content for drafting their letters. Your child can't assume his or her favorite teachers know everything about his or her life and accomplishments. (See Chapter 9 for more about how to get great recommendations.)

As I mentioned in the last chapter, June and July are the best months for your child to do any college visits. Your child should take the tours, attend the information sessions, ask questions, and talk to students. While visiting, your child should also take time stop by each school's admissions office and get on the mailing list. (See Chapter 31 for more on college visits.)

At the colleges your child is most interested in, try to schedule on-campus interviews to coincide with your June or July visits. The alternative is trying to work in an interview during August or during the fall semester, which could mean missing classes.

After your child's college visits and interviews, he or she will need to narrow the list of potential colleges (see Chapter 32), request applications from each of the remaining candidates, and send each his or her exam scores.

If your child has determined which college is his or her first choice, he or she should strongly consider applying early decision. We'll discuss that option in greater detail in Chapter 33.

The summer after junior year is an ideal time for your child to begin drafting college essays. The earlier your child starts on these essays, the more time he or she will have for review and revision, which is necessary for creating compelling essays that effectively tie every element of your child's profile together. Your child should aim to have his or her personal essay and additional information section of the application completed in August. Your child should also try to have a handful of supplementary essays completed (based on his or her list of colleges) before the fall semester begins.

In addition to these written components, your child should take the time to complete the common application and the applications to three or more top college choices before school starts.

This may seem like a lot of work. It is. But as your child enters his or her senior year, all the work will have been worth it. With so much of the application process completed or underway, your child will be able to focus on high academic performance and an amazing last year of high school filled with great experiences.

Chapter 28:
Senior Year

Your child's senior year will be one of his or her busiest—but also one of the most exciting and rewarding.

By following the guidance in the previous three chapters, your child will be able to enjoy a much less stressful senior year since your child will have already done many of the things most students wait to do. For your child, senior year can be an amazing, memorable experience marked by relative calm and a growing excitement for college instead of panic and stress.

The biggest responsibilities facing your child this year include keeping grades up and submitting his or her applications. Then, after waiting patiently, your child will receive responses from colleges. If your child is accepted through early decision, the choice is already made. But if he or she receives multiple regular decision acceptance letters, deciding which college to attend is, perhaps, the most significant choice of his or her life thus far.

So, what are the last steps your child must take on the way to those acceptance letters?

Academic Planning

As your child selects courses for senior year, he or she should strive to make it as demanding as possible. To gain admission to top colleges, your child will need to take a number of specific AP courses or their equivalents: English, a foreign language, history (e.g., United States History, World History, etc.), math, and science. Your child has likely taken some of these classes already, but if not, he or she must take them this year.

Regarding AP math, your child should take at least AP Calculus AB since for many top colleges, AP Calculus is a must. If, however, your child is going into a field that requires advanced math (e.g., computer science, engineering, aeronautics, etc.), he or she should actually take AP Calculus BC.

Colleges will definitely consider your child's grades senior year, so now is not the time for your child to take it easy. Getting solid grades senior year will demonstrate to colleges that your child cares about his or her high school success and is determined to finish well.

Even if your child has been accepted through early decision, grades matter—a top college might rescind your child's admission if his or her grades decline. If, on the other hand, your child did not gain early acceptance, he or she needs to keep focused on maintaining good grades for the sake of his or her regular decision applications.

Standardized Testing

If your child is particularly unhappy with one or more standardized test scores, fall of senior year is his or her last chance to push the score higher. Taking the ACT, SAT, or SAT Subject Tests senior year is generally inadvisable, but if your child spent considerable time preparing over the summer with the goal of improving a score, he or she should take the opportunity to do so.

Extracurricular Activities

If your child has not already focused on making one of his or her extracurricular pursuits stand out through some pinnacle accomplishment (which we discussed in the previous chapter), he or she should do so early in senior year. The first few months of senior year represent a final opportunity for your child to complete a project or achieve some major goal and include the accomplishment on his or her application. Once your child applies, however, he or she may still send admissions officers updates regarding any new, significant accomplishments.

Your child may be tempted to drop extracurricular activities during senior year after achieving a prestigious award, accomplishing an important goal, or even just submitting his or her application. For the same basic reasons your child needs to keep his or her grades up during senior year, he or she should be careful about dropping activities. Doing so may make it look like the only reason he or she participated in an extracurricular activity was to pad his or her résumé. Your child needs to maintain active leadership involvement in his or her extracurricular activities throughout senior year.

If your child is planning to play sports at a Division I or Division II school, he or she will need to register with the NCAA. While there is no deadline, your child should consider registering in the fall.

College Applications

Before finalizing and submitting applications, your child should consider one more visit to his or her high school guidance counselor. During this meeting, your child should walk through his or her personal essay and some supplemental essays as well as discuss his or her list of colleges.

Your child will also want to talk to his or her counselor about any early decision or early action applications and get feedback on whether applying early makes sense given his or her specific circumstances.

In addition to talking with his or her counselor, your child should politely inquire about the recommendations he or she requested from two favorite teachers at the end of last school year. Teachers are often inundated with such requests, and so it is important to be patient, not pushy. But a friendly reminder may be an important step in ensuring the recommendations are sent on time—particularly for any early decision applications.

If the colleges your child is applying to consider additional recommendations, your child should consider seeking a supplementary recommendation from someone who has had the opportunity to get to know your child from a different perspective than his or her teachers and counselor. In rare cases, this may be another teacher, but more likely it will be someone from your child's extracurricular pursuits, someone your child interned under, or an employer. Supplemental letters of recommendation should be sent to any school that indicates it will consider additional recommendations in the admission process.

For colleges that accept additional recommendations, admissions officers generally appreciate those recommendations that offer different insights into who the applicant is and what he or she has accomplished. The fact that another person is willing to recommend your child may, in itself, demonstrate the value your child would bring to college, but the stronger the connection and the higher the praise, the more value the recommendation has.

Before submitting any applications, your child should note any special circumstances regarding his or her education. Anything out of the ordinary, like homeschooling or homebound instruction, online education, part time attendance at a performing arts conservatory, etc., should be mentioned. Your child could send this information directly to the admissions officers of the colleges to which he or she is applying, or your child could provide this information in his or her résumé.

If your child will be applying through early decision or early action, he or she will need to complete any final elements of these applications and be sure to send them before the deadline, which is typically in early to mid November.

For regular decision applications, your child has a little more time to finish writing and reviewing any remaining supplemental essays.

As your child enters December, he or she needs to be focused on finishing all of the elements of each application to ensure everything is in order and ready to submit. If possible, your child should tie up any loose ends early in the month, take some time to proofread each element, and submit the applications before January 1—preferably submitting all applications one or more days ahead of the deadline.

If at any point after submitting an application your child has a significant update, he or she should not hesitate to send an email or letter to each admissions office to keep the colleges informed. Your child should use these correspondences to demonstrate sustained interest in the school and how he or she will add even more value based on the newly provided information.

Your child should take care, however, not to needlessly or flippantly send updates—doing so only if something significant has changed (e.g., winning an award, starting or finishing a major project, etc.). If a college is your child's first choice, he or she might mention that as well—but only if it is true—and that if accepted, he or she will attend.

College Decision

If your child is admitted through an early decision application, congratulations! His or her college decision has already been made, he or she has been admitted, and your child should now notify the other schools to which he or she applied of the decision.

If your child is not accepted via early decision but is offered admission through early action, again, congratulations! Your child may still have decisions to make, but he or she has at least one viable option. At this point, your child should contact his or her safety colleges and let them know of the early admission offer.

Apart from being admitted through early decision, your child will have to be patient and wait until late spring to hear back from colleges. With one or more acceptance letters in hand, your child can take a deep breath. Congratulations!

Now for the last consequential decision of your child's high school career—which admissions offer to accept. To aid in his or her decision, your child should attend accepted student overnight and weekend events. Your child should enjoy these activities but must remember that colleges may rescind his or her admission if he or she engages in inappropriate behavior or if his or her grades slip.

While enjoying accepted student events, your child should take the opportunity to talk to students on campus and learn more about the campus culture, professors, programs, clubs, and services offered by the school.

You should take time to talk to your child about his or her admissions success—congratulating him or her but also being realistic. Talk about which school your child would prefer to attend and then discuss finances and financial aid offers. Sometimes financial aid offers can be negotiated based on the other packages your child has been offered, so don't be afraid to call the financial aid office of your child's top choice to see if they can improve their offer (see Chapter 34).

The last thing your child will need to do is submit his or her decision by the May 1 deadline. And again, congratulations!

The Waitlist

If your child is placed on the waitlist of one or more colleges, your child should indicate to the admissions office whether he or she wishes to remain on the waitlist. If so, your child should schedule a meeting with his or her guidance counselor to discuss the situation. Your child's counselor may be able to find out more information from the college, perhaps even learning what his or her chances of admission from the waitlist are, which would help inform your child's decision making.

While discussing the situation with his or her counselor, your child should also ask about what he or she might do to improve his or her chances. Your child may be able to submit some additional material or notify the admissions office of some accomplishment that might help make admission from the waitlist more likely.

At some point, however, your child will have to consider whether to remain on the waitlist or enroll at one of the colleges that accepted his or her application.

Chapter 29:
Summer Before College

Once your child has been accepted into a top college and graduated high school, much of the hard work and challenge leading up to his or her college education is over. But that doesn't mean he or she should coast through the summer before college. Instead, your child should make the most of his or her summer by spending extra time with family and friends, refining any underdeveloped skills, preparing his or her résumé for internships and jobs, and beginning the transition to college life.

Spend Extra Time with Family & Friends

Especially if your child will be attending college far from home, the summer before he or she leaves is a great time to focus on family. Make it a priority to spend quality time together at local events or go on a special family vacation. Also, the summer before freshman year in college is likely one of your child's last opportunities to really spend time with high school friends, and so he or she should take whatever opportunities are available to enjoy time with his or her peers.

Refine Underdeveloped Skills

While your child might take the opportunity over the summer to catch up on some leisure reading, he or she should also take time to consider his or her weaknesses and take steps to hone some skills. If your child struggles with time management, he or she might read or listen to a few books on how to better manage his or her time. Your child might participate in a writing workshop, work through online tutorials for Microsoft Office (e.g., Word, PowerPoint, Excel), read a book on money management, or take an online course covering research methods and tools.

Prepare a Résumé for Internships & Jobs

If your child has not yet created a résumé, summer before freshman year is the time to do so. A résumé is not a static document—it should change as your child develops new skills, greater work experience, and higher levels of education. This means that if your child created a résumé for the admissions process, at the very least it needs to be updated to show he or she has graduated and is enrolled in college.

As your child develops or refines his or her résumé, he or she should focus on his or her successes and accomplishments, using numbers to demonstrate impact. Your child should also try to highlight his or her skills throughout the résumé, not just in a succinct list. For example, if your child helped make marketing materials for a nonprofit during an internship, instead of saying, "Created marketing materials," he or she might say, "Designed PowerPoint pitch presentation and two-page brochure in Adobe InDesign." Using specific details within his or her experience shows not only that your child has certain skills, but that he or she has applied these skills in a real-world setting to accomplish something.

Your child should also highlight any public service, community projects, or nonprofits he or she has been involved with. Again, the focus should be on impact and measurable results.

As your child prepares to use this résumé for internship and job applications, he or she should take time to go back over it and custom tailor it for each specific role.

Transition toward College Life

Obviously, the summer before college is a time of transition for your child. He or she is going to have increased freedom as well as increased responsibility. Summer is a good time for your child to tie up loose ends and prepare for new responsibilities.

For example, your child might take time throughout the summer to organize his or her room, update his or her wardrobe, and detail his or her car (getting any necessary maintenance done, as well). Your child should also check to ensure his or her bank account is easily accessible at college—local and regional banks may not have a branch near the school, and if that is the case, your child should consider setting up an account at a national bank with branches at home and at school.

If your child is employed, he or she will want to have a conversation with his or her employer to schedule your child's last day of work. Not only is it polite to give plenty of notice, but leaving on a positive note is important because employers can make excellent references.

Summer is also a great time for your child to research community organizations he or she is interested in, both on and off campus. For example, your child might want to look for a place to volunteer on weekends, a student organization in which to participate, or a place to worship.

Additionally, your child may need to shop for clothing and accessories (particularly with presentations and interviews in mind), a college planner, a laptop, dorm-room or apartment furnishings, etc. Your child might also consider packing everything he or she won't need until arriving on campus in advance to reduce the stresses of leaving for school.

As your child prepares to depart for college, you should discuss expectations about communication, holidays, finances, grades, etc. The more you discuss and the better you understand one another, the less potential for unnecessary tension.

Enjoy Summer Responsibly

Just as most colleges can rescind your child's acceptance for poor academic performance before high school graduation, colleges can rescind acceptance based on behavior. Your child should be careful about what he or she posts online—even posting memes as jokes or commenting on friends' posts can result in a college revoking your child's admissions offer if they deem the content inappropriate. And getting arrested, depending on the charges, can result in a rescind letter as well.

Your child should have fun and enjoy his or her summer, but that doesn't mean behaving irresponsibly.

Section Seven:

Strategy

Chapter 30:
Selecting Potential Colleges

During your child's junior year, he or she should begin the process of creating a list of colleges he or she might apply to. The goal of this initial list is to narrow your child's options to one to two dozen choices. This list will later be narrowed even further to somewhere around 10 to 12 colleges (see Chapter 32).

Your child will need to have a diverse and balanced list of options that match his or her personality, preferences, interests, strengths, and goals. The list will need to include schools that vary in their selectivity—from statistical reaches to safety schools—and that range in cost.

Developing such a list may seem like a daunting task, but as your child considers his or her own personality, interests, social needs, academics, and goals, creating a list of suitable matches won't be as difficult as it may seem.

Your Child's Profile

Before your child determines whether a particular college is a good fit, he or she should engage in some introspection to determine what exactly a good fit might look like. This doesn't mean your child needs to know everything about him or herself, or that he or she has to have everything figured out. Self-discovery is a lifelong process, but your child should reflect on what currently makes him or her tick.

The more your child knows about him or herself, the better equipped he or she will be to ask relevant questions about a college and find pertinent answers.

Practically speaking, this means your child should strive to know what he or she wants to accomplish in college and, generally, how to accomplish it. In so doing, your child will be able to rule out colleges that don't align with his or her goals. For example, if your child wants to pursue computer science, schools with fewer computer science courses will be less appealing than those with strong computer science programs.

By comparing his or her priorities against what colleges offer, your child will be able to quickly spot colleges that don't fit as well as those that do.

So, as your child considers his or her personality, interests, community, academics, and goals, he or she should try to identify any personal priorities along the way. Your child should consider what he or she must have in a college—his or her highest priorities. If a college doesn't fit your child's must-have priorities, it is not an option. But your child should also consider any lesser priorities—programs or features he or she would appreciate having but could live without.

Values, Interests, & Preferences

Your child's unique way of looking at and interacting with the world and other people is an important consideration when selecting a college. Will your child thrive in larger or smaller class sizes? Does your child like to get away for an hour or two to walk somewhere quiet and peaceful, or would he or she prefer to be in a crowded café?

Your child should try to identify any important priorities related to his or her lifestyle and find colleges that fit those preferences. The same is true of his or her interests. Your child should jot down a list of the activities he or she enjoys and would like to pursue in college.

Your child should weigh his or her values, interests, and needs against the college's core identity and set of priorities. For instance, if your child is politically conservative, he or she might think about whether a college is known for being conservative, liberal, or somewhere in between. If your child is intent on championing a particular social issue or has a fairly unique interest, such as competing in robotics challenges or participating in renaissance faires, he or she might consider whether the college has any related student-led organizations.

Your child should also consider his or her physical, emotional, and spiritual needs and whether the college or surrounding community will be able to meet those needs.

Community

Every college community is different, but so is every student's concept of an ideal community. Your child will need to determine how much weight to place on a college's proximity to family and friends. Your child might also consider his or her social interactions in and out of high school and assess what opportunities to interact with others he or she would like to have at college.

Academics

One of the primary concerns for where your child goes to college is whether or not the school has a program that fits his or her academic interests. Your child should clearly list the academic subjects he or she wishes to focus on in college.

Goals

Your child should consider his or her goals for college—and for his or her career after graduation. What does your child want to learn and experience? What does he or she hope to gain from attending a top-tier school?

There's nothing wrong with dreaming, even if the plan changes somewhere along the way. But your child should try to think in general rather than specific terms—identify priorities. For example, instead of trying to determine exactly what kind of business he or she will pursue after graduating, your child should acknowledge that studying business is a top priority because he or she wants to eventually found and run a company.

School Profiles

Before your child can assess which schools align with his or her priorities, he or she will need to gather some basic information about the schools.

Location

Where the college is located has a substantial impact on the character of the college. A college's location will determine the surrounding geography, the climate, the area demographics, and the local amenities.

Not only does location affect the character of the college itself, but it also defines the college's proximity to home.

As your child considers the location of a college, he or she should try to identify any personal priorities. Perhaps your child will want to stay closer to home. Or maybe cold, snowy winters sound unappealing. Your child may prioritize the amenities offered by a larger city—museums, theaters, major retail outlets, and all the services he or she may need while away. On the other hand, your child might want a quieter environment with plenty of nearby places to get away from all the noise.

Funding: Public or Private

The character of a school is greatly affected by how it is funded. State funded colleges and universities tend to have lower tuition costs and much larger enrollment. On the other hand, private colleges tend to enroll fewer students, and while tuition may be higher, they tend to offer more financial aid. The number of programs offered by a college will also be affected by whether it is public or private—as will the nature of those programs.

Your child should be less concerned about whether the school is public or private and more interested in what that means for the education experience at the college. Does your child want smaller or larger class sizes? More programs and larger classes may, for instance, mean less access to professors. Does that matter to your child?

Cost

Cost may not be an issue for your family, but if it is, you will need to discuss how much a school's cost will affect your child's chances of attending.

As mentioned above, cost is largely a function of whether a school is public or private—but every school is different, and the financial aid opportunities at each school will be unique to each student. For example, a public college that offers in-state tuition may be much more accessible than a public college in another state.

The cost of a school will also be affected by your child's grades, test scores, accomplishments, and other factors that may result in a larger financial aid package from the school, scholarships, or grants.

For now, your child should simply note what a college's tuition and financial aid options are to ensure cost remains part of the equation.

Size

Like cost, size is largely a function of whether a school is public or private. Many of the top colleges have total undergraduate enrollment of around four to six thousand, while some have tens of thousands of students.

The size of a college influences just about every aspect of the institution. Larger and smaller schools each have their strengths and weaknesses—so a college's size isn't so much about being better or worse as it is about preference.

For instance, larger schools tend to have more majors, higher athletics rankings, and a broader range of opportunities. Smaller schools, however, tend to have a stronger sense of community, smaller class sizes, and more accessible professors.

History

Each school has a unique history that has profound influence on its nature and character. Perhaps this is most obvious in historically black or women's colleges. But beyond the obvious, each school has strengths and weaknesses, quirks, traditions—all of which relate to the history, development, and track record of the college.

If your child plays a particular sport, for example, he or she may prioritize the historic strength of that sport at a college. Or, perhaps, your child might prioritize colleges that have historically strong participation in fraternities and sororities.

Your child should ask, What is the college best known for? What is its longtime strength? What's its best team?

Culture & Diversity

A campus's culture is largely a function of its composition—the character of the staff and students, their backgrounds, interests, and lifestyles. As a result, the demographics of a college strongly influence its culture.

For example, a school with a large subset of international students changes the flavor of that campus—and, by virtue of the different backgrounds and perspectives of these students, a different learning experience for everyone.

A school's diversity—in terms of gender, ethnicity and race, religion, politics, socioeconomic status, age, etc.—are all factors for your child to consider.

The culture of a college is also influenced by what organizations and groups are active on campus. Fraternities and sororities, clubs, political groups, social activism groups, etc., all contribute to a school's unique culture.

Academics

The education a college offers is likely one of the most significant factors in deciding which colleges are good fits for your child and which are not. When considering a school's academics, your child should certainly look at the majors, minors, concentrations, and courses the school offers. Does the college match your child's academic interests and goals?

In addition to these details, your child ought to consider the big picture. Can students easily transfer from one of the university's colleges to another? Does the school employ an open curriculum or are there certain core course requirements? How are classes structured and taught?

Your child should also look for any unique educational opportunities or partnerships the school may have with other U.S. schools, foreign universities, or any local businesses or organizations. Such programs could greatly enrich your child's education and offer unique opportunities that will set him or her apart when he or she starts looking for a job after graduating.

Extracurricular Activities

All through high school, your child has developed a focused interest and deep commitment to a handful of activities—many of which he or she may want to continue to pursue in college. Your child will want to assess what extracurricular activities, volunteer opportunities, clubs, etc., are available on campus.

Your child might also want to look beyond the campus for local service organizations and places to worship. He or she should also consider what recreational and entertainment opportunities exist.

Although your child may not have a lot of spare time, knowing what he or she can fill that time with may be important.

Athletics

Athletics is an area of particular interest for many students. Your child should consider what priority he or she places on college athletics. Does the school's NCAA division matter? Is a particular sport important? What priority does your child place on the availability of intramural sports opportunities?

Listing Possible Choices

By engaging in self-reflection and considering what colleges have to offer, your child will have likely begun to develop a strong sense of what he or she values most. These priorities will guide the process of creating a list of schools.

You'll want to work with your child to develop criteria that a college must meet in order to make it onto his or her list. These criteria should be based on the priorities your child has identified through self-reflection and by researching various colleges. For example, your child might determine that for a college to make it onto the list, it must have a specific major.

So, consider your child's priorities to develop criteria, then use these criteria and your child's academic record to develop a list of colleges that match your child's priorities. The list should include a range of colleges from safety schools to reach schools and will likely represent various price points. The key is to create a balanced list of colleges, any of which your child would be excited to attend.

Target Number

How many schools should your child add to his or her initial list? There is no specific number, but at this point, more is better. Later, after your child has had a chance to visit some schools and finalize test scores, he or she will need to refine this list.

This list should include several safety schools—colleges to which your child should have little difficulty gaining admissions based on his or her academic performance and test scores—as well as a number of target schools and some reach schools. For this rough draft, your child should aim to have about two dozen colleges listed, and it should include only schools your child thinks he or she would like to attend. Having so many options on the initial list leaves room to eliminate colleges once your child is ready to refine the list (see Chapter 32).

Cost

If cost is an issue, be careful not to exclude a college based on tuition without also considering potential financial aid.

Honestly assess what you and your family can contribute to your child's education expenses and make sure you discuss this important financial information with your child. What you can afford should be clear before your child sends out any applications—and it would be wise to talk about it before your child even develops a list of potential college choices.

When considering finances for college, you'll need to keep in mind not only your anticipated income, but also the scholarships and grants your child may be eligible to receive. These opportunities vary from college to college, and some of the most selective colleges have the most generous aid opportunities. At this point, your child should include schools of varying costs and with varying opportunities for financial aid (for more discussion of financial aid, see Chapter 34). Also, you should discuss with your child whether loans are an option and might consider applying for local, regional, or national scholarships.

Selectivity

As mentioned earlier, your child needs to consider selectivity when developing a list of colleges. For this initial list, this means selecting a handful of safety schools, several target schools, and some reaches.

These terms will mean different things for different students. One student's target school might be another's reach—it all depends on the strength of one's profile. As a result, your child should strive to develop the strongest profile possible so his or her list of options is filled with top-tier colleges.

That said, your child will want to include some safe options in his or her list. Simply put, a safety school is one that your child is likely to gain admission to because his or her academic record is above the average range for incoming freshman. Safety schools help keep your child's college options open if he or she does not gain admission to a more selective institution.

That doesn't mean these colleges should be weak choices—in fact, they should be school's your child wouldn't mind attending barring any better choices. So, safety schools should still fit your child's priorities and meet his or her criteria.

In addition to a handful of safety schools, your child needs a strong list of target colleges. These are schools whose admission statistics match your child fairly well. If, for instance, your child's GPA and test scores fall squarely within the GPA and test score range for a school's first-year admits, this is a target school for your child. Your child's initial list should include several target schools.

Reach schools are those to which your child has a lower statistical likelihood of being admitted. This may have little to do with your child's level of academic success—many of the most selective colleges reject a large number of applicants with perfect SAT scores. The primary issue is that these schools only accept a couple thousand students but receive five to 10 times the number of applications.

To determine whether a school is a reach for your child, start by taking the acceptance rate of the college and comparing it to where your child would rank in the average applicant pool. For example, University of Pennsylvania admits about 9% of applicants. If your child is not within the top 9% of all applicants, this school would be classified as a reach. (See Appendix II for admissions statistics.)

The problem with statistics is they tend to give only a partial picture. Top-tier colleges generally admit every really stand-out student who applies. That's why your child must differentiate him or herself—doing so brings statistical reaches much closer to your child's grasp.

After adding a few reach schools to the list, your child should have something to work with as he or she conducts additional research and plans visits.

Chapter 31:
Visiting Colleges

Before finalizing any decisions regarding which top college best fits your child's personality, interests, and goals, he or she should consider visiting the college to get a better sense of what the college is actually like. By touring the campus, seeing the classrooms, visiting the libraries, and meeting students and faculty, your child will not only get a feel for what he or she likes and doesn't like in a particular college, but also what he or she wants and doesn't want in any college.

While a number of resources can help your child get acquainted with a school—such as virtual tours, blogs, and even conversations with alumni—nothing can adequately substitute for an on-campus visit.

In this chapter, we'll discuss some important considerations for planning college visits and then examine strategies for making the most of your child's time on campus.

Planning a College Visit

One of the keys to planning successful college visits is starting early. As mentioned briefly in Chapter 27, your child should probably wait until early summer after junior year to do any official college visits—but that doesn't mean your child can't begin planning visits to colleges to which he or she is likely to apply. Generally, this means planning for visits sometime during spring of junior year.

Earlier than that, however, your child could still consider taking advantage of any opportunities to visit college campuses while in the area on vacations or while attending sporting or fine arts events. Even if your child doesn't have much time to explore the campus, he or she should at least take a few moments to visit the admissions office for information.

If your child decides he or she wants to visit a college during the spring, he or she should check his or her high school policy regarding time off for college visits.

When planning college visits, you and your child will need to discuss a number of factors, including how much time you have, the distances you're willing to travel, and how much you are willing to spend. Since one of the main purposes of visiting college campuses is to help your child refine his or her preliminary college list, your child should visit as many of his or her top safety, target, and reach schools as possible. But he or she does not need to visit every college on the initial list. In fact, carefully choosing which colleges to visit should provide enough information for your child to refine his or her list down to 10–12 choices.

Get to Know the School

While visiting college campuses may be exciting and enjoyable for your child, the main goal of the visit is getting to know the school well enough to make an informed choice about that school. And in getting to know one school, your child will develop insight into colleges in general that will likely help your child refine his or her initial list of schools.

So, one of the primary tasks for your child during a campus visit is to be engaged and pay attention. Getting to know the school requires open eyes and a bit of curiosity. Your child should take in the campus, watch students and faculty, and try to get a feel for the overall culture and atmosphere of the college.

Attend the Information Session & Take the Tour

Your child should take advantage of any opportunities provided by the school to get to know the college better, which primarily take the form of information sessions and tours. Your child should also ask question, talking to an admissions officer, tour guide, students, and even faculty as opportunities presents themselves.

Each college will have different policies regarding admission information sessions and tours—some will require reservations while others will not. Reservation requirements for tours may also depend on group size. If your child needs a reservation for an admission information session or tour but is unable to make one for the time he or she will be on campus, your child should check to see if the college has a self-guided tour option and be sure to visit the admissions office for information.

As opportunities arise, your child should be sure to ask admissions officers any questions he or she may have about the application process, college mission and goals, and campus life. Your child should try to avoid asking questions that are easily researched online. Instead, your child might ask questions about what the admissions officer looks for in applications and essays, how applicants' financial aid requirements affect admissions decisions, the kind of students that seem to thrive on campus, what changes are taking place at the school, the unique opportunities available to students of the college, etc.

During tours, your child should feel free to ask questions of the tour guide. Typically, campus tours are led by current students, and so this gives your child an opportunity to get some unique insights into student life and campus culture. Tour guides are typically honest and relatively transparent with visitors—but they are also expected to portray the college in a positive light, which your child should keep in mind.
Just because a student is a tour guide, however, does not mean the student knows everything. If your child has a specific question about the

college, he or she should ask; the tour guide may or may not know the answer. Some of the best questions your child can ask the tour guide are those that shed light on what it's like to be a student at the college. Your child should ask questions about why the tour guide chose to enroll at the college, what he or she enjoys most about the school, what surprised him or her, and other questions about life on campus.

During the tour, your child should be considerate of other visitors and allow them to ask their questions, too.

Spend Unscheduled Time Exploring Campus

In addition to attending the information session and taking the tour, your child should take time to explore the campus on his or her own. Your child might scan some bulletin boards to get a sense of upcoming activities, watch how students interact with one another and with faculty members, and ask any questions he or she might have along the way.

Your child doesn't necessarily have to talk at length with any one student—he or she can just ask a single question. If that question leads to more conversation, that's great. Your child should simply introduce him or herself as a visitor and ask if the student would be willing to answer a question. Then, your child should ask a question about the student's experience—why he or she chose to attend this particular college, what he or she is studying, where he or she studies, what social life is like on campus, what he or she likes and doesn't like about campus, etc.

This is your child's opportunity to get a glimpse of what life is like at this particular school from the perspective of a current student. Unlike with the tour guide, who is supposed to keep things positive, a candid conversation with a random student will provide a more balanced view of the school.

Visit Top Choices a Second Time, If Possible

If your child is planning to apply to a college through an early decision program, he or she should try to make a second visit to the college sometime during fall of senior year—prior to applying. If possible, your child should spend the night at the school, ask a lot of questions, and be sure to visit some classes. Since early decisions are binding, your child should be fairly certain that the college is his or her first choice. If your child is accepted under early decision, he or she may want to visit one more time during spring of senior year to further familiarize him or herself with campus and best prepare for returning in the fall as a student.

If not accepted through an early decision program, your child should wait for regular decision acceptance letters and then consider visiting the colleges to which he or she is most likely to enroll. Many of the colleges have admissions events for admitted students, and these would be good opportunities for your child to make the second visit. Visiting again allows your child to more carefully consider what each college has to offer, compare them, and make a more informed decision.

Nearly a year will have passed from the time your child initially visits a school and when he or she receives acceptance letters, and in that time, your child will have grown and matured and may have even changed in significant ways. A second visit helps give your child additional confidence about his or her choice.

Document the Visit

Whenever your child visits a college campus, he or she should carefully process all he or she learns. While visiting, your child will take in a lot of information and form several impressions. Without documenting what he or she learns, your child is likely to get schools confused when thinking back on visits—especially if he or she did several visits over a short span of time.

Immediately following a visit, your child should try to write down things he or she liked and didn't like about the school, what stood out, and any other thoughts about the experience. The more specific the notes, the more useful they will be in the future. Remember, nearly a year will pass between campus visits and acceptance letters. Your child will want detailed notes.

As a parent, you are likely to be eager to find out what your child thought of a school. Be careful not to overwhelm your child or overstep. Keep conversations casual and follow your child's lead as he or she processes each visit. Use these conversations as opportunities to help your child work through his or her experience at each college, offering feedback and suggestions along the way.

When you have the chance, make your own notes based on your observations—not necessarily of the school itself, but of your child's reaction to the school. Then, when your child is making decisions about which colleges to remove from his or her list, you can offer meaningful insights about how your child reacted to a college.

Remember that the purpose of these visits is for your child to familiarize him or herself with the schools he or she is considering and then using what your child learns to refine the list. The more you and your child document along the way, the easier it will be to make decisions about which schools to keep on the list and which to remove.

Beyond taking notes, making lists, and otherwise writing about the visit, your child should take pictures of whatever stands out. Your child should start with a picture that includes the name of the school so he or she can distinguish where one visit ends and the next begins.

Also, your child should consider keeping a folder for each school, using it to compile all of the documents he or she receives while on campus— maps, itineraries, admissions information, business cards, and any other handouts.

While your child should document each visit the same day, he or she should wait until the visit is over. Your child should spend his or her time on campus observing and interacting, not distracted with writing down everything he or she sees. Just because the purpose of the visit is to get information doesn't mean the visit can't be enjoyed.

Chapter 32:
Refining the List

Once your child has visited all the schools he or she is able to visit and has conducted further research on each of the colleges on his or her list, he or she needs to take time to refine the preliminary list of colleges, narrowing the selections down to about 10 to 12 colleges. This refined list represents the colleges to which your child intends to apply.

In this chapter, we'll discuss how to go from a preliminary list of approximately two dozen colleges to a list of about 10–12. Your child will do this by reviewing his or her initial list and marking those that should obviously remain or be removed. Then, your child will need to balance the list for selectivity and cost, ultimately arriving at a list of no fewer than about six colleges, but no more than about 12.

Review the Initial List

Applying to too many schools with too little research can make the selection process so much more difficult if admitted to a large number of colleges. So, by doing some initial research and creating a preliminary list (see Chapter 30), your child will have already made this refining process much easier.

Now that your child has visited some colleges and conducted additional research, he or she may be able to make some easy changes to the preliminary list of schools. Your child should take time to consider the colleges he or she visited—it may now be obvious that some of these schools are great fits and should remain on the list. Likewise, your child may have discovered that some of the schools really aren't for him or her and can remove them from the list.

Also, since developing the initial list of schools, your child may have changed his or her mind about what major to pursue. If your child is adamant about a particular major and a college on the list has nothing like it, he or she should remove that college from the list.

Your child should also consider his or her motives for having certain colleges on the list. If he or she added colleges strictly because someone else wanted him or her to do so and your child has no real interest in attending, he or she should remove the college from the list. Also, your child may have placed a college on the list with the sole intention of seeing whether he or she is accepted. This is often called "trophy hunting," and if that's all your child is doing, he or she should remove the college from the list.

As your child reviews his or her initial list, he or she should cut the list down to about 12 schools, but shouldn't cut it down past six. If your child cuts too many, he or she will need to add the best of those he or she cut back onto the list.

After your child conducts this review of his or her preliminary list, he or she should double check the list by asking two simple questions: Am I genuinely interested in this college? If so, why? If your child cannot provide a good answer for why a college is still on his or her list, it should be removed. This doesn't mean your child has to know precisely what he or she wants in a college, but it does mean he or she should be able to articulate what he or she likes about a specific school.

For example, your child may be drawn to the state-of-the-art research facilities at a particular college, or to a school's charm and atmosphere, or to the unique programs and opportunities available at a specific school. As long as your child can say why he or she really likes a given college, it should remain on the list. If your child can't explain what draws him or her to a school, it should be crossed off.

275

Factor in Selectivity

While refining his or her list, your child should keep a balance of safety, target, and reach schools. The fewer schools on the list, the more the list needs to be weighted toward safety and target schools. The larger the list, the more reach schools he or she can afford to pursue. Generally speaking, this means keeping at least three safety schools and three target schools on the list, adding no more than one or two of each as well as two or three reach schools. So, as your child makes cuts to the list, he or she should take a balanced approach, cutting some of each level of selectivity—not a bottom up approach that removes mostly safety and target schools.

If your child has a great list of safety and target schools, he or she should definitely include some reach schools on his or her list. Adding reach schools is not risky as long as your child's list includes schools to which he or she is almost certain to gain admission. As long as that's the case, including dream schools is not only safe to do, but a good idea. Your child will have worked hard to create a compelling application, and there is no reason to only play it safe. So, your child should apply to three or more safety schools and three or more target schools, but should also apply to at least one reach school.

Students with fewer resources and less guidance—or who are the first in their families to apply to college—tend to avoid applying to more selective colleges even though they actually have the potential to be admitted. In fact, since top colleges consider an applicant's context, such students may have better chances of gaining admission to selective colleges than academically equivalent students with more resources and college-educated parents. So, even if your child isn't confident about applying to a highly selective college, he or she should do so anyway as long as he or she will also be applying to several safety and target schools.

Factor in Cost

The other big factor that you and your child will need to discuss while refining the list is cost. If you were actively engaged during the development of the preliminary list, cost has likely already been considered—but you may not have ruled out certain colleges on the basis of cost.

At this stage of the process, you and your child need to reassess which colleges are within an acceptable financial range and which are not. Those that aren't may need to be removed from the list. If, however, a college is nearly within an acceptable price range, your child should consider keeping the college on the list and, if accepted, see what financial aid is available. The key is having several backup options in case the financial aid packages from more expensive schools are not sufficient.

Narrow the List to 10–12 Schools

After your child has refined his or her list based on college visits, research, and preferences as well as selectivity and cost, he or she should arrive at a list of 10–12 schools, preferably—but at least six. The specific number, however, is not as important as the schools on the list. For example, a list of 10 reach schools would not be reasonable. Nor would a list of 10 safety schools.

So, instead of focusing too much on the number of schools, your child should focus on having a good balance of schools—enough that he or she is going to have at least one acceptance letter in the spring.

But your child's refined college list should not just be about ensuring admission somewhere—though that is important. Your child should develop a list that opens him or her up to the best possible opportunities. And that is why 10–12 schools is a good number. Too few schools on the list and your child is either sacrificing safety or opportunity—or both.

Too many schools on the list and your child won't be able to give each application the attention it needs.

In order for your child to have compelling applications, he or she must compile a strong list of colleges. The better suited the list is to your child and the more familiar your child is with each college, the better his or her applications will be. Refining the preliminary list into the best possible list of colleges for your child is challenging and time-consuming, but it is also one of the most important aspects of the application process, and your child must take it seriously.

Chapter 33:
Regular Decision, Early Decision, & Early Action

As discussed briefly in Chapter 2, your child's chances of being admitted can be significantly influenced by when he or she applies. By applying early decision to the college at the top of his or her list, your child can double or even triple his or her admissions odds.

In this chapter, we'll discuss the differences between regular decision, early decision, and early action and some related strategic considerations.

Application Deadlines

Not all colleges have the same application deadlines, and so your child should research the specific deadlines for each college to which he or she plans to apply. This is also important for your child to note in the materials he or she gives his or her counselor, teachers, and anyone else writing letters of recommendation. At some colleges, regular decision deadlines are at the end of November. At others, the deadline is as late as the middle of January. For most top colleges, however, the deadline is January 1.

All of the parts of your child's application—the transcript, test scores, essays, and recommendations—should be in motion long before the deadline. Some of these elements, like test scores, can be completed during junior year, while others, like essays and short answers, might not be done until late in the summer before senior year. But by fall of senior year, your child should be putting finishing touches on his or her application—not getting started.

Starting late and rushing can result in unnecessary errors, poor decisions, lower quality recommendations, and technological failures leading to missed deadlines. Starting early is key. Once your child has determined to keep a college on his or her list, he or she should start preparing application materials specific to that college.

Regular Decision

Regular decision applications are those that undergo the normal admissions process during spring of an applicant's senior year. Such applications are weighed against all others in the general application pool and offer no distinct admissions advantage.

Early Decision

Early decision applications are binding in that if your child is accepted to the college, he or she must enroll. As a result, a student can only submit an early decision application to a single college—and it should be his or her top choice.

Fewer students apply early decision to each school, and so your child's application is weighed against a smaller pool of applications. Most top colleges, however, have higher standards for early decision applications. Despite that, applying early decision will in most cases give your child a significantly higher chance of being admitted to his or her top college.

Below are several of the most selective colleges and their regular decision admission rates compared to their early application admission rates:

Institution	Regular Decision*	Early Admission
Stanford	4.7%	9.2%
Harvard University	5.2%	14.5%
Yale University	6.9%	17.1%
MIT	7.1%	7.8%
Northwestern University	9.0%	32.6%
Johns Hopkins University	11.8%	30.6%
Williams College	14.6%	35.3%

* Regular Decision and Early Admissions statistics given above are for the class of 2021.

Besides MIT, where early decision doesn't make as significant a difference, most of the colleges listed above have early decision rates from 5% to 23% higher than regular decision rates. The institutions in this list are representative of other top colleges that offer early decision programs, but be sure to review Appendix II for more comprehensive admissions statistics.

Colleges typically send notices to early decision applicants by the middle of December. In addition to being either accepted or rejected, a student's application may be deferred to the regular decision application pool and will be reconsidered through the normal admissions process.

If admitted through early decision, your child must notify the other colleges to which he or she applied of his or her enrollment to the early decision school.

In addition to standard early decision applications (also known as "Early Decision I"), some colleges offer "Early Decision II" programs, which are the same as early decision programs except that they have later deadlines. In fact, if your child's early decision application is rejected or deferred to regular decision, he or she may be able to apply to another school through its Early Decision II program.

Applying early decision does have certain financial ramifications: if accepted, your child is required to enroll. But unlike regular decision acceptances, which include financial aid packages that might influence your child's decision, early decision means accepting whatever financial aid is offered sight unseen.

Early Action

Early action applications have similar deadlines and notification periods to early decision programs, but unlike early decision, early action applications are nonbinding. So, even if your child is accepted to a college through an early action program, he or she will still be able to apply to other colleges and will be able to make his or her decision about which college to attend by the regular deadline.

A variant early action program known as single choice early action allows applicants to submit an early, nonbinding application, but may only do so at one school. If your child submits a single choice early action application, he or she may not apply early decision or early action to any other school—but if accepted, he or she can wait to decide whether to enroll until hearing back from all the colleges to which he or she applied regular decision and can consider financial aid in the decision.

Application Strategies

The increased acceptance rates for early applications are significant, so if your child is able to prepare a compelling admissions profile in time for early application, he or she should apply early wherever possible. Doing so will make your child's application even more effective.

Below, we'll discuss some basic strategic considerations for applying early decision, early action, and regular decision.

If Financially Possible, Apply Early Decision

Unless you cannot afford to pay full tuition and your child has to wait until he or she hears back from a college about financial aid, your child should apply early decision to his or her top choice college, assuming that college offers an early decision program.

Also, if your child is planning to apply as a recruited athlete or legacy student, he or she should research whether the college requires him or her to do so through early decision. At University of Pennsylvania, for example, legacies are given more consideration if applying early decision. And many top colleges require athletic recruits to apply early decision.

Apply Early Action

Whether or not your child applies early decision, he or she should consider applying early action to one or more schools. By applying early action, your child not only has higher chances of being admitted, but will also be able to review financial aid packages with time to consider additional scholarships and grants before enrolling.

Check for Special Deadline Policies

Once your child has refined his or her college list, he or she needs to look carefully at the application deadlines and policies to ensure he or she is aware of any special requirements. For example, some colleges have priority and preferred deadlines, which are earlier than the standard regular decision deadline. To remain competitive, your child should submit his or her application by the priority or preferred date.

Some colleges have what's known as a rolling admissions policy, which means application decisions are made as applications are received. If your child is applying to a college with a rolling admissions policy, applying early is obviously in your child's best interest.

Don't Apply Early at the Expense of a Strong Application

If your child plans to apply early—for an early decision or early action program, to meet a priority or preferred date, to be competitive at a school with a rolling admissions policy, or simply to be early—he or she must carefully weigh the advantages of being early against the quality of his or her application. Your child should not submit a rushed application. If his or her essays aren't ready, he or she should take the time to polish them. If he or she needs to take the ACT or SAT again, better to push that score up and apply regular decision.

Starting the application process early, however, is the best option, because it makes all the other options possible. So, while your child shouldn't apply early at the expense of a strong application, he or she should start preparing his or her application with enough time to both make it stand out and submit it early.

Chapter 34:
Financial Aid

The costs of an education at a top college can be sizeable. For many parents, paying a quarter of a million dollars for their child's education is an insurmountable obstacle. What many do not know, however, is that some of the most selective schools in the nation are also some of the most generous.

For example, Harvard claims that "Ninety percent of American families would **pay the same or less** to send their children to Harvard as they would a **state school**" (emphasis in the original).[22] In fact, families with incomes below $65,000 are not expected to contribute at all. The same is true of Yale and Stanford, and many top colleges have similar policies.

So, while each institution is different, generous financial aid in the form of scholarships and grants are fairly common for lower income applicants.

You and your child need to have a frank conversation about finances, and if aid is needed, your child will need to take the time to research the specific financial aid opportunities at each college to which he or she plans to apply. By selecting colleges with need-blind admissions policies, merit-based scholarships, and need-based grants—and by pursuing other scholarship and grant opportunities—your child may be able to mitigate some or all of his or her college expenses.

Select the Right Colleges

If cost is a factor, part of your child's strategy lies in selecting the right colleges. As discussed in Chapters 30 and 32, your child should develop a list of colleges that include a range of costs and financial aid opportunities.

Some of the financial aid criteria your child should consider when selecting colleges include the following:

- Is the college need-blind (does not consider financial need when making admissions decisions)?
- Does the college offer merit scholarships? If so, are scholarships awarded based on the college application or must additional materials (e.g., forms, essays, etc.) be submitted?
- Does the college offer need-based grants or student loans?

From a financial aid perspective, your child should consider selecting at least one safety school that is also totally within your price range. This school will serve as a backup in case the other colleges to which your child is accepted don't offer enough financial aid.

Apply for Application Fee Waivers

Depending on your level of financial need, your child may be eligible for application fee waivers. These waivers can be obtained through the Common Application, the College Board, the National Association for College Admission Counseling (NACAC), or even the colleges to which your child plans to apply. Generally speaking, if your child qualifies for free and reduced price school meals, he or she will qualify for an application fee waiver.

Seek Merit-Based Scholarships

For applicants with exceptional academic, leadership, or extracurricular achievements, many colleges offer merit-based scholarships. As part of your child's application strategy, he or she should consider applying to at least some schools that offer merit-based financial aid. Merit scholarships vary in size, with some scholarships paying for a portion of tuition and others covering all tuition costs, room and board, and other fees.

Many merit scholarships are awarded based on a student's application and do not require applicants to submit additional forms, essays, or other material. If your child is applying to such a college, this is all the more reason to develop a compelling admissions profile. The stronger your child's application, the higher his or her chances of receiving merit-based scholarship money.

At some colleges, merit-based financial aid requires an additional application and often an essay. If your child is accepted to such a school and needs additional financial aid, he or she should certainly take the time to apply for a merit scholarship. When applying to receive a merit-based scholarship, your child should apply all the principles of developing a compelling admissions profile to his or her scholarship application. Your child should present a compelling narrative that highlights his or her major achievements and demonstrates his or her value to the college.

Some colleges offer scholarships to athletic recruits, and so if your child is an athlete looking to be recruited by a top college, he or she might consider those that offer athletic scholarships. Ivy League schools and some other top colleges do not offer athletic scholarships, but many top-tier schools do.

Take Advantage of Need-Based Grants

As the term suggests, a need-based grant is based solely on the applicant's level of need and does not require repayment. Many top colleges offer generous need-based grants that, depending on your household income, may cover most if not all of the costs related to your child's education at a top-tier school. Unlike merit-based scholarships, need-based grants do not take your child's academic record, test scores, or other accomplishments into consideration—they are based on family income.

While many of the nation's most selective schools do not offer merit-based financial aid, most offer need-based aid that doesn't leave applicants hundreds of thousands of dollars in debt. Many of the Ivy League schools, for instance, are committed to meeting 100% of a student's demonstrated financial need. For most top colleges, you can quickly and easily get an idea of how much you will be expected to contribute by visiting the financial aid pages of their websites. Some even have online financial aid calculators.

If you plan to apply for need-based financial aid, you will need to complete the Free Application for Federal Student Aid (FAFSA) as well as any college-specific financial aid forms. College-specific applications may vary, and so you'll need to follow instructions carefully and avoid making assumptions based on the policies of other colleges.

Need-Blind Admissions

Colleges that practice need-blind admissions do not consider whether or not an applicant can afford the cost of attendance in their admissions decisions. For colleges that do not have need-blind admissions policies, the ability or inability to pay tuition and other expenses may be factored into the decision to accept or reject an application.

Not all selective colleges are need-blind, so you and your child should research each college's policy before applying.

Negotiate for Better Financial Aid

If your child receives multiple acceptance letters, he or she may be able to negotiate to increase his or her financial aid. Colleges want to protect their enrollment yield, and so with multiple options, your child may have some leverage. So, before you and your child cross a college off the list due to insufficient financial aid, consider asking for more.

Specifically, if one college has offered your child a larger financial aid package than a college higher on your child's list, he or she should consider contacting the admissions office of the preferred college. During this call, your child needs to explain that without additional financial aid, he or she will be unable to afford the cost of attendance and that he or she will have to enroll at a college that offered more aid. Requests for additional aid will carry more weight if your child received a larger offer from a comparable school in terms of selectivity and national rank—but in any case, it doesn't hurt to ask.

Generally, colleges want to see that a request for additional aid is about making enrollment at that college feasible, not just cheaper because your child wants to get the best deal. Trying to play one college's financial aid office against another's often leads only to frustration for all parties, but it may instead lead to a bidding war that results in a better aid package. That isn't the norm, however, and colleges typically won't improve financial aid offers unless your child offers a compelling reason for them to do so.

Negotiating for a better financial aid package may or may not result in more aid, but a college will not rescind your child's admission based on such a request, and so your child has nothing to lose.

Seek Outside Scholarships

If your child's financial aid offers don't completely cover his or her cost of attendance, he or she may be able to rely on scholarships from other organizations to offset college costs. A host of national, merit-based scholarship funds exist—too many to consider here. Instead of focusing on specific scholarships, then, we'll consider some basic strategies for finding scholarships and submitting compelling applications.

Don't Limit Yourself

Since there are no limits to how much scholarship money your child can receive, he or she should pursue as many scholarships as desired.

Start Early

Your child should begin searching for scholarships as early as freshman year. Since these scholarships are based on merit and accomplishment, not only do they offer financial benefits, but depending on how prestigious and selective, they could also help strengthen your child's admissions profile.

Early recognition can open doors to additional opportunities, which often has a compounding effect.

Search Locally

Your child should ask his or her guidance counselor about any local businesses or organizations that offer scholarships to local students.

Use Scholarship Search Engines

The College Board website has a scholarship search engine that produces search results based on a number of factors, including your child's year in high school, demographics, interests, and more. A number of other similar tools are available online.

Search Regularly

Your child will be busy all throughout high school, and searching for scholarships can take time. Instead of spending a lot of time at once looking for a suitable scholarship opportunity, you and your child should regularly spend small portions of time looking for scholarships.

Don't Reinvent the Wheel

Many of the same elements found in a compelling admissions profile can be incorporated into scholarship applications. Your child should try to avoid making extra work for him or herself by applying for scholarships that don't require a great deal of additional time and effort.

Apply to a Variety of Scholarships

While your child may be drawn to prestigious national scholarships—and should certainly consider applying—he or she should not ignore smaller local, regional, or niche opportunities. The smaller the number of applicants, the greater your child's chances of being awarded scholarship funds. Over the course of four years, several small scholarships can amount to significant financial aid.

Chapter 35:
Avoiding Common Admission Mistakes

In this chapter, we'll consider some of the common mistakes applicants make throughout the admissions process. Most of these mistakes can be easily avoided, and while some of them are more serious than others, each of them can have a significant adverse affect on your child's chances of being admitted to a top college.

Spending Time on Too Many Unrelated Activities

Your child should focus on a handful of meaningful activities that fit his or her theme and narrative. Having a focused list of extracurricular activities is much more valuable than having a well-rounded list.

Failing to Take Required Classes

If your child wants to be admitted to a top college, he or she must meet all the academic requirements of that college. Failing to take a required course will result in rejection—your child must carefully research the high school course requirements of each college to which he or she plans to apply.

Exaggerating, Lying, or Otherwise Attempting to Deceive

More than just about anything else, admissions officers value transparency, honesty, and integrity. Intentional dishonesty is a certain path to rejection. So, while your child may be tempted to lie about his or her ethnicity, how many hours he or she spent on activities, whether or not he or she toured the college, and other details on his or her application or brought up during an interview, it is imperative that your child is totally truthful.

Waiting until the Last Minute to Submit Applications

While your child shouldn't rush to submit an application, he or she shouldn't wait until the last minute, either.

Wasting Summers

The temptation to take it easy during summer is great, but if your child is serious about gaining admission to a top college, he or she cannot afford to waste a summer. He or she needs to spend the summer reading, learning, researching, preparing for the SAT, interning, working, or otherwise engaging in activities that will strengthen his or her admissions profile.

Taking Classes Online Instead of at School

Taking courses online is not a problem if your child's high school does not offer the course or if your child has special scheduling considerations that make taking a particular course impossible (e.g., part-time conservatory attendance or an internship). If, however, your child opts to take a course online instead of at his or her high school because he or she is concerned about getting a poor grade and is looking for an easier option, this could reflect poorly on your child.

Failing to Adequately Prepare for the ACT or SAT

To do well on the ACT or SAT, your child will likely need to invest considerable time and energy. Failing to do so will mean retaking the test, which is allowed and acceptable—to a point. If unsatisfied with his or her first ACT or SAT score, your child needs to make sure he or she dedicates adequate time to prepare before taking the test again. Taking entrance exams more than twice can raise concerns.

Confusing One College with Another

As your child prepares his or her application for each college, he or she must ensure that the essay does not accidentally include the name of another college to which he or she is applying.

Also, whether in his or her application or during an interview, your child should take care not to mistakenly refer to a program, professor, or student-led organization that exists at another college but not the one in question.

Being Passive & Letting Mom or Dad Do Everything

Your child should neither expect nor allow you to take over any part of the admissions process—you aren't the applicant. Don't make calls your child should be making; admissions officers might take note. And don't sit in on admissions interviews. Your child needs to demonstrate independence, responsibility, and maturity.

Making Decisions Based on What Others Want

Your child will likely face pressure from several people to apply to certain colleges. Friends might try to convince your child to pursue the same colleges they are applying to, relatives might pressure your child to apply to their alma maters, and even teachers or guidance counselors might weigh in. Your child needs to make decisions that are best for him or herself—not based on what others want.

Focusing Too Much on a Single School

Your child may be determined to attend a particular school, but focusing too much on a single application can have disastrous results. Your child cannot let hopes of attending his or her dream college interfere with researching other potential schools, creating a strong list of colleges, and submitting applications to these other schools on time.

Failing to Get to Know a School before Enrolling

Once your child receives acceptance letters, he or she needs to take time to get to know each school before making any decisions. If your child didn't previously have the opportunity to visit any of the schools that accepted his or her application, he or she should do so before enrolling. Accepted student events are great opportunities for your child to take last looks at his or her top choices.

Applying Early Decision When Uncertain

If your child is not sure about a college, he or she should not apply early decision. Better for your child to apply regular decision and be rejected than to be accepted early decision and forced to attend a school he or she does not like or that doesn't offer the major, minor, or other academic program your child planned to pursue.

Letting Grades Slip or Dropping Courses Once Accepted

Once your child is accepted, he or she may be tempted to let grades go (senioritis) or switch from an advanced course to something easier. Top colleges expect your child to be the same applicant at the end of senior year as he or she was at the time of his or her application. While colleges don't often send rescind letters without warning, once your child is warned, it may be too late to course correct. Your child needs to maintain his or her academic performance all the way through graduation.

Speaking or Acting in an Unbecoming Manner

Another way for your child to earn a rescind letter—or not be accepted in the first place—is to speak or behave in an inappropriate manner. Top colleges have little tolerance for bigotry, hate speech, excessive lewdness, and illegal activity. Your child needs to be careful not to list an inappropriate email address on his or her application, wear clothing with explicit content to admissions interviews, or include obscene, bigoted, or otherwise inappropriate language in his or her essays.

Additionally, your child's social media accounts are likely to be visited by admissions officers, and what they discover can have serious adverse consequences. Your child needs to ensure his or her social media profiles and posts won't hurt his or her chances of being admitted.

Even after being accepted, any inappropriate behavior online could be noticed by a college—your child needs to carefully guard his or her online image.

Section Eight:

Appendices

Appendix I:
References

1. "First Destination Report: Class of 2016." Yale University. http://ocs.yale.edu/sites/default/files/files/OCS%20Stats%20pages/Public%20-%20Final%20Class%20of%202016%20Report%20(6%20months).pdf

2. "Average and Median Amounts of Net Compensation." United States Social Security Administration. Accessed July 2017. https://www.ssa.gov/oact/cola/central.html

3. "Household Income: 2015." United States Census Bureau. Accessed July 2017 https://www.census.gov/content/dam/Census/library/publications/2016/demo/acsbr15-02.pdf

4. *Integrated Postsecondary Education Data System.* National Center for Education Statistics. Accessed July 2017. https://nces.ed.gov/ipeds/Home/UseTheData

5. "Concordance Tables." The College Board. May 2016. Accessed July 2017. https://collegereadiness.collegeboard.org/pdf/higher-ed-brief-sat-concordance.pdf

Note

The current SAT statistics from the Integrated Postsecondary Education Data System (IPEDS) uses the old SAT with a maximum score of 2400. Statistics for the new SAT, with a maximum score of 1600, are calculated by adjusting the data from IPEDS using the Concordance Tables provided by the College Board. Average scores are given as the mean of a college's 25th and 75th percentile scores.

6. Malcolm Gladwell. *Outlier: The Story of Success.* New York: Hachette Book Group, 2008.

7. "The Common Application Announces 2017-2018 Essay Prompts." The Common Application. February 2017. Accessed July 2017. http://www.commonapp.org/whats-appening/application-updates/common-application-announces-2017-2018-essay-prompts

8. "Fast Facts: Back to School Statistics (2016)." National Center for Education Statistics. Accessed July 2017. https://nces.ed.gov/fastfacts/display.asp?id=372

9. "AP Students – AP Courses and Exams for Students." The College Board. Accessed July 2017. https://apstudent.collegeboard.org/home

10. "International Education – International Baccalaureate." Accessed July 2017. http://www.ibo.org/

11. "The ACT Test." ACT, Inc. Accessed July 2017. http://www.act.org/

12. "SAT." The College Board. Accessed July 2017. https://collegereadiness.collegeboard.org/sat

13. "A Brief History of the SAT." *Frontline.* Public Broadcasting Service (PBS). Accessed July 2017. http://www.pbs.org/wgbh/pages/frontline/shows/sats/where/history.html

14. "SAT Subject Tests." The College Board. Accessed July 2017. https://collegereadiness.collegeboard.org/sat-subject-tests/

15. "PreACT." ACT, Inc. Accessed July 2017. http://www.act.org/content/act/en/products-and-services/preact.html

16. "PSAT/NMSQT and PSAT 10." The College Board. Accessed July 2017. https://collegereadiness.collegeboard.org/psat-nmsqt-psat-10

17. "ACT Aspire." ACT, Inc. Accessed July 2017. http://www.act.org/content/act/en/products-and-services/act-aspire.html

18. Michele A Hernandez. *A is for Admission: The Insider's Guide to Getting into the Ivy League and Other Top Colleges*. New York: Grand Central Publishing, 2009.

19. Bill Pennington. "A Rare Glimpse Inside the Ivy League's Academic Index." *New York Times*. January 10, 2012. Accessed July 2017. https://thechoice.blogs.nytimes.com/2012/01/10/ivy-academic-index/

20. David Freed and Alexander Koenig. "Taking on the AI." *The Harvard Crimson*. May 30, 2013. Accessed July 2017. http://www.thecrimson.com/article/2013/5/30/harvard-academic-index-explanation/

21. "Passion." Merriam-Webster Dictionary. Accessed July 2017. https://www.merriam-webster.com/dictionary/passion

22. "Fact Sheet." Harvard College, Griffin Financial Aid Office. Accessed July 2017. https://college.harvard.edu/financial-aid/how-aid-works/fact-sheet

Works Consulted

Aayush Upadhyay. *Behind The Ivy Curtain: A Data Driven Guide to Elite College Admissions*. Self-published, 2015.

Allen Cheng. "How to Get Into Harvard and the Ivy League, by a Harvard Alum." PrepScholar. May 30, 2015. http://blog.prepscholar.com/how-to-get-into-harvard-and-the-ivy-league-by-a-harvard-alum

Deborah Bedor. *Getting IN by Standing OUT: The New Rules for Admission to America's Best Colleges*. Charleston, South Carolina: Advantage Media Group, 2015.

Greg Kaplan. *Earning Admission: Real Strategies for Getting into Highly Selective Colleges*. Self-published, 2016.

Michele A Hernandez. *A is for Admission: The Insider's Guide to Getting into the Ivy League and Other Top Colleges*. New York: Grand Central Publishing, 2009.

Robin Mamlet and Christine VanDeVelde. *College Admission: From Application to Acceptance, Step by Step*. New York: Random House, 2011.

Appendix II:
Admissions Statistics

Boston College

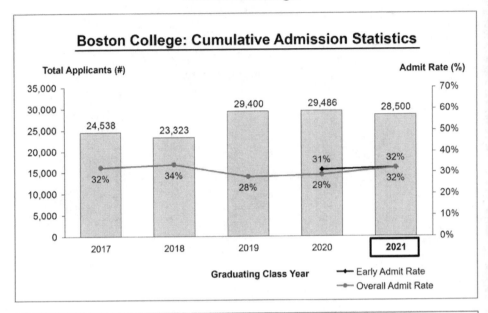

Boston College: Cumulative Admission Statistics

Boston College: ACT / New SAT Statistics

ACT	Average	25th Percentile	75th Percentile
Composite	32	30	33

New SAT	Average	25th Percentile	75th Percentile
Math	720	660	770
Reading	36	33	38
Writing	36	35	38
Composite	1440	1350	1510

* Note that all ACT / New SAT statistics given in Appendix II are as of the Class of 2021.

Boston College is a highly competitive school and its admissions statistics make Boston College one of the 50 most competitive schools for undergraduate admissions globally. Similar to the trends across all top schools, Boston College acceptance rates have continued to decline over the past 8 years and will almost certainly continue to do so into the future.

The Class of 2021 was one of the most challenging year to be admitted to Boston College ever. For the Class of 2021, 28,500 students applied to Boston College of which 9,200 students were accepted, yielding an overall acceptance rate of 32.3%. Overall applications decreased by 3.3% over last year (2020 to 2021) from 29,486 to 28,500.

For the Class of 2021, 2,900 students were admitted through the early admissions process. Total early applications totaled 9,000, yielding an early acceptance rate of 32.2%. Early applications increased by 4.7% over last year (2020 to 2021) from 8,600 to 9,000.

Boston College: Current Student Population

Total Enrollment	13,906	
Undergrad Enrollment	9,088	
Freshmen	2,113	
Male/Female	47%	53%
From Out of State	77%	
From Public High School	51%	
Undergrads Live on Campus	85%	
African American	4%	
Asian	9%	
Caucasian	62%	
Hispanic	10%	
Native American	<1%	
Mixed (2+ Ethnicities)	2%	
International	4%	
Countries Represented	94	

Founded in 1863, Boston College has maintained its Roman Catholic Jesuit religious roots and has become one of America's leading private research universities. Boston College is now ranked thirty-first among national universities by U.S. News & World Report. Over recent years the university's students have received a number of prestigious academic scholarships including Rhodes Scholarships, Marshalls, Goldwaters and Fulbright grants and more.

Boston College is well known for its extremely competitive Presidential Scholar scholarship program which is awarded to only fifteen people, equal to less than a one percent acceptance rate. Some of the university's most popular majors include Economics, Finance, Communication, Biology, Political Science, Psychology, English, Nursing, Applied Psychology & Human Development, and Accounting. Boston College is also known as a university with high research activity. It has highly ranked graduate programs including the Lynch School of Education, Boston College Law School and the Carroll School of Management.

An example of notable alumni in the areas of education, law and business include Peter Dervan, former Chairman, Division of Chemistry and Chemical Engineering at the California Institute of Technology; Brigida Benitez, President, Hispanic Bar Association and proposed alternative nominee for the United States Supreme Court; and Nikesh Arora, President, Global Sales Operations and Business Development at Google. In all, Boston College has more than 160,000 alumni worldwide, and maintains one of the largest alumni association among Catholic universities in the world.

Boston College has eight schools and colleges that enroll 14,100 students with 9,000 of those being undergraduate students. There are 4,500 graduate and professional students and 600 students in the Woods College of Advancing Studies that make up the remainder. Boston College's undergraduate programs consist of its College of Arts & Sciences, Carroll School of Management, Connell School of Nursing, Lynch School of Education and Woods College of Advancing Studies.

Although Boston College has no fraternities or sororities on campus, the university has more than 200 clubs and organizations broken up into the following categories: Academic/Pre-Professional, Campus Ministry, Honor Societies, Intercultural, Music, Art and Performance, Political, Publications and Media, Service and Specific Issues. When it comes to sports, the Boston College Eagles boast one of the highest graduation rates for student-athletes in the country.

Brown University

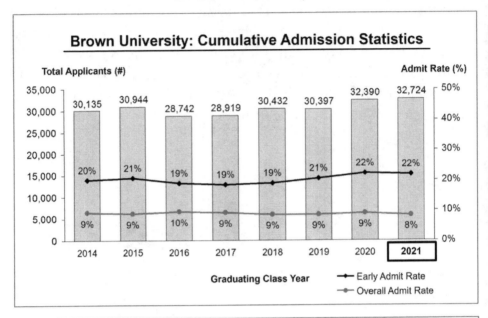

Brown University: ACT / New SAT Statistics

ACT	Average	25th Percentile	75th Percentile
Composite	32	31	34

New SAT	Average	25th Percentile	75th Percentile
Math	750	720	790
Reading	38	36	40
Writing	37	36	40
Composite	1500	1440	1580

Brown University is an Ivy League School and its admissions statistics fall in the middle of all Ivy League Schools. Similar to the trends across all top schools, Brown University acceptance rates have continued to decline over the past 8 years and will almost certainly continue to do so into the future.

The Class of 2021 was the single most challenging year to be admitted to Brown University ever. For the Class of 2021, 32,724 students applied to Brown University of which 2,722 students were accepted, yielding an overall acceptance rate of 8.3%. Overall applications increased by 1% over last year (2020 to 2021) from 32,390 to 32,724.

For the Class of 2021, 695 students were admitted through the early admissions process. Total early applications totaled 3,170, yielding an early acceptance rate of 21.9%. Early applications increased by 4.6% over last year (2020 to 2021) from 3,030 to 3,170.

Brown University: Current Student Population

Total Enrollment	8,786	
Undergrad Enrollment	6,380	
Freshmen	1,507	
Male/Female	48%	52%
From Out of State	95%	
From Public High School	63%	
Undergrads Live on Campus	79%	
African American	6%	
Asian	12%	
Caucasian	45%	
Hispanic	10%	
Native American	0%	
Mixed (2+ Ethnicities)	4%	
International	11%	
Countries Represented	105	

Brown University has one of the most generous student financial aid programs in the world.

Approximately 46% of current Brown University students are receiving some amount of financial aid. What this statistic also tells us is that approximately 54% of Brown students come from families likely in the top tax brackets, with families earning a minimum of $250,000 in annual household income. For the recently admitted Class of 2018, an even higher 67% of students applied for financial aid.

In the U.S. today, the percentage of households with this level of income or above is approximately 4%. Therefore, we can conclude that on the whole, students in Ivy League schools are ~25 times more likely to come from households with a minimum of $250,000 in annual household income compared with students in the U.S. population at large.

What this means is that although the Ivy League is becoming more and more accessible to lower income families, it is still ~50% comprised of students from the wealthiest households in the U.S. and abroad.

It is no surprise that students from these wealthy families end up in the Ivy League and other highly selective schools. These students are groomed from an early age and have access to tremendous resources including standardized test preparation courses, unique internship/research opportunities and access to college admission strategy consulting firms such as Ivy League Prep to give them the "edge" needed to gain admission to these highly selective schools and surpass the competition.

Brown University is the nation's seventh oldest institution of higher education and the third oldest in New England. As a liberal arts university, its education offered encourages leading-edge scholarship, research, and opportunities for community-based service learning. Brown University is most known for its unconventional curriculum designed to encourage students to pursue their passion without fear of punishment for exploring the wrong path. The university offers more than 6,000 students the ability to design their own studies, with almost eighty concentrations in forty-four different academic areas, as well as an opportunity for independent study. Some of Brown's strongest and most popular programs include Biology/ Biological Sciences, History,

Economics; English, Political Science, and International Relations and Affairs. The university also offers 37 Division I sports teams, with standout programs including the men's and women's rowing teams, men's soccer, football and equestrian.

Brown University's graduates earn some of the highest salaries in the country. The university is currently ranked in a tie for eighth place as one of the institutions with the highest paid graduates, more than a third of who accept business and management positions in Corporate America. Brown was also ranked third in the Princeton Review's list of America's Happiest College Students in 2012.

Columbia University

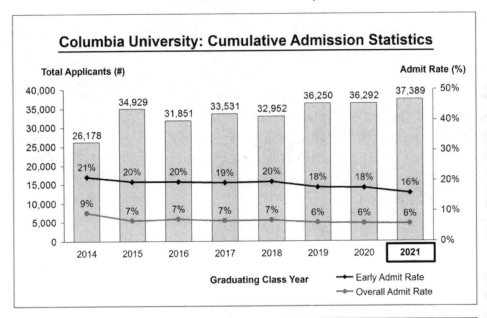

Columbia University: ACT / New SAT Statistics

ACT	Average	25th Percentile	75th Percentile
Composite	34	32	35

New SAT	Average	25th Percentile	75th Percentile
Math	770	730	800
Reading	38	37	40
Writing	38	37	40
Composite	1530	1470	1590

Columbia University is an Ivy League School and its admissions statistics make it one of the most competitive Ivy League Schools. Similar to the trends across all top schools, Columbia University acceptance rates have continued to decline over the past 8 years and will almost certainly continue to do so into the future.

The Class of 2021 was the single most challenging year to be admitted to Columbia University ever. For the Class of 2021, 37,389 students applied to Columbia University of which 2,185 students were accepted, yielding an overall acceptance rate of 5.8%. Overall applications increased by 3.0% over last year (2020 to 2021) from 36,292 to 37,389.

For the Class of 2021, 650 students were admitted through the early admissions process. Total early applications totaled 4,086, yielding an early acceptance rate of 15.9%. Early applications increased by 16.1% over last year (2020 to 2021) from 3,520 to 4,086.

Columbia University: Current Student Population

Total Enrollment	6,027	
Undergrad Enrollment	6,027	
Freshmen	1,391	
Male/Female	53%	47%
From Out of State	75%	
From Public High School	63%	
Undergrads Live on Campus	94%	
African American	12%	
Asian	18%	
Caucasian	34%	
Hispanic	14%	
Native American	2%	
Mixed (2+ Ethnicities)	4%	
International	12%	
Countries Represented	87	

Founded by King George II of England, Columbia University is an Ivy League university located in Morningside Heights, in Upper Manhattan, New York. Established in 1754, it is the oldest institution of higher learning in New York. First known as King's College, today it is officially known as Columbia University.

Columbia University excels in both the sciences and liberal arts. In 1767, Columbia became the first American medical school to grant the MD, and in 1928, the university's coalition with The Presbyterian Hospital formed the first medical center to combine teaching, research, and patient care.

Columbia University's colleges and law school have developed a fairly impressive list of United States Legislator alumni, including nine supreme court justices, more than thirty-five governors, and the university's first President of the United States of America, Barack Obama.

Columbia University enrolls approximately 7,900 students in undergraduate programs, 5,400 students in graduate programs, and 12,000 students in professional programs. The university's various schools include Columbia's School of the Arts, School of International and Public Affairs, School of Public Health, School of Engineering & Applied Science and their School of General Studies which includes its Post-baccalaureate Premedical Program. Some of Columbia's most respected graduate schools include its Graduate School of Arts & Sciences and Graduate School of Business.

Columbia has nearly 500 clubs and organizations, including Pre-professional clubs such as the Charles Drew Premedical Society, Columbia Pre-Law Society, and the Columbia Women's Business Society. Columbia also has many student organizations centered around politics, music, media and publications such as the Columbia Political Review, Musical Theatre Society, Columbia Television, and Echoes (Barnard College Literary Magazine), respectively.

Cornell University

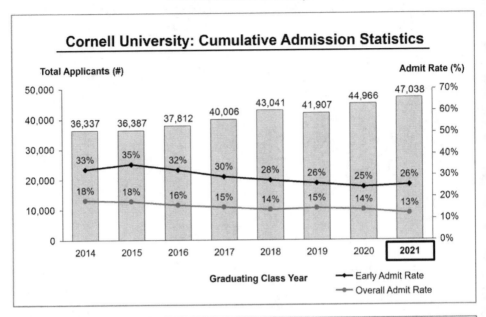

Cornell University: Cumulative Admission Statistics

Cornell University: ACT / New SAT Statistics

ACT	Average	25th Percentile	75th Percentile
Composite	32	30	34

New SAT	Average	25th Percentile	75th Percentile
Math	760	710	790
Reading	37	35	39
Composite	1480	1410	1570

Cornell University is an Ivy League School and its admissions statistics make it the least competitive Ivy League School. Similar to the trends across all top schools, Cornell University acceptance rates have continued to decline over the past 8 years and will almost certainly continue to do so into the future.

The Class of 2021 was the single most challenging years to be admitted to Cornell University ever. For the Class of 2021, 47,038 students applied to Cornell University of which 5,889 students were accepted, yielding an overall acceptance rate of 12.5%. Overall applications increased by 4.6% over last year (2020 to 2021) from 44,966 to 47,038.

For the Class of 2021, 1,378 students were admitted through the early admissions process. Total early applications totaled 5,384, yielding an early acceptance rate of 25.6%. Early applications increased by 10.6% over last year (2020 to 2021) from 4,866 to 5,384.

Cornell University: Current Student Population

Total Enrollment	21,131	
Undergrad Enrollment	14,167	
Freshmen	3,282	
Male/Female	50%	50%
From Out of State	66%	
Undergrads Live on Campus	57%	
African American	6%	
Asian	16%	
Caucasian	46%	
Hispanic	9%	
Native American	<1%	
Mixed (2+ Ethnicities)	4%	
International	9%	
Countries Represented	77	

Founded in 1865, Cornell is a privately endowed research university situated on a picturesque 745-acre campus in Ithaca, New York. Ithaca is said to be one of the top 100 places to live in the U.S., and is renowned for its restaurants, among other things. Ithaca is also a top-10 recreation city, ranked as one of the best 'green' places to live. It's not hard to see why nearly 21,500 aspiring students enroll at this top-ranked national university every year.

Cornell considers itself different from other Ivy League universities, having set out to make "contributions in all fields of knowledge in a manner that prioritizes public engagement to help improve the quality of life in our state, the nation, the world."

As a research university, Cornell is ranked fourth in the world and is known for having the largest number of graduates who go on to pursue doctorates in engineering or in the natural sciences at American institutions. Cornell also ranks fifth in the world in producing graduates who pursue doctorates in any field at American institutions. Additionally, Cornell established the first four-year schools of hotel administration and industrial and labor relations. It awarded the world's first degree in journalism and was the first American university to offer a major in U.S. Studies.

Notable alumni include Hotels.com founder David Litman; Founder, Chairman, and CEO of HEI Hotels & Resorts, Gary Mendell; Dutch architect, journalist, screenwriter and Pritzker Architecture Prize winner Rem Koolhaas, and political commentator Bill Maher. There are currently forty-three Nobel laureates affiliated with Cornell, either as faculty members or alumni.

Cornell has fourteen colleges and schools. The Ithaca campus hosts 14,393 students in seven undergraduate schools and the four graduate and professional schools host 5,023 students & 2,177 students, respectively. An additional two medical graduate and professional schools are located in New York City, and one in Doha, Qatar, making Cornell's total student enrollment approximately 21,593.

Cornell's "Big Red Bears" have an NCAA Division I athletics program with thirty-six varsity sports including lacrosse, hockey, wrestling, football, men' s basketball and women' s ice hockey.

On the twenty-four page list of Cornell University's student organizations, there's something for practically anyone—from the Cornell Beekeeping Club, to the A Cappella Advisory Council, to the public service group A Global Friendship CIO, to the performers known as the Absolute Zero Breakdance Club and even the professionals in the Cornell Accounting Association, just to name a few.

Dartmouth College

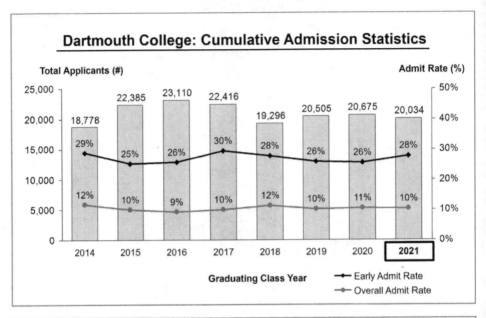

Dartmouth College: Cumulative Admission Statistics

Total Applicants (#)   Admit Rate (%)

Graduating Class Year	2014	2015	2016	2017	2018	2019	2020	2021
Total Applicants	18,778	22,385	23,110	22,416	19,296	20,505	20,675	20,034
Early Admit Rate	29%	25%	26%	30%	28%	26%	26%	28%
Overall Admit Rate	12%	10%	9%	10%	12%	10%	11%	10%

— Early Admit Rate
— Overall Admit Rate

Dartmouth College: ACT / New SAT Statistics

ACT	Average	25th Percentile	75th Percentile
Composite	32	30	34

New SAT	Average	25th Percentile	75th Percentile
Math	750	700	790
Reading	37	35	40
Writing	37	36	40
Composite	1500	1410	1580

Dartmouth College is an Ivy League School and its admissions statistics fall in the middle of all Ivy League Schools. Similar to the trends across all top schools, Dartmouth College acceptance rates have continued to decline over the past 8 years and will almost certainly continue to do so into the future.

The Class of 2021 was one of the most challenging years to be admitted to Dartmouth College ever. For the Class of 2021, 20,034 students applied to Dartmouth College of which 2,092 students were accepted, yielding an overall acceptance rate of 10.4%. Overall applications decreased by 3.1% over last year (2020 to 2021) from 20,675 to 20,034.

For the Class of 2021, 555 students were admitted through the early admissions process. Total early applications totaled 1,999, yielding an early acceptance rate of 27.8%. Early applications increased by 3.7% over last year (2020 to 2021) from 1,927 to 1,999.

Dartmouth College: Current Student Population

Total Enrollment	6,144	
Undergrad Enrollment	4,193	
Freshmen	1,113	
Male/Female	50%	50%
From Out of State	96%	
From Public High School	55%	
Undergrads Live on Campus	86%	
African American	7%	
Asian	14%	
Caucasian	48%	
Hispanic	8%	
Native American	3%	
Mixed (2+ Ethnicities)	6%	
International	8%	
Countries Represented	70	

Dartmouth College is located in rural Hanover, New Hampshire on a beautiful 200-acre campus. Established in 1769, Dartmouth is one of America's oldest colleges and one of the oldest in the world. One of the eight Ivy League schools, Dartmouth has a tradition of striving for the highest educational standards with proven success, especially in the areas of engineering, business, medicine and the arts & sciences.

Dartmouth has received outstanding recognition for its undergraduate liberal arts programs and graduate education programs. It has three well-known leading professional schools: the Geisel School of Medicine, the Thayer School of Engineering, and the Tuck School of Business. The Carnegie Foundation is one of the university's supporters, and calls it a "top university with a high level of research activity."

Notable Dartmouth alumni include author Dr. Seuss, actress Meryl Streep, poet Robert Frost, two former Secretaries of the U.S. Treasury and three Nobel laureates.

Today, Dartmouth has 6,300 students enrolled. The forty departments of the undergraduate schools enroll 4,200 members of the total. The graduate schools of arts & sciences, medicine, engineering, and business account for the remaining 2,100 students.

Dartmouth has more than 160 student organizations on campus, including those dedicated to academic competition, cultural awareness, pre-professional preparation, community service and philanthropy. Dartmouth has thirty-four intercollegiate varsity sports teams including sixteen women's teams, sixteen men's teams and two co-ed teams. The Dartmouth "Big Green" play in the Ivy League, the Eastern Collegiate Athletic conference and the NCAA Division I conference. Recent student surveys indicate that 75% of Dartmouth undergraduates participate to some degree in the school's athletics.

Some famous Dartmouth campus traditions include campus-wide "big weekends" or "party weekends" which occur every academic term. In the fall, winter, spring, and summer respectively, these weekends include Homecoming (officially Dartmouth Night Weekend), Winter Carnival, Green Key, and Tubestock, the last of which has been canceled indefinitely and replaced in 2006 by an event called Fieldstock.

Duke University

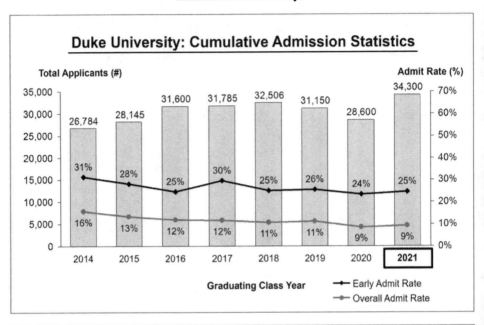

Duke University: ACT / New SAT Statistics

ACT	Average	25th Percentile	75th Percentile
Composite	34	32	35

New SAT	Average	25th Percentile	75th Percentile
Math	780	750	800
Reading	38	37	40
Writing	38	37	40
Composite	1540	1480	1590

Duke University is a highly competitive school and its admissions statistics make Duke University one of the 50 most competitive schools for undergraduate admissions globally. Similar to the trends across all top schools, Duke University acceptance rates have continued to decline

over the past 8 years and will almost certainly continue to do so into the future.

The Class of 2021 was one of the most challenging years to be admitted to Duke University ever. For the Class of 2021, 34,300 students applied to Duke University of which 3,174 students were accepted, yielding an overall acceptance rate of 9.3%. Overall applications increased by 19.9% over last year (2020 to 2021) from 28,600 to 34,300.

For the Class of 2021, 861 students were admitted through the early admissions process. Total early applications totaled 3,516, yielding an early acceptance rate of 24.5%. Early applications increased by 1.8% over last year (2020 to 2021) from 3,455 to 3,516.

Duke University: Current Student Population

Total Enrollment	15,427	
Undergrad Enrollment	6,680	
Freshmen	1,724	
Male/Female	50%	50%
From Out of State	89%	
From Public High School	67%	
Undergrads Live on Campus	82%	
African American	10%	
Asian	21%	
Caucasian	47%	
Hispanic	7%	
Native American	1%	
Mixed (2+ Ethnicities)	2%	
International	8%	
Countries Represented	89	

Duke University is a private research university that traces its roots back to 1838 when it was called Trinity College. It was in 1924 when James B. Duke created a philanthropic foundation under the family name entitled The Duke Endowment that Trinity College officially became Duke University. During that time, Duke University underwent major changes, both physically and academically. The original old campus became known as the East Campus and the university's new Gothic-style architecture side became known as the West Campus. Duke's original East Campus served as Duke's College for women until 1972 when the campuses were integrated and made co-ed. The East Campus is now the home for all first-year students. Forbes recently ranked Duke University thirteenth in Research Universities and second in the South on its list of Top Colleges. Duke University's mission is to "offer a unique and compelling combination of academic achievement, engagement with society, and athletic accomplishment at the highest."

Some of Duke University's most popular undergraduate programs are in the areas of science (biomedical engineering, biology, and psychology), economics and public policy. With regard to science, Duke University is also known to host the world's largest protected population of endangered primates, including 200 lemurs at the university's Lemur Center. With regard to academics, Duke Libraries rank among the nation's top ten private research library systems.

Duke University has produced a great many notable alumni, and when speaking of some of today's most recognizable and relevant to current public policy issues, the likes of Charlie Rose, Ron Paul and Jeffrey Zients should be mentioned. Also worth noting is Melissa Gates, Cofounder of the Bill & Melinda Gates Foundation and wife of Bill Gates. The foundation donates large sums of money to the school annually. Ironically, Timothy Cook CEO of Apple Inc. is also a notable Duke University Alumni.

Approximately 15,467 students annually attend Duke's ten schools and colleges including; Trinity College of Arts & Sciences, School of Law, Divinity School, Graduate School, School of Medicine, School of

Nursing, Pratt School of Engineering, Fuqua School of Business, Sanford School of Public Policy and the Nicholas School of the Environment.

Duke University competes in 26 NCAA Division I varsity sports and has numerable recent championships in both basketball and lacrosse. Duke University Press puts out about 120 new books every year, in addition to publishing more than thirty scholarly journals covering areas such as the humanities, social sciences, law, medicine, the sciences and mathematics. Duke University is also home to more than 400 recognized clubs, living groups, and other organizations.

Emory University

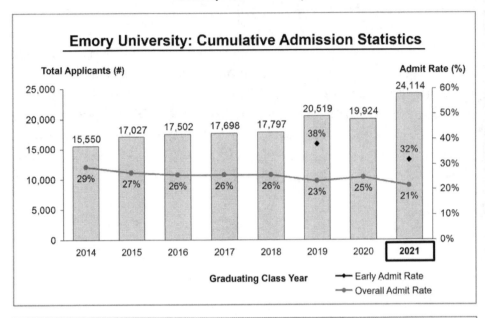

Emory University: Cumulative Admission Statistics

Total Applicants (#) / Admit Rate (%)

Graduating Class Year	Total Applicants	Overall Admit Rate	Early Admit Rate
2014	15,550	29%	
2015	17,027	27%	
2016	17,502	26%	
2017	17,698	26%	
2018	17,797	26%	
2019	20,519	23%	38%
2020	19,924	25%	
2021	24,114	21%	32%

Emory University: ACT / New SAT Statistics

ACT	Average	25th Percentile	75th Percentile
Composite	31	29	33

New SAT	Average	25th Percentile	75th Percentile
Math	720	670	780
Reading	35	33	38
Writing	36	35	38
Composite	1430	1350	1520

Emory University is a highly competitive school and its admissions statistics make Emory University one of the 50 most competitive schools for undergraduate admissions globally. Similar to the trends across all top schools, Emory University acceptance rates have continued to decline

over the past 8 years and will almost certainly continue to do so into the future.

The Class of 2021 was one of the most challenging year to be admitted to Emory University ever. For the Class of 2021, 24,114 students applied to Emory University of which 5,172 students were accepted, yielding an overall acceptance rate of 21.4%. Overall applications increased by 21% over last year (2020 to 2021) from 19,924 to 24,114.

For the Class of 2021, 474 students were admitted through the early admissions process. Total early applications totaled 1,493, yielding an early acceptance rate of 31.7%.

Emory University: Current Student Population

Total Enrollment	13,893	
Undergrad Enrollment	7,441	
Freshmen	1,342	
Male/Female	45%	55%
From Out of State	73%	
From Public High School	61%	
Undergrads Live on Campus	68%	
African American	10%	
Asian	23%	
Caucasian	41%	
Hispanic	5%	
Native American	<1%	
Mixed (2+ Ethnicities)	1%	
International	12%	
Countries Represented	101	

Emory College was founded in 1836 in Oxford, Georgia. Named after a bishop who dreamed of an American educational system that would that mold character as well as intellect, Emery College struggled to survive for many years, but by 1914 was looking to expand. Since that time,

Emory University has become highly recognized internationally for its outstanding liberal arts colleges and graduate and professional schools, and is known to be one of Southeast America's leading places of study and application in the area of health care. Former U.S. President Jimmy Carter, physician and CNN chief health correspondent Sanjay Gupta and activist and Nobel Peace Prize winner Desmond Tutu have all taught at Emory.

Some of Emory University's notable alumni in the areas of science and health care include British physician, anthropologist, biographer, author and international civil servant, Peter Bourne and American physician, professional soccer player, United States Navy officer, and NASA astronaut, Sonny Carter. Others outside the field of science and medicine include President and Chief Operating Officer of Aflac U.S., Paul Amos II; Chairman of the Board, President and Chief Executive Officer of MetLife, C. Robert Henrikson, and founder of Callaway Golf, Ely Callaway.

Emory University has approximately 7,836 undergraduates who attend classes on its 630-acre campus. Four of Emory University's nine schools and colleges serve both undergraduates and graduates.

When it comes to tradition, Emory University does not fall short. There are even events that commemorate its beginning. For instance, the Founder's Week custom is an academic festival held between the annual academic celebrations of Opening Convocation and Commencement. It commemorates the first meeting of the Board of Trustees on Feb. 6, 1837. Many other traditions exist as well, such as "Dooley's Week," a tradition that takes place every year, and is named for Dooley, a skeleton and "Lord of Misrule" who remains steeped in Emory legend.

Georgetown University

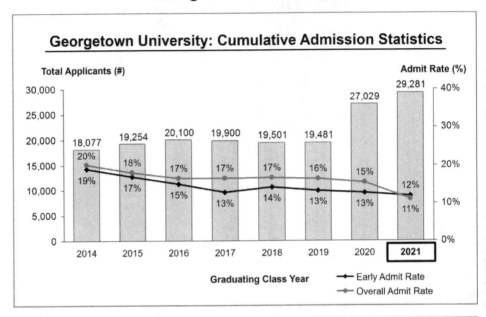

Georgetown University: Cumulative Admission Statistics

Total Applicants (#) — Admit Rate (%)

Graduating Class Year	Total Applicants	Early Admit Rate	Overall Admit Rate
2014	18,077	19%	20%
2015	19,254	17%	18%
2016	20,100	15%	17%
2017	19,900	13%	17%
2018	19,501	14%	17%
2019	19,481	13%	16%
2020	27,029	13%	15%
2021	29,281	11%	12%

Georgetown University: ACT / New SAT Statistics

ACT	Average	25th Percentile	75th Percentile
Composite	32	30	34

New SAT	Average	25th Percentile	75th Percentile
Math	730	690	770
Reading	37	35	39
Composite	1460	1390	1550

Georgetown University is a highly competitive school and its admissions statistics make Georgetown University one of the 50 most competitive schools for undergraduate admissions globally. Similar to the trends across all top schools, Georgetown University acceptance rates have

continued to decline over the past 8 years and will almost certainly continue to do so into the future.

The Class of 2021 was the single most challenging year to be admitted to Georgetown University ever. For the Class of 2021, 29,281 students applied to Georgetown University of which 3,219 students were accepted, yielding an overall acceptance rate of 11.0%. Overall applications increased by 8.3% over last year (2020 to 2021) from 27,029 to 29,281.

For the Class of 2021, 931 students were admitted through the early admissions process. Total early applications totaled 7,822, yielding an early acceptance rate of 11.9%. Early applications increased by 11.3% over last year (2020 to 2021) from 7,027 to 7,822.

Georgetown University: Current Student Population

Total Enrollment	17,130	
Undergrad Enrollment	7,590	
Freshmen	1,698	
Male/Female	45%	55%
From Out of State	99%	
From Public High School	50%	
Undergrads Live on Campus	68%	
African American	6%	
Asian	9%	
Caucasian	61%	
Hispanic	7%	
Native American	<1%	
Mixed (2+ Ethnicities)	3%	
International	10%	
Countries Represented	138	

Established in 1789 by founder John Carroll, Georgetown is a private research university on a fifty-four building, 104-acre campus.

Georgetown has four undergraduate schools, three graduate and professional schools and many specialized institutes that it uses to administer the approximate 180 academic programs it covers. Georgetown also has campuses in Italy, Turkey and Qatar, as well as a law campus on Capitol Hill.

Georgetown has long played a major role in producing international and domestic policy makers. The list of notable government officials is seemingly endless and worldwide. The list ranges from no fewer than the likes of seven presidents of various countries other than the Unites States, one U.S. President (Bill Clinton), and at least twenty-six U.S. heads of state. Also on the list of notable alumni are numerable royalty from many countries around the world.

Georgetown is made up of approximately 17,357 students annually; roughly 7,552 of which make up the university's undergraduate population. Georgetown schools include Georgetown College, Robert E. McDonough School of Business, Edmund A. Walsh School of Foreign Service, Georgetown Law, Graduate School of Arts and Sciences, School of Medicine, School of Nursing and Health Studies, School of Continuing Studies, and the McCourt School of Public Policy.

Georgetown's motto is *Utraque Unum*, meaning "both into one". The blue and gray Hoyas cheer *Hoya Saxa* meaning "what rocks" as the mascot Jack the Bulldog does his part to stir up the crowd at any of the twenty-nine varsity team Division I intercollegiate athletics events of which Georgetown is a participant. Approximately 800 student-athletes compete in the various varsity sports programs at Georgetown.

Harvard University

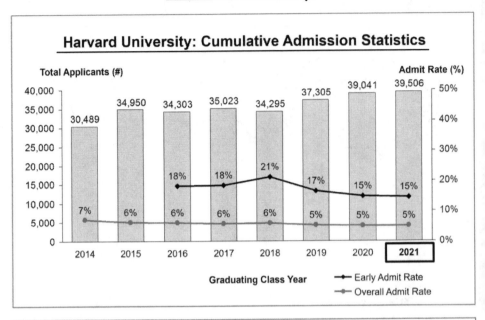

Harvard University: Cumulative Admission Statistics

Total Applicants (#) — Admit Rate (%)

Graduating Class Year	2014	2015	2016	2017	2018	2019	2020	2021
Total Applicants	30,489	34,950	34,303	35,023	34,295	37,305	39,041	39,506
Early Admit Rate			18%	18%	21%	17%	15%	15%
Overall Admit Rate	7%	6%	6%	6%	6%	5%	5%	5%

— Early Admit Rate
— Overall Admit Rate

Harvard University: ACT / New SAT Statistics

ACT	Average	25th Percentile	75th Percentile
Composite	34	32	35

New SAT	Average	25th Percentile	75th Percentile
Math	770	730	800
Reading	39	37	40
Writing	38	37	40
Composite	1540	1470	1600

Harvard University is an Ivy League School and its admissions statistics make it one of the most competitive Ivy League Schools. Similar to the trends across all top schools, Harvard University acceptance rates have continued to decline over the past 8 years and will almost certainly continue to do so into the future.

The Class of 2021 was one of the most challenging year to be admitted to Harvard University ever. For the Class of 2021, 39,506 students applied to Harvard University of which 2,056 students were accepted, yielding an overall acceptance rate of 5.2%. Overall applications increased by 1.2% over last year (2020 to 2021) from 39,041 to 39,506.

For the Class of 2021, 938 students were admitted through the early admissions process. Total early applications totaled 6,473, yielding an early acceptance rate of 14.5%. Early applications increased by 4.9% over last year (2020 to 2021) from 6,173 to 6,473.

Harvard University: Current Student Population

Total Enrollment	10,569	
Undergrad Enrollment	6,676	
Freshmen	1,675	
Male/Female	50%	50%
From Out of State	86%	
Undergrads Live on Campus	98%	
African American	7%	
Asian	18%	
Caucasian	45%	
Hispanic	9%	
Native American	<1%	
Mixed (2+ Ethnicities)	5%	
International	10%	
Countries Represented	109	

Harvard College, founded on September 8, 1636 in Cambridge, Massachusetts, is the oldest college in the United States, and is one of the oldest universities in the world. Harvard is a founding member of the Ivy League and has become one of the most prestigious and respected educational institutions globally.

Harvard graduates include some of the world's wealthiest and most influential people. In the media, Harvard alumni include Facebook founder Mark Zuckerberg and television and movie stars Bill O'Reilly, Tommy Lee Jones and Matt Damon. Harvard also has many alumni in the financial and political arenas including recent Federal Reserve Chairman Ben Bernanke, current CEO of Goldman Sachs, Lloyd Blankfein, Vice President Al Gore, and the current President of Mexico, Felipe Calderon.

Harvard College treasures its smaller, liberal arts college image and has approximately 6,500 undergraduates, maintaining a nearly 50/50 male-to-female ratio. The relatively small classes average forty or fewer students, allowing students tremendous access to Harvard faculty, which includes several Nobel Laureates.

As a whole, Harvard University has ten graduate and professional schools offering graduate studies. Some of Harvard's most famous graduate and professional schools include Harvard Law School, Harvard Divinity School, Harvard Medical School and the renowned Harvard Business School.

The Harvard Crimson are the athletic teams of Harvard University and are comprised of forty-two Division I intercollegiate varsity teams, more than any other Division I college. Approximately eighty percent of current undergraduate students participate in some form of athletic activity, primarily at the Club or Varsity Levels. The great Harvard vs. Yale football rivalry, more commonly known as "The Game", began in 1875. Harvard is also credited with building the first-ever concrete athletic stadium in 1903.

Harvard sponsors more than fifty cultural, ethnic and international organizations. There are also more than 400 student-run organizations including orchestras, chamber music ensembles, a Capella groups, newspapers, political publications, humor magazines, ethnic publications, economic journals, finance and investment clubs, and improve comedy groups.

Johns Hopkins University

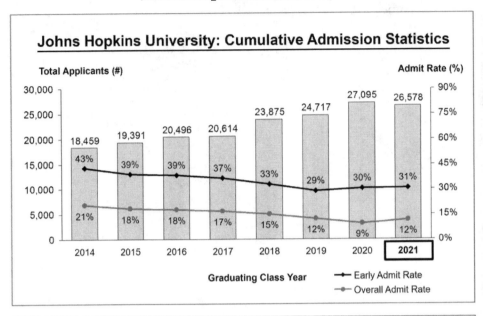

Johns Hopkins University: Cumulative Admission Statistics

Total Applicants (#)   **Admit Rate (%)**

Graduating Class Year	2014	2015	2016	2017	2018	2019	2020	2021
Total Applicants	18,459	19,391	20,496	20,614	23,875	24,717	27,095	26,578
Early Admit Rate	43%	39%	39%	37%	33%	29%	30%	31%
Overall Admit Rate	21%	18%	18%	17%	15%	12%	9%	12%

→ Early Admit Rate
→ Overall Admit Rate

Johns Hopkins University: ACT / New SAT Statistics

ACT	Average	25th Percentile	75th Percentile
Composite	33	32	34

New SAT	Average	25th Percentile	75th Percentile
Math	760	740	800
Reading	38	37	39
Writing	37	36	39
Composite	1510	1460	1570

Johns Hopkins University is a highly competitive school and its admissions statistics make Johns Hopkins University one of the 50 most competitive schools for undergraduate admissions globally. Similar to the trends across all top schools, Johns Hopkins University acceptance

rates have continued to decline over the past 8 years and will almost certainly continue to do so into the future.

The Class of 2021 was one of the most challenging year to be admitted to Johns Hopkins University ever. For the Class of 2021, 26,578 students applied to Johns Hopkins University of which 3,133 students were accepted, yielding an overall acceptance rate of 11.8%. Overall applications decreased by 1.9% over last year (2020 to 2021) from 27,095 to 26,578.

For the Class of 2021, 591 students were admitted through the early admissions process. Total early applications totaled 1,934, yielding an early acceptance rate of 30.6%. Early applications increased by 0.3% over last year (2020 to 2021) from 1,929 to 1,934.

Johns Hopkins University: Current Student Population

Total Enrollment	7,047	
Undergrad Enrollment	5,066	
Freshmen	3,576	
Male/Female	53%	47%
From Out of State	90%	
From Public High School	68%	
Undergrads Live on Campus	53%	
African American	5%	
Asian	20%	
Caucasian	51%	
Hispanic	9%	
Native American	<1%	
Mixed (2+ Ethnicities)	4%	
International	9%	
Countries Represented	71	

In 1876, Johns Hopkins University became the first university in the United States to be modeled after European research institutions.

Located in Baltimore, MD, the private research university aims to encourage research and the advancement of individual scholars, who by their excellence would advance the sciences they pursue, and the society in which they dwell. After more than 130 years in academia, it can certainly be said it has accomplished its original purpose, and much more. Johns Hopkins University currently claims the first place title for university research funding for the last thirty-four years running.

Johns Hopkins University's official current mission is "to educate its students and cultivate their capacity for life-long learning, to foster independent and original research, and to bring the benefits of discovery to the world." From the arts and music to humanities and natural sciences, engineering, international studies, business, medicine and more, Johns Hopkins University has become one of the most recognized education and research universities in the world. Two of the university's most popular current majors are International Studies and Writing Seminars. Others include Bioengineering and Biomedical Engineering, Neuroscience, Public Health, and Cell/Cellular and Molecular Biology.

When it comes to Johns Hopkins' International Studies and Writing Seminar majors, the school has a long list of notable alumni that includes the likes of Caryle Murphy, MA, SAIS 1987 Pulitzer Prize-winning journalist and long-time international reporter for The Washington Post, Jody Williams, MA, SAIS 1984 and founding coordinator of the International Campaign to Ban Landmines (ICBL) and winner of the 1997 Nobel Peace Prize; and Kathleen Schalch, MA, SAIS '88 and NPR business reporter. All are graduates of SAIS, Johns Hopkins University's Nitze School of Advanced International Studies.

Johns Hopkins University has a student population of approximately 20,871. Approximately 6,023 of those are undergraduates. The student-faculty ratio is about 10:1 and more than 3/4 of all classes have fewer than twenty students, providing more than ample attention to each and every attendee.

When it comes to activities outside of the classroom, more than two-thirds of the student body participate in at least one volunteer activity. Additionally, more than half of all undergraduates live in one of the ten residence halls or apartment buildings on the 140-acre campus. It can be seen how the collegiate social life flourishes with inner activity among the students who attend this prestigious university.

Johns Hopkins University competes in NCAA Division III athletics, with the exception of the men's and women's lacrosse teams, which are Division I.

Massachusetts Institute of Technology (MIT)

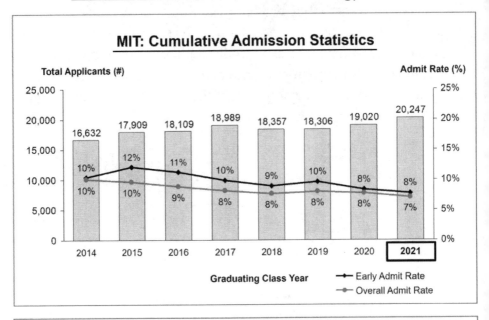

MIT: Cumulative Admission Statistics

Total Applicants (#)

Admit Rate (%)

Graduating Class Year		

Early Admit Rate
Overall Admit Rate

MIT : ACT / New SAT Statistics

ACT	Average	25th Percentile	75th Percentile
Composite	34	33	35

New SAT	Average	25th Percentile	75th Percentile
Math	780	770	800
Reading	38	36	40
Writing	37	36	40
Composite	1520	1480	1590

Massachusetts Institute of Technology is a highly competitive school and its admissions statistics make Massachusetts Institute of Technology one of the 50 most competitive schools for undergraduate admissions globally. Similar to the trends across all top schools, Massachusetts Institute of Technology acceptance rates have continued to decline over the past 8 years and will almost certainly continue to do so into the future.

The Class of 2021 was the single most challenging years to be admitted to Massachusetts Institute of Technology ever. For the Class of 2021, 20,247 students applied to Massachusetts Institute of Technology of which 1,438 students were accepted, yielding an overall acceptance rate of 7.1%. Overall applications increased by 6.5% over last year (2020 to 2021) from 19,020 to 20,247.

For the Class of 2021, 657 students were admitted through the early admissions process. Total early applications totaled 8,394, yielding an early acceptance rate of 7.8%. Early applications increased by 8.1% over last year (2020 to 2021) from 7,767 to 8,394.

Massachusetts Institute of Technology: Current Student Population

Total Enrollment	10,894	
Undergrad Enrollment	4,348	
Freshmen	1,128	
Male/Female	55%	45%
From Out of State	92%	
From Public High School	66%	
Undergrads Live on Campus	90%	
African American	7%	
Asian	24%	
Caucasian	36%	
Hispanic	15%	
Native American	1%	
Mixed (2+ Ethnicities)	3%	
International	10%	
Countries Represented	92	

Incorporated by the Commonwealth of Massachusetts on April 10, 1861, MIT officially opened its doors in 1865, situated on 168 acres in Cambridge, MA. Ranked first in the World University rankings for 2014/15 and second in the University Subject rankings for 2014/15, when it comes to all things related to technology, the independent, coeducational, and privately endowed university is one of the most respected educational institutions in the world.

MIT was founded by William Barton Rogers (a distinguished natural scientist) on the premise that professional competence is best fostered by joining teaching & research, and by focusing attention on real-world problems. Since that time, the official mission of MIT has become to advance knowledge and to educate students in science, technology, and other areas of scholarship that will best serve the nation and the world.

Today, MIT is known for having produced eighty Nobel laureates, fifty-six National Medal of Science winners, twenty-eight National Medal of Technology and Innovation winners, and forty-three MacArthur Fellows. The eighty Nobel laureate alumni are largely in the fields of economics, chemistry and physics.

The top employment sector for MIT undergraduates after graduation is computer technology. Approximately twenty-eight percent of all undergraduates were hired by companies such as Google, Oracle, McKinsey, Morgan Stanley, Accenture, Amazon, AthenaHealth, ExxonMobil, Microsoft, Boston Consulting Group, Goldman Sachs, Palantir and Shell. Twenty-one percent of all masters graduates went into various fields of engineering and twenty-five percent of all doctoral graduates went into education.

There are 1,319 students who attend MIT's five schools, which include the School of Science, MIT Sloan School of Management, School of Humanities, Arts, and Social Sciences, School of Engineering and the

School of Architecture and Planning. Approximately 4,512 of the students are undergraduates.

Nearly all first-year students live in one of MIT's residence halls. After the first year, students may then choose to remain on campus or to move into one of the thirty-six MIT-affiliated fraternities, sororities, and living groups.

MIT also has various award-winning extracurricular programs, from the arts to athletics and recreation programs. MIT also prides itself on computer hacking.

New York University

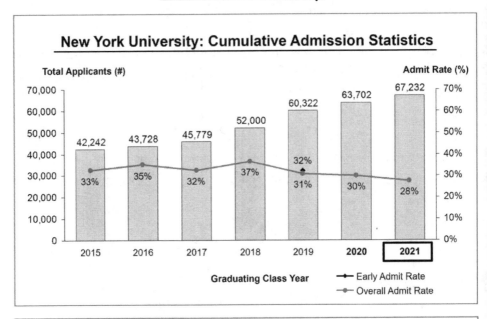

New York University: Cumulative Admission Statistics

Total Applicants (#) / Admit Rate (%)

Graduating Class Year	Total Applicants	Overall Admit Rate	Early Admit Rate
2015	42,242	33%	
2016	43,728	35%	
2017	45,779	32%	
2018	52,000	37%	
2019	60,322	31%	32%
2020	63,702	30%	
2021	67,232	28%	

New York University: ACT / New SAT Statistics

ACT	Average	25th Percentile	75th Percentile
Composite	30	28	32

New SAT	Average	25th Percentile	75th Percentile
Math	710	650	760
Reading	35	33	37
Writing	36	34	37
Composite	1410	1320	1500

New York University is a highly competitive school and its admissions statistics make New York University one of the 50 most competitive schools for undergraduate admissions globally. Similar to the trends across all top schools, New York University acceptance rates have

continued to decline over the past 8 years and will almost certainly continue to do so into the future.

The Class of 2021 was the single most challenging years to be admitted to New York University ever. For the Class of 2021, 67,232 students applied to New York University of which 18,520 students were accepted, yielding an overall acceptance rate of 27.5%. Overall applications increased by 5.5% over last year (2020 to 2021) from 63,702 to 67,232.

New York University: Current Student Population

Total Enrollment	43,911	
Undergrad Enrollment	22,280	
Freshmen	4,870	
Male/Female	40%	60%
From Out of State	73%	
From Public High School	65%	
Undergrads Live on Campus	47%	
African American	4%	
Asian	19%	
Caucasian	41%	
Hispanic	9%	
Native American	<1%	
Mixed (2+ Ethnicities)	2%	
International	10%	
Countries Represented	129	

Founded in 1831, New York University was built on Albert Gallatin's idea to create "a system of rational and practical education fitting for all and graciously opened to all." Since that time, NYU has become one of the largest private research universities in the United States and is one of only sixty member institutions distinguished in the Association of American Universities.

Centralized in the heart of Manhattan's Greenwich Village, NYU is in one of the most creative and lively communities in all New York. In addition to the Manhattan campus, NYU also has a Brooklyn campus, and Abu Dhabi and Shanghai also serve as extensions campuses for the university.

New York University states its mission to be "a top quality international center of scholarship, teaching and research". NYU has continually achieved its goal by maintaining its ability to attract and retain outstanding faculty who are leaders in their fields and who are able to encourage students through creative programs that create an intellectually rich environment.

Although NYU has a number of popular majors, such as degrees in Social Sciences, Business, General Studies and Humanities (just to name a few), NYU is most widely known for its exceptional ability to attract top talent interested in drama and film. The renowned Tisch School of the Arts offers both undergraduate and graduate programs in acting, dance, dramatic writing, film, television and more.

Notable alumni from the Tisch School include popular celebrities such as directors Martin Scorsese and Spike Lee; actor, writer and director, Woody Allen; and actresses Whoopi Goldberg and Angelina Jolie, plus many, many more.

NYU enrolls approximately 40,000 students annually in its eighteen schools and colleges. When NYU began in 1831, it started with a mere fourteen professors and lecturers. Today, the university has more than 3,100 full-time members throughout its various departments including the humanities department; sciences and social sciences departments; law, medicine and business departments; education; fine arts, studio arts, performing arts and cinematic arts departments; music; social work and more.

Both students and faculty have access to a full range of extracurricular activities and services that bolster the excitement of the university's academic culture. From medical attention to discount theater tickets, to academic facilities including nine libraries and dozens of specialized centers, to student services, residence halls and dining locations that everyone has access to—NYU has practically everything one could want or need in a university.

Northwestern University

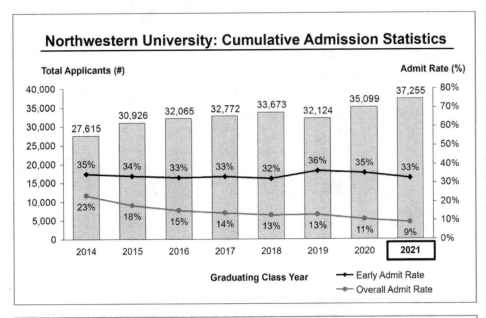

Northwestern University: ACT / New SAT Statistics

ACT	Average	25th Percentile	75th Percentile
Composite	33	31	34

New SAT	Average	25th Percentile	75th Percentile
Math	770	740	800
Reading	38	37	39
Composite	1510	1480	1580

Northwestern University is a highly competitive school and its admissions statistics make Northwestern University one of the 50 most competitive schools for undergraduate admissions globally. Similar to the trends across all top schools, Northwestern University acceptance

rates have continued to decline over the past 8 years and will almost certainly continue to do so into the future.

The Class of 2021 was the single most challenging years to be admitted to Northwestern University ever. For the Class of 2021, 37,255 students applied to Northwestern University of which 3,371 students were accepted, yielding an overall acceptance rate of 9%. Overall applications increased by 6.1% over last year (2020 to 2021) from 35,099 to 37,255.

For the Class of 2021, 1,100 students were admitted through the early admissions process. Total early applications totaled 3,376, yielding an early acceptance rate of 32.6%. Early applications increased by 11.7% over last year (2020 to 2021) from 3,022 to 3,376.

Northwestern University: Current Student Population

Total Enrollment	20,959	
Undergrad Enrollment	8,485	
Freshmen	2,107	
Male/Female	48%	52%
From Out of State	75%	
From Public High School	65%	
Undergrads Live on Campus	65%	
African American	6%	
Asian	19%	
Caucasian	56%	
Hispanic	7%	
Native American	<1%	
Mixed (2+ Ethnicities)	3%	
International	6%	
Countries Represented	42	

Northwestern University is a private research university founded in 1851. In 1853, the founders purchased an additional 379-acre tract of land on the shores of Lake Michigan, where they established the first campus. In 1855, they began their first classes with a mere two faculty members and ten students. Since then, Northwestern University has been built-up, and now offers roughly 150 majors from twelve schools and colleges, including their graduate and professional programs.

Northwestern University is known for its engineering, arts and communications programs. A few notable alumni in the area of communications are Peter Alexander, national correspondent, NBC News; Steve Bell, former correspondent for ABC News; and David Barstow, Pulitzer Prize-winning reporter for The New York Times.

Northwestern University has three main campuses in the U.S., with two of the campuses located on Lake Michigan and a third campus in Chicago. A satellite campus is also located in Doha, Qatar. The university enrolls more than 8,000 full-time undergraduates and 8,000 full-time graduate students. When part-time students are included, Wake University's total enrollment reaches 21,000. Northwestern has 3,344 full time faculty members, many of whom are distinguished Tony Award Winners, MacArthur Fellowship winners and more.

Northwestern has hundreds of campus organizations that meet a variety of student interests. The university is also filled with a large number of traditions and historical artifacts, such as "The Rock", a huge purple-and-white quartzite boulder set in the middle of campus, which dates back from hundreds of millions of years ago. It was moved from Devil's Lake, Wisconsin as a gift from the class of 1902.

When it comes to sports, Northwestern University is a Division I school in the Big Ten athletic conference. Of notable recognition is Northwestern's women's lacrosse team which has won multiple NCAA national championships.

Princeton University

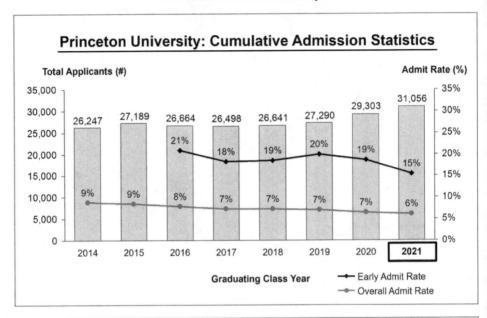

Princeton University: Cumulative Admission Statistics

Total Applicants (#)

Admit Rate (%)

Graduating Class Year	2014	2015	2016	2017	2018	2019	2020	2021
Total Applicants	26,247	27,189	26,664	26,498	26,641	27,290	29,303	31,056
Early Admit Rate			21%	18%	19%	20%	19%	15%
Overall Admit Rate	9%	9%	8%	7%	7%	7%	7%	6%

→ Early Admit Rate
→ Overall Admit Rate

Princeton University: ACT / New SAT Statistics

ACT	Average	25th Percentile	75th Percentile
Composite	33	32	35

New SAT	Average	25th Percentile	75th Percentile
Math	770	730	800
Reading	38	37	40
Writing	38	37	40
Composite	1520	1470	1590

Princeton University is an Ivy League School and its admissions statistics make it one of the most competitive Ivy League Schools. Similar to the trends across all top schools, Princeton University acceptance rates have continued to decline over the past 8 years and will almost certainly continue to do so into the future.

The Class of 2021 was the single most challenging year to be admitted to Princeton University ever. For the Class of 2021, 31,056 students applied to Princeton University of which 1,890 students were accepted, yielding an overall acceptance rate of 6.1%. Overall applications increased by 6.0% over last year (2020 to 2021) from 29,303 to 31,056.

For the Class of 2021, 770 students were admitted through the early admissions process. Total early applications totaled 5,003, yielding an early acceptance rate of 15.4%. Early applications increased by 18.3% over last year (2020 to 2021) from 4,229 to 5,003.

Princeton University: Current Student Population

Total Enrollment	7,859	
Undergrad Enrollment	5,249	
Freshmen	1,303	
Male/Female	51%	49%
From Out of State	83%	
From Public High School	59%	
Undergrads Live on Campus	98%	
African American	7%	
Asian	17%	
Caucasian	48%	
Hispanic	8%	
Native American	<1%	
Mixed (2+ Ethnicities)	4%	
International	10%	
Countries Represented	91	

Chartered in 1746, Princeton University is located in central New Jersey, and is the fourth oldest college in the United States and one of the oldest in the world. Princeton has a diverse campus community that enables students to learn from one another as they pursue academics and can choose from a plethora of extracurricular activities available to them.

Notable Princeton alumni include President and CEO of Forbes, Inc., Steve Forbes; environmental activist, attorney and best-selling author Ralph Nader; former CEO and executive chairman of Google, Eric Schmidt; CEO of Hewlett-Packard, Meg Whitman; and founder and CEO of Amazon.com, Jeff Bezos.

Princeton is known for its Institute for Advanced Study of Physics, made famous by the work of renowned scientist and Nobel Prize winning physicist Albert Einstein. Princeton also has a very strong English department and the creative writing program offers undergraduates the opportunity to learn from some of today's most respected writers including Jeffrey Eugenides, Chang-rae Lee, Paul Muldoon and Joyce Carol Oates.

Today, Princeton has more than 1,100 faculty members, approximately 5,200 undergraduate students, and 2,600 graduate students. Minority and international students represent approximately forty percent of the undergraduate student body.

Princeton's largest lecture hall seats 480 students, but most classes are broken up into smaller groups, with upper-level courses primarily offered in a seminar-style format, offering a high level of personalized attention.

Princeton has thirty-four departments and forty-seven interdepartmental certificate programs from which students may pursue either a Bachelor of Arts (B.A.) or Bachelor of Science in Engineering (BSE) degree. Princeton is considered to be a liberal arts university rather than a professional university, although it does offer many pre-professional courses to its students. Princeton differs from its fellow Ivy League peers as it does not have a law school or a business school.

When it comes to sports, the Princeton Tigers are an NCAA Division I, Ivy League school with 38 varsity teams.

One other unique aspect of Princeton are the eating clubs—private clubs resembling both college dining halls and social houses, where the majority of Princeton upperclassmen eat their meals. Each club occupies a large colonial style mansion on Prospect Avenue, one of the main roads that runs through the Princeton campus. The exception is the Terrace Club, which is just around the corner on Washington Road.

Stanford University

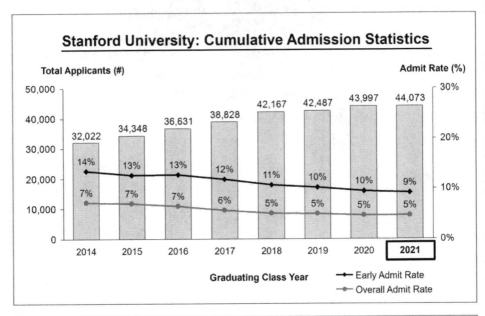

Stanford University: Cumulative Admission Statistics

Total Applicants (#)   Admit Rate (%)

Data points by year (Graduating Class Year):

Year	Total Applicants	Early Admit Rate	Overall Admit Rate
2014	32,022	14%	7%
2015	34,348	13%	7%
2016	36,631	13%	7%
2017	38,828	12%	6%
2018	42,167	11%	5%
2019	42,487	10%	5%
2020	43,997	10%	5%
2021	44,073	9%	5%

Legend: Early Admit Rate, Overall Admit Rate

Stanford University: ACT / New SAT Statistics

ACT	Average	25th Percentile	75th Percentile
Composite	33	31	35

New SAT	Average	25th Percentile	75th Percentile
Math	770	730	800
Reading	38	37	40
Writing	38	36	40
Composite	1520	1450	1590

Stanford University is a highly competitive school and its admissions statistics make Stanford University one of the 50 most competitive schools for undergraduate admissions globally. Similar to the trends across all top schools, Stanford University acceptance rates have

continued to decline over the past 8 years and will almost certainly continue to do so into the future.

The Class of 2021 was one of the most challenging year to be admitted to Stanford University ever. For the Class of 2021, 44,073 students applied to Stanford University of which 2,050 students were accepted, yielding an overall acceptance rate of 4.7%. Overall applications increased by 0.2% over last year (2020 to 2021) from 43,997 to 44,073.

For the Class of 2021, 721 students were admitted through the early admissions process. Total early applications totaled 7,822, yielding an early acceptance rate of 9.2%. Early applications remained flat over last year (2020 to 2021) from 7,822 to 7,822.

Stanford University: Current Student Population

Total Enrollment	19,945	
Undergrad Enrollment	7,603	
Freshmen	1,707	
Male/Female	52%	48%
From Out of State	54%	
From Public High School	58%	
Undergrads Live on Campus	91%	
African American	9%	
Asian	21%	
Caucasian	39%	
Hispanic	13%	
Native American	<1%	
Mixed (2+ Ethnicities)	11%	
International	7%	
Countries Represented	83	

Stanford University is a beautifully manicured university campus on 8,180 acres of prime real estate located in the heart of the Silicon Valley in Northern California. Established in 1885 and first opened in 1891, the private research university has nearly 700 buildings to accommodate its 7,018 undergraduate students and 9,118 graduate students annually.

Known as one of the world's leading research universities, Stanford has also recently bolstered its prominence for entrepreneurship in high-tech, due largely to its relationship with Silicon Valley. Stanford is well known to excel equally in humanities, social sciences, engineering and the sciences, in general.

When it comes to Stanford's fame for having a connection with entrepreneurial excellence, it can be said that Stanford is second to none. From Google founders Sergey Brin and Larry Page to Yahoo! co-founder, Jerry Yang, Stanford's trend of feeding Silicon Valley with the best minds in the business has been consistently top-notch. Some of Stanford's illustrious alumni include Carly Fiorina, CEO of Hewlett-Packard from 1999–2005; Brian Acton, co-founder of WhatsApp; Kurt Akeley, co-founder of Silicon Graphics and Jim Allchin, co-President of Microsoft, just to name a few.

Right in line with its tradition of producing outstanding entrepreneurs, Stanford University is considered to have the number one business graduate school in the United States, the Stanford Graduate School of Business. The university's six other schools are also some of the most highly respected schools in the country, including Stanford School of Earth, Energy and Environmental Sciences; Stanford Graduate School of Education; Stanford School of Humanities and Sciences; Stanford Engineering; Stanford Law and Stanford Medicine.

Outside of the classroom, Stanford features a massive list of things to do and see. In April of 2011, Stanford earned its 100th NCAA team national title. Foster field, the recently-built stadium completed in 2006, is home to Cardinal Football and seats an unbelievable 50,000 fans. When it comes to basketball and volleyball, Stanford University also shares an equal amenity with the beautiful Maples Pavilion. Sunken Diamond is the place to go for baseball lovers, and when it comes to water sports, dive into Avery Aquatic Center, one of the finest water centers in the nation.

Tufts University

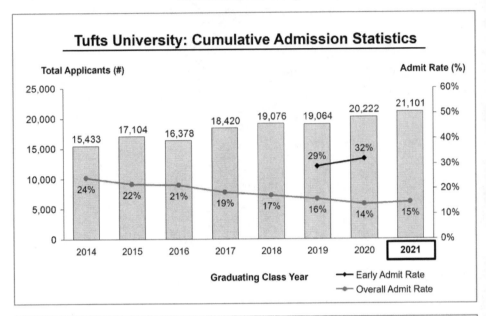

Tufts University: Cumulative Admission Statistics

Total Applicants (#) — Admit Rate (%)

Graduating Class Year	Total Applicants	Overall Admit Rate	Early Admit Rate
2014	15,433	24%	
2015	17,104	22%	
2016	16,378	21%	
2017	18,420	19%	
2018	19,076	17%	
2019	19,064	16%	29%
2020	20,222	14%	32%
2021	21,101	15%	

Tufts University: ACT / New SAT Statistics

ACT	Average	25th Percentile	75th Percentile
Composite	32	30	33

New SAT	Average	25th Percentile	75th Percentile
Math	750	720	780
Reading	37	36	39
Writing	37	36	39
Composite	1490	1440	1550

Tufts University is a highly competitive school and its admissions statistics make Tufts University one of the 50 most competitive schools for undergraduate admissions globally. Similar to the trends across all top schools, Tufts University acceptance rates have continued to decline

over the past 8 years and will almost certainly continue to do so into the future.

The Class of 2021 was one of the most challenging year to be admitted to Tufts University ever. For the Class of 2021, 21,101 students applied to Tufts University of which 3,128 students were accepted, yielding an overall acceptance rate of 14.8%. Overall applications increased by 4.3% over last year (2020 to 2021) from 20,222 to 21,101.

For the Class of 2021, 574 students were admitted through the early admissions process.

Tufts University: Current Student Population

Total Enrollment	10,777	
Undergrad Enrollment	5,194	
Freshmen	1,319	
Male/Female	49%	51%
From Out of State	77%	
From Public High School	59%	
Undergrads Live on Campus	64%	
African American	4%	
Asian	10%	
Caucasian	57%	
Hispanic	7%	
Native American	<1%	
Mixed (2+ Ethnicities)	3%	
International	7%	
Countries Represented	93	

Tufts University, located in the Medford/Somerville area of Massachusetts, is a private research university founded in 1852 when Boston businessman Charles Tufts donated the land for what was first called Tufts College. Tufts University has other local campuses as well, including a health sciences campus in Boston's Chinatown neighborhood, and a veterinary medicine school in the suburb of Grafton. The mission of the university was to be a "source of illumination, as a beacon standing on a hill, where its light cannot be hidden, its influence will naturally work like all light; it will be diffusive."

Tufts is recognized by the Carnegie Foundation as a Research University with "very high research activity" and is well known internationally for its School of Arts and Sciences in which 90% of all Tuft university students are enrolled. Tufts is also well-known for its internationalism and study abroad programs, with a huge percentage of all Tufts students studying abroad in places such as China, Oxford, Ghana, Paris, and Chile. One of many notable Tuft graduates is eBay founder Pierre Omidyar, but the university has a long tradition of hiring notable faculty as well, such as Allan M. Cormack, physicist, Nobel Prize recipient, and inventor of the CAT scan; Ayesha Jalal, historian of South Asia, MacArthur fellow, and Carnegie scholar; and Barry Trimmer, professor of Biology, and inventor (along with David Kaplan) of the world's first soft-bodied robot.

Tufts University enrolls 5,131 undergraduates, and 10,819 students in all. The university has a faculty and staff of 4,500 that work in and oversee the university's six libraries and four campuses at Medford/Somerville, Boston, Grafton, and Talloires, France.

Tufts University's colors are brown and blue, and Jumbo the elephant is the university mascot. Tuft has various university traditions, some of which are about 160 years old. One of the most popular at football games and homecoming is singing the Tufts Fight Song which was written in 1912 by Elliot W. Hayes.

University of Notre Dame

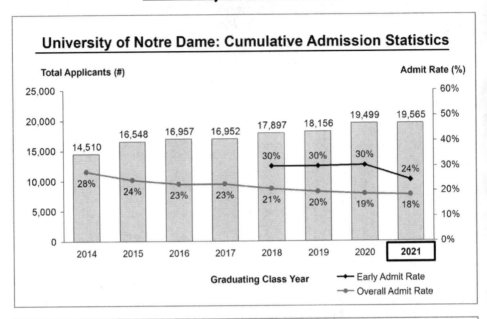

University of Notre Dame: Cumulative Admission Statistics

ACT	Average	25th Percentile	75th Percentile
Composite	33	32	34

New SAT	Average	25th Percentile	75th Percentile
Math	750	710	780
Reading	37	35	39
Writing	37	35	39
Composite	1490	1410	1550

University of Notre Dame is a highly competitive school and its admissions statistics make University of Notre Dame one of the 50 most competitive schools for undergraduate admissions globally. Similar to the trends across all top schools, University of Notre Dame acceptance

rates have continued to decline over the past 8 years and will almost certainly continue to do so into the future.

The Class of 2021 was the single most challenging year to be admitted to University of Notre Dame ever. For the Class of 2021, 19,565 students applied to University of Notre Dame of which 3,600 students were accepted, yielding an overall acceptance rate of 18.4%. Overall applications increased by 0.3% over last year (2020 to 2021) from 19,499 to 19,565.

For the Class of 2021, 1,470 students were admitted through the early admissions process. Total early applications totaled 6,020, yielding an early acceptance rate of 24.4%. Early applications increased by 13.1% over last year (2020 to 2021) from 5,321 to 6,020.

University of Notre Dame: Current Student Population

Total Enrollment	12,004	
Undergrad Enrollment	8,452	
Freshmen	2,020	
Male/Female	54%	46%
From Out of State	92%	
From Public High School	50%	
Undergrads Live on Campus	81%	
African American	3%	
Asian	6%	
Caucasian	74%	
Hispanic	9%	
Native American	<1%	
Mixed (2+ Ethnicities)	3%	
International	3%	
Countries Represented	87	

Founded in 1842 and located in St. Mary's, IN, Notre Dame is a private research university, ranked eighth according to Forbes, which resides on what is said by many to be one of the most beautiful university settings in the entire United States. Notre Dame is known as a traditional university that still welcomes change, as well as a university that, as the university states, is "dedicated to religious belief no less than scientific knowledge". Forty fellowships from the National Endowment for the Humanities have been extended to Notre Dame faculty members over recent years.

When it comes to the university's "scientific knowledge", the National Science Foundation ranks Notre Dame as one of the top three U.S. universities in the study of low-energy nuclear physics research. Notable Notre Dame alumni in such related areas of study include three NASA astronauts, Kevin Ford, Michael Good and Jim Wetherbee, as well as Former Flight Director of the Johnson Space Center, Annette Hasbrook.

Notre Dame comprises a student body that draws students from nearly every state in the U.S. and 100 other countries. Eighty percent of the undergraduate students live on campus, and eighty percent of those are also involved in community volunteer activities. Notre Dame's graduation rate of ninety-six percent is exceeded only by Harvard and Yale.

Notre Dame does not have any social fraternities or sororities and uses the university residence halls for many social activities. Notre Dame participates in NCAA Division I athletics and regularly ranks in the Learfield Sports Directors' Cup standings of the best overall athletic programs.

University of Pennsylvania

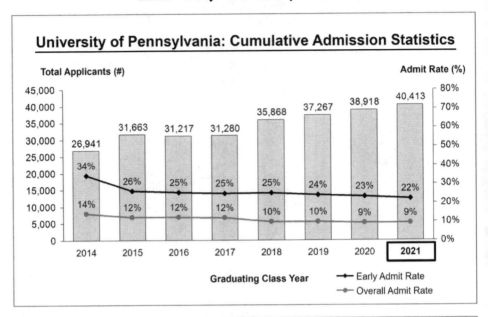

University of Pennsylvania: Cumulative Admission Statistics

ACT	Average	25th Percentile	75th Percentile
Composite	32	31	34

New SAT	Average	25th Percentile	75th Percentile
Math	760	730	800
Reading	37	36	39
Writing	38	36	40
Composite	1510	1450	1570

University of Pennsylvania is an Ivy League School and its admissions statistics fall in the middle of all Ivy League Schools. Similar to the trends across all top schools, University of Pennsylvania acceptance rates have continued to decline over the past 8 years and will almost certainly continue to do so into the future.

The Class of 2021 was the single most challenging years to be admitted to University of Pennsylvania ever. For the Class of 2021, 40,413 students applied to University of Pennsylvania of which 3,699 students were accepted, yielding an overall acceptance rate of 9.2%. Overall applications increased by 3.8% over last year (2020 to 2021) from 38,918 to 40,413.

For the Class of 2021, 1,354 students were admitted through the early admissions process. Total early applications totaled 6,147, yielding an early acceptance rate of 22.0%. Early applications increased by 6.7% over last year (2020 to 2021) from 5,762 to 6,147.

University of Pennsylvania: Current Student Population

Total Enrollment	19,919	
Undergrad Enrollment	9,779	
Freshmen	2,421	
Male/Female	49%	51%
From Out of State	81%	
From Public High School	57%	
Undergrads Live on Campus	56%	
African American	7%	
Asian	19%	
Caucasian	46%	
Hispanic	8%	
Native American	<1%	
Mixed (2+ Ethnicities)	2%	
International	11%	
Countries Represented	126	

The University of Pennsylvania was founded by Benjamin Franklin and George Whitefield in 1740 on the premise that educational programs should be focused as much on practical education for commerce and public service, as they should on the classics and theology. Now ranked number twelve on Forbes' list of top colleges, The University of

Pennsylvania (UPenn) is also number six on the list of top research schools in the United States.

UPenn's medical, dental, business, law, engineering, communications, and nursing schools all claim notable graduates. The University of Pennsylvania has placed prominent figures in practically every field imaginable. UPenn is even able to claim twenty-five billionaire alumni, including both Warren Buffett and Donald Trump.

Approximately 21,441 full-time students attend UPenn's four undergraduate schools, and twelve graduate and professional schools each year. A major research university, UPenn is furnished with 141 research centers and institutes. Its research budget is $851 million and it has a research community of nearly 11,000.

The UPenn athletes, better known as the Quakers, have a couple of time-honored traditions that they share with their fans: "The Line'"; a 24-hour overnight camp-out for choice basketball season tickets, or the "there's the toast" tradition, where at all home football games the Quaker mascot directs the crowd to toss pieces of toast onto the playing field, resulting in about 30,000 slices of bread per game on the sidelines.

University of Southern California

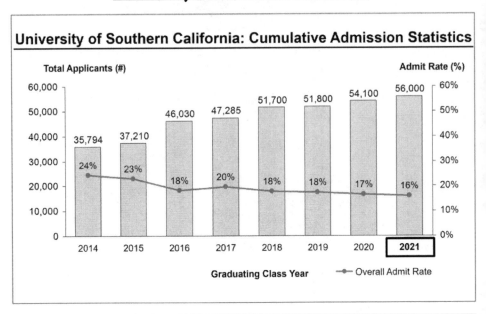

University of Southern California: Cumulative Admission Statistics

Total Applicants (#) — Admit Rate (%)

Graduating Class Year	Total Applicants	Overall Admit Rate
2014	35,794	24%
2015	37,210	23%
2016	46,030	18%
2017	47,285	20%
2018	51,700	18%
2019	51,800	18%
2020	54,100	17%
2021	56,000	16%

University of Southern California: ACT / New SAT Statistics

ACT	Average	25th Percentile	75th Percentile
Composite	32	30	33

New SAT	Average	25th Percentile	75th Percentile
Math	740	670	780
Reading	36	33	38
Writing	37	35	38
Composite	1450	1360	1540

University of Southern California is a highly competitive school and its admissions statistics make University of Southern California one of the 50 most competitive schools for undergraduate admissions globally. Similar to the trends across all top schools, University of Southern

California acceptance rates have continued to decline over the past 8 years and will almost certainly continue to do so into the future.

The Class of 2021 was the single most challenging year to be admitted to University of Southern California ever. For the Class of 2021, 56,000 students applied to University of Southern California of which 8,980 students were accepted, yielding an overall acceptance rate of 16.0%. Overall applications increased by 3.5% over last year (2020 to 2021) from 54,100 to 56,000.

University of Southern California: Current Student Population

Total Enrollment	44,000	
Undergrad Enrollment	19,000	
Freshmen	3,068	
Male/Female	55%	45%
From Out of State	44%	
From Public High School	63%	
Undergrads Live on Campus	30%	
African American	5%	
Asian	20%	
Caucasian	41%	
Hispanic	13%	
Native American	<1%	
Multiple Ethnicities	6%	
International	14%	
Countries Represented	65	

The University of Southern California (USC) is a private research university founded in 1880. Located on a beautiful 229-acre campus, USC is near the heart of the recently gentrified downtown Los Angeles, and a short distance from the Pacific Ocean.

USC was ranked twenty-third in the National University Rankings in 2014 by U.S. News, but USC's Annenberg School for Communication and Journalism is ranked 1st in the nation by USA Today's "Top Journalism Schools" of 2014. The university has become known for its Business Administration and Management, Speech Communication and Rhetoric, and Accounting programs, which have produced many Californian regional business leaders and professionals. In fact, of the more than 365,000 current USC alumni that can be found in positions of leadership globally, nearly an amazing 50% of them live in California.

Some of USC's alumni include the current owner of Los Angeles Dodgers, Frank McCourt Jr.; owner of the Los Angeles Lakers, Jerry Buss; and Chairman/CEO of Trader Joe's, Dan Bane.

USC has 43,000 undergraduate, graduate and professional students attending the university's 230+ programs. A little more than half of that figure is made up of graduate and professional students who are studying in fields such as business, law, engineering, architecture, pharmacy, public policy, and social work. USC also offers doctoral degrees in humanities, social sciences, medicine and dentistry.

The USC Trojans are an NCAA DIVISION I-A school in football, basketball, baseball, cross country and track. The university is known for their cross-town rivalry with UCLA, and the annual football game between the two schools is one of the most watched football games around the country. When it comes to clubs and organizations, USC has musical groups, performing arts organizations and an ROTC program, as well as journalism and publication organizations. In line with the university's number one rank in journalism, the school publishes The Southern California Review. Headed by Los Angeles Times book critic David Ulin, along with The New Yorker staff writer Dana Goodyear and run by MPW students, it has been publishing both fiction and poetry since 1982 and now also publishes creative nonfiction and short dramatic forms.

Vanderbilt University

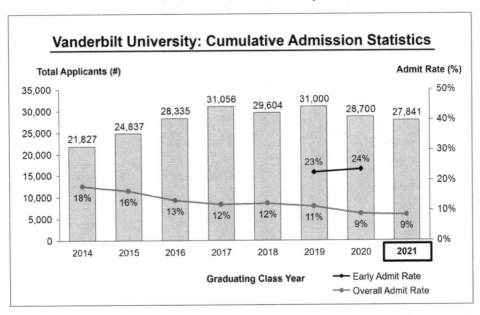

Vanderbilt University: Cumulative Admission Statistics

Total Applicants (#) — Admit Rate (%)

Graduating Class Year	2014	2015	2016	2017	2018	2019	2020	2021
Total Applicants	21,827	24,837	28,335	31,056	29,604	31,000	28,700	27,841
Overall Admit Rate	18%	16%	13%	12%	12%	11%	9%	9%
Early Admit Rate						23%	24%	

Vanderbilt University: ACT / New SAT Statistics

ACT	Average	25th Percentile	75th Percentile
Composite	34	32	35

New SAT	Average	25th Percentile	75th Percentile
Math	780	750	800
Reading	39	37	40
Writing	38	36	39
Composite	1530	1480	1590

Vanderbilt University is a highly competitive school and its admissions statistics make Vanderbilt University one of the 50 most competitive schools for undergraduate admissions globally. Similar to the trends across all top schools, Vanderbilt University acceptance rates have

continued to decline over the past 8 years and will almost certainly continue to do so into the future.

The Class of 2021 was the single most challenging year to be admitted to Vanderbilt University ever. For the Class of 2021, 27,841 students applied to Vanderbilt University of which 2,382 students were accepted, yielding an overall acceptance rate of 8.6%. Overall applications decreased by 3% over last year (2020 to 2021) from 28,700 to 27,841.

Vanderbilt University: Current Student Population

Total Enrollment	12,836	
Undergrad Enrollment	6,817	
Freshmen	1,601	
Male/Female	50%	50%
From Out of State	89%	
From Public High School	58%	
Undergrads Live on Campus	86%	
African American	7%	
Asian	7%	
Caucasian	62%	
Hispanic	8%	
Native American	<1%	
Mixed (2+ Ethnicities)	4%	
International	5%	
Countries Represented	96	

Nashville, Tennessee is home to Vanderbilt University. Founded in 1873, this private research university was built on a vision by Cornelius Vanderbilt to "contribute to strengthening the ties that should exist between all sections of our common country". Today, Vanderbilt is not only recognized around the country, but around the world as a top research university that offers undergraduate programs in various areas, including the liberal arts and sciences, music, human development, engineering and education.

When it comes to Vanderbilt University recognition, the university is nationally known for its schools of business, having one of the top graduate schools of education in the nation and for having a distinguished medical center.

Some of the most notable alumni in those recognized areas are Muhammad Yunus, Ph.D. who won the Nobel Peace Prize in 2006 for establishing the Grameen Bank; Stanley Cohen, a Medical Center faculty member who won a Nobel Prize in Medicine in 1986; and Earl Sutherland Jr., another Medical Center faculty member who in 1971 also won a Nobel Prize in Medicine.

Vanderbilt enrolls 6,767 full-time undergraduate students, eighty-six percent of whom live on campus. Vanderbilt's undergraduate student-to-faculty ratio is 8:1, which is spread over its wide array of colleges and schools, including Vanerbilt College of Arts and Science, Blair School of Music, Divinity School, School of Engineering, Law School, School of Medicine, School of Nursing, Owen Graduate School of Management and the Peabody College of Education and Human Development.

Vanderbilt University has more than 500 clubs and organizations, including fifteen sororities and seventeen fraternities. Student housing includes twenty-six fraternity and sorority houses as well as thirty-nine residence halls and apartments that can accommodate 5,448 students.

The university has a variety of traditions, both recent and well-aged. Some of these traditions include Movie Night, Maggie Moo's, and Commons Lawn, "where Sunday nights are filled with ice cream, movies, and friends". There are also more physically interactive traditions such as the Founders Walk, "which is an old Vanderbilt tradition to welcome new first-year and transfer students where walkers trek the outskirts of campus and end up at Wilson Lawn, but not before encountering a

HUGE crowd of our student groups lining the final stretch, cheering and welcoming everyone to campus."

Wake Forest University

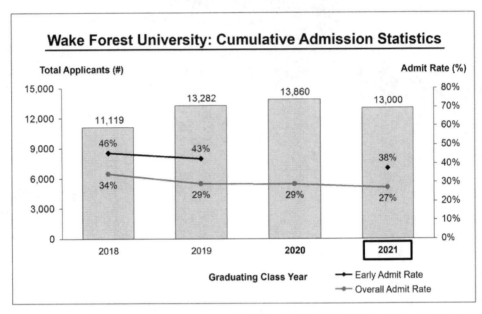

Wake Forest University: Cumulative Admission Statistics

Total Applicants (#) / Admit Rate (%)

- 2018: 11,119 — 46% (Early), 34% (Overall)
- 2019: 13,282 — 43% (Early), 29% (Overall)
- 2020: 13,860 — 29% (Overall)
- 2021: 13,000 — 38% (Early), 27% (Overall)

Graduating Class Year

→ Early Admit Rate
→ Overall Admit Rate

Wake Forest University: ACT / New SAT Statistics

ACT	Average	25th Percentile	75th Percentile
Composite	30	28	31

New SAT	Average	25th Percentile	75th Percentile
Math	690	630	750
Reading	34	32	37
Writing	35	33	37
Composite	1380	1290	1470

Wake Forest University is a highly competitive school and its admissions statistics make Wake Forest University one of the 50 most competitive schools for undergraduate admissions globally. Similar to the trends across all top schools, Wake Forest University acceptance rates have

continued to decline over the past 8 years and will almost certainly continue to do so into the future.

The Class of 2021 was the single most challenging years to be admitted to Wake Forest University ever. For the Class of 2021, 13,000 students applied to Wake Forest University of which 3,500 students were accepted, yielding an overall acceptance rate of 26.9%. Overall applications decreased by 6.2% over last year (2020 to 2021) from 13,860 to 13,000.

For the Class of 2021, 750 students were admitted through the early admissions process. Total early applications totaled 2,000, yielding an early acceptance rate of 37.5%.

Wake Forest University: Current Student Population

Total Enrollment	7,351	
Undergrad Enrollment	4,775	
Male/Female	48%	52%
From Out of State	77%	
From Public High School	65%	
Undergrads Live on Campus	68%	
African American	8%	
Asian	5%	
Caucasian	78%	
Hispanic	5%	
Native American	<1%	
Mixed (2+ Ethnicities)	2%	
International	2%	
Countries Represented	27	

Founded in 1834, not far from the Blue Ridge Mountains in Winston-Salem, North Carolina, Wake Forest University is a private research university that incorporates the kind of charismatic personal attention often found at liberal arts colleges but offers both undergraduate programs leading to the Bachelor of Arts and Bachelor of Science degrees.

Wake Forest has made one of its on-going goals to educate global leaders with innovative training in the form of liberal arts. The university's School of Business is considered one which develops "relevant business skills and helps students to find their passion".

Some of the most recognized Wake Forest alumni who have made an immense impact in the field of business include Charlie Ergen, co-founder and CEO of Dish Network; Zach Klein, co-founder of Vimeo; D. Wayne Calloway, Former CEO of PepsiCo; Jabez A. Bostwick, American businessman and founding partner of Standard Oil, and a number of others.

The total enrollment at Wake Forest University is 7,591, with 1,288 of that being freshmen. Total undergraduate enrollment is 4,812 and the remaining enrollment of 2,779 makes up the graduate and professional school numbers.

Wake Forest has forty undergraduate and graduate departments that cover a variety of majors and minors. The university also has interdisciplinary programs, service-learning programs, co-curricular programs, and research opportunities.

Wake Forest University competes in eighteen Division I sports in the Atlantic Coast Conference (ACC) and offers intramural sports and outdoor trips such as kayaking on the New River, hang-gliding and sky-diving. The university has over 150 chartered student organizations in a number of categories such as Civic Engagement, Cultural & Multicultural, Fraternities, Philanthropy and Fundraising, Professional and more.

Williams College

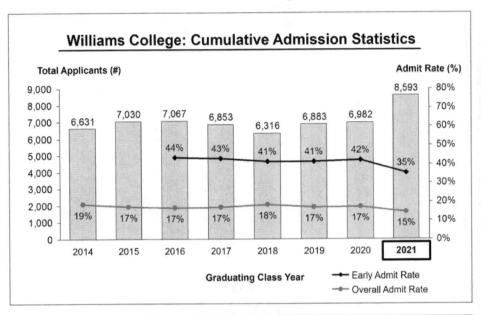

Williams College: Cumulative Admission Statistics

Total Applicants (#) — Admit Rate (%)

Graduating Class Year	Total Applicants	Early Admit Rate	Overall Admit Rate
2014	6,631		19%
2015	7,030		17%
2016	7,067	44%	17%
2017	6,853	43%	17%
2018	6,316	41%	18%
2019	6,883	41%	17%
2020	6,982	42%	17%
2021	8,593	35%	15%

Williams College: ACT / New SAT Statistics

ACT	Average	25th Percentile	75th Percentile
Composite	32	31	34

New SAT	Average	25th Percentile	75th Percentile
Math	730	690	780
Reading	38	36	40
Writing	37	36	40
Composite	1490	1410	1570

Williams College is a highly competitive school and its admissions statistics make Williams College one of the 50 most competitive schools for undergraduate admissions globally. Similar to the trends across all top schools, Williams College acceptance rates have continued to decline

over the past 8 years and will almost certainly continue to do so into the future.

The Class of 2021 was the single most challenging years to be admitted to Williams College ever. For the Class of 2021, 8,593 students applied to Williams College of which 1,253 students were accepted, yielding an overall acceptance rate of 14.6%. Overall applications increased by 23.1% over last year (2020 to 2021) from 6,982 to 8,593.

For the Class of 2021, 257 students were admitted through the early admissions process. Total early applications totaled 728, yielding an early acceptance rate of 35.3%. Early applications increased by 24.4% over last year (2020 to 2021) from 585 to 728.

Williams College: Current Student Population

Total Enrollment	2,109	
Undergrad Enrollment	2,053	
Freshmen	551	
Male/Female	47%	53%
From Out of State	70%	
From Public High School	60%	
Undergrads Live on Campus	99%	
African American	11%	
Asian	13%	
Caucasian	65%	
Hispanic	10%	
Native American	1%	
Mixed (2+ Ethnicities)	5%	
International	6%	
Countries Represented	79	

Williams College is located in Williamstown, Massachusetts and is situated between the foothills of the Berkshire Mountains and the fringes of urban settings. Established in 1793, Forbes ranks Williams College as the number one top college in America, first in private colleges, first in the Northeast and third in Grateful Grads, as of 2015. The elite school has thirty-six majors available with no required courses; the exception being that all students must complete three arts and humanities courses, three social sciences courses and three science and math courses.

Williams College is known to attract talented, highly motivated students and faculty. Williams College is also known to be first for many things, such as being the world's first society of alumni, the first to wear caps and gowns for graduations, and the first to host an intercollegiate baseball game. More than 60% of Williams College graduates have gone on to earn at least one graduate or professional degree, with the most popular degrees being in the areas of management, education, law, and health care.

Some of Williams' most notable alumni include: Kristin Forbes, Associate Professor of International Management at the MIT Sloan School of Management, and Member of the Council of Economic Advisers—confirmed by the United States Senate in 2003, she is the youngest person to ever hold this position; Morris Leopold Ernst, lawyer and co-founder of the American Civil Liberties Union, and Jonathan Fielding, M.D., Director of the Los Angeles County Department of Public Health.

The undergraduate enrollment at Williams College is approximately 2,000 students, with a student-faculty ratio of about 7:1. Williams College has three academic divisions (languages and the arts, social sciences, and science and mathematics) that encompass its twenty-five departments, thirty-six majors, and several concentrations and special programs. Williams College has Oxford-style tutorials that require heavy student participation.

Although fraternities have been phased out since 1962, Williams has about 150 student organizations with about 96% of all students participating in at least one extracurricular activity such as the Williams College Law Society, Williams College Literary Review, Williams College Medical Reserve Corps and the Williams College Nordic Ski Club.

Washington University in St. Louis

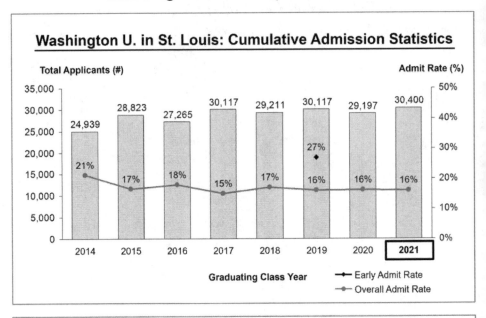

Washington U. in St. Louis: Cumulative Admission Statistics

Total Applicants (#) — Admit Rate (%)

Graduating Class Year	2014	2015	2016	2017	2018	2019	2020	2021
Total Applicants	24,939	28,823	27,265	30,117	29,211	30,117	29,197	30,400
Overall Admit Rate	21%	17%	18%	15%	17%	16%	16%	16%
Early Admit Rate						27%		

Washington U. in St. Louis: ACT / New SAT Statistics

ACT	Average	25th Percentile	75th Percentile
Composite	33	32	34

New SAT	Average	25th Percentile	75th Percentile
Math	770	740	800
Reading	38	37	39
Writing	38	36	39
Composite	1510	1460	1570

Washington University in St. Louis is a highly competitive school and its admissions statistics make Washington University in St. Louis one of the 50 most competitive schools for undergraduate admissions globally. Similar to the trends across all top schools, Washington University in St.

Louis acceptance rates have continued to decline over the past 8 years and will almost certainly continue to do so into the future.

The Class of 2021 was one of the most challenging years to be admitted to Washington University in St. Louis ever. For the Class of 2021, 30,400 students applied to Washington University in St. Louis of which 4,864 students were accepted, yielding an overall acceptance rate of 16%. Overall applications increased by 4.1% over last year (2020 to 2021) from 29,197 to 30,400.

Washington University: Current Student Population

Total Enrollment	13,908	
Undergrad Enrollment	7,239	
Freshmen	1,633	
Male/Female	48%	52%
From Out of State	93%	
From Public High School	57%	
Undergrads Live on Campus	79%	
African American	6%	
Asian	15%	
Caucasian	58%	
Hispanic	4%	
Native American	<1%	
Mixed (2+ Ethnicities)	3%	
International	7%	
Countries Represented	90	

Located in St. Louis, Missouri and founded in 1853, Washington University is a private research institution that considers itself a medium-sized, independent university. The university enrolls 7,336 undergraduates annually on a semester-based schedule.

Washington University recently ranked first in social work, second in best college dorms and fifth as the best undergraduate business school.

The university makes it their mission "to discover and disseminate knowledge, and protect the freedom of inquiry through research, teaching, and learning."

Just two of the many alumni who have contributed to the university's reputation for service to society include forerunner of feminist thought in American sociology, Jessie Shirley Bernard, and American civil rights activist, author, civil servant and sociologist, Joyce Ann Ladner.

Washington University has more than 150 buildings on its 2,300 acre campus which accommodates its undergraduate population, along with an additional 6,500 graduate students and about 1,000 non-traditional students (enrolled for evening and weekends).

The list of Washington University traditions is lengthy. Keeping up the school's image through the promotion of social issues, the Dance Marathon benefits the Children's Miracle Network. The All Student Theatre takes students from every major in the university and gives them the opportunity to produce and perform a play at Beaumont Pavilion.

Yale University

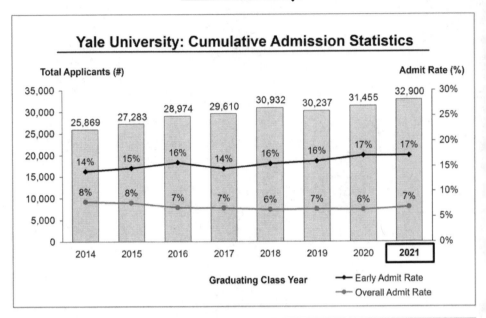

Yale University: ACT / New SAT Statistics

ACT	Average	25th Percentile	75th Percentile
Composite	33	31	35

New SAT	Average	25th Percentile	75th Percentile
Math	770	740	800
Reading	39	38	40
Writing	38	37	40
Composite	1540	1490	1600

Yale University is an Ivy League School and its admissions statistics make it one of the most competitive Ivy League Schools. Similar to the trends across all top schools, Yale University acceptance rates have continued to decline over the past 8 years and will almost certainly continue to do so into the future.

The Class of 2021 was one of the most challenging years to be admitted to Yale University ever. For the Class of 2021, 32,900 students applied to Yale University of which 2,272 students were accepted, yielding an overall acceptance rate of 6.9%. Overall applications increased by 4.6% over last year (2020 to 2021) from 31,455 to 32,900.

For the Class of 2021, 871 students were admitted through the early admissions process. Total early applications totaled 5,086, yielding an early acceptance rate of 17.1%. Early applications increased by 9.1% over last year (2020 to 2021) from 4,662 to 5,086.

Yale University: Current Student Population

Total Enrollment	11,875	
Undergrad Enrollment	~6,200*	
Freshmen	~1,550	
Male/Female	50%	50%
From Out of State	94%	
From Public High School	55%	
Undergrads Live on Campus	88%	
African American	6%	
Asian	15%	
Caucasian	47%	
Hispanic	10%	
Native American	1%	
Mixed (2+ Ethnicities)	6%	
International	10%	
Countries Represented	108	

*Assumes four years of freshmen enrollment at 1,550

Founded in 1701, Yale University ranks third among U.S. universities listed in the 2015 edition of *Best Colleges and National Universities.*

Some of the university's most popular majors include Economics, Political Science and Government. As such, Yale's alumni make up some of the most influential public figures, policy makers and foreign relations experts in the United States. More U.S. presidents have attended Yale University than any other university in the U.S., including Gerald Ford, George H. W. Bush, Bill Clinton, and George W. Bush.

Located in New Haven, Connecticut, Yale University is comprised of Yale College (for undergraduates), the Graduate School of Arts and Sciences, and thirteen other professional schools. Together, the student population of all Yale schools is approximately 5,379 undergraduate students, 6,501 graduate and professional students, and 2,135 international students. There is an approximate 50/50 male-to-female ratio among students.

The university is known for its small class sizes and offers hundreds of seminars capped at just twelve students. There are approximately six students for every faculty member, which contributes to more than 75% of all Yale classes having less than twenty students per class. Yale students are assigned to live in one of twelve residential colleges, each run by an appointed master and dean. The most famous residential colleges are Branford, Silliman, Saybrook and Davenport Colleges. The residential college system is a central part of every undergraduate student's social experience at Yale, as each residential college has its own dining hall, gymnasium, entertainment complex, and student café. Additionally, each of the campus Cultural houses, such as the Asian American Cultural Center and the Latino Cultural Center, provide a way for students to express cultural identity on campus.

Yale features thirty sports programs for both men and women. Popular sports include basketball, volleyball, golf, ice hockey and soccer. There are also many less-conventional sport offerings as well, including inner-tubing, water polo and dodge ball, as well as a coed sailing program.

Appendix III:
Testimonials

"Your approach – bringing creativity and entrepreneurial shrewdness to the equation – was greatly appreciated. I see my son continuing to build on these skills that will continue to serve him well in the future"
—*Parent (North Carolina), Son Admitted to New York University (NYU)*

"The way you logically approached the situation and laid out a roadmap for success made perfect sense and allowed me to focus my time on activities that really maximized my chances of admission"
—*Daniel (New York), Admitted to Williams College*

"I am still on cloud nine: my daughter Alexandra, was just admitted via the Early Action application program to Harvard College, her top choice. This would not have been possible without the advice and personal guidance of Sam Silverman over the past several years. Not only did Sam get our oldest daughter into Harvard, but he also removed the stress and confusion from the college application process that my husband and I would have gone through otherwise. Sam's approach to the college application process is strategic, logical, and above all made sense to our family. Sam works with a select clientele who are passionate about providing their children with the best opportunities to attend top colleges and universities. My husband and I could not be happier with our experience working with Sam and are so grateful for his support and guidance toward Alexandra during a crucial time in her life. If we had to do it again, we would work with Sam without a moment's hesitation. We enthusiastically recommend Sam to any parent who feels that their child's school's college guidance department may not appreciate their child's special needs, talent or desire to gain admission to their "reach" school. Dreams do come true with proper planning, guidance and enthusiasm provided by knowledgeable and experienced college counselors like Sam Silverman."
—*Parent (Florida), Daughter Admitted to Harvard University*

"Sam did an incredible job guiding me through the admissions process. From sharing award program ideas I should apply for to editing my resume, to helping me think through what my essay and short answer topics should be. I could not have done it without him"
—*Margaret (Connecticut) Admitted to American University*

"In short, by hiring Sam, you will help your child gain admission to colleges/universities that otherwise would be out of reach, and remove all of the stress that comes down on involved parents who want to give their child the best possible education, but are not sure where to begin."
—*Parent (Massachusetts), Daughter Admitted to every college applied to*

"Not only was I admitted to one of my top choices, but I also received over $35K in scholarship awards thanks to your guidance in developing my extra-curricular activities and making my admissions profile truly one-of-a-kind. I cannot thank you enough, my family is overjoyed."
—*Natasha, (Florida) Admitted to Washington University in St. Louis*

"With college counseling, Sam knows all the tricks of the trade to place your child in the best possible position to gain admission to their desired college or university. For those parents who are not sure where to begin, or what to do in general, Sam Silverman is the answer. With his individualized advice and customized planning techniques, your child will have the best chance of seeing their collegiate dreams come true."
—*Parent (Florida), Daughter Admitted to Georgetown University*

"I did not know what we were missing until we began working with Sam. His value was helping us to develop and execute a unique extracurricular project that gave our son the "edge" that he needed to be competitive in today's highly selective admissions process and gain admission to Stanford."
—*Parent (California), Son Admitted to Stanford University*

"When I began preparing my law school application materials, I was thrilled to find that you had expanded to graduate school admissions as well. Your comments and suggestions on my law school application, resume, and personal statement were invaluable, and they helped me tell my story to law schools across the country. This week I heard back from several law schools and again was admitted to my top choice, Stetson University College of Law where I will be starting law school in the fall. I cannot thank you enough for all of your help and support. You are the first person I think of when I need advice on important decisions and I am very grateful that you have always been there for me. I look forward to returning back to North Palm Beach after graduation next month and catching up with you in person over the summer."

—*Jacyln (Florida), Admitted to Stetson University College of Law*

"Sam began working with my oldest daughter when she was in 10th grade, now she is attending college in the U.S. and he is working with my two younger daughters 8th and 9th grade respectively...I could not be happier with his help and the impact he has had on the way my daughters approach their schoolwork and prepare for applying for college."

—*Parent (England), Daughter Admitted to Elon University*

"Sam worked closely with my older son to help him differentiate himself among other applicants when it came time to put together his college applications. Sam helped my son present his athletic, academic, and community service accomplishments to my son's top choices for college. Today my son is currently enrolled in a top undergraduate business school and still connects with Sam to better navigate business school and internship opportunities. Sam uses a pragmatic, "work-smarter" approach to all that he does – an approach that is extremely effective in helping to develop a student's profile for college admission. It is not only about the amount of time that one spends to prepare for the admissions process, but also the quality and focus of the preparation that counts. Most importantly, Sam is extremely committed to the future of his students and is 110% invested in their application process. He takes the

time to understand his client's interests and to locate and recommend the next steps needed to help his client accomplish his or her goals."
—*Parent (Florida), Son Admitted to U. Michigan Ross School of Business*

"I still cannot believe that I got into Dartmouth- - my dream school around the corner...I cannot thank you enough for helping me through crunch time and making sure that I spent my time effectively."
—*Michael (North Carolina), Admitted to Dartmouth College*

"Ryan and I really appreciate the unbelievable responsiveness and professionalism you portrayed during the college admission process. I believe that your guidance, professionalism and accessibility have given Ryan the opportunity to attend some of the best schools in the country. Your skill and experience in project management exemplifies excellence and has been a great lesson for my son. He was notified this week that NYU Abu Dhabi is interested in him attending and they have selected him to participate in a fully paid candidate weekend prior to admission."
—*Parent (South Carolina), Son Admitted to New York University Abu Dhabi*

"Thank you for the brilliant admissions counseling meeting with Kelly. She is only a freshman, but you really inspired her and it shows. I cannot thank you enough."
—*Parent (Massachusetts), Current Client*

"I am a graduating senior this year and a few months ago, I gained admission to my dream school—Harvard College. Working closely with Sam Silverman the past three years helped turn this childhood dream into a reality. Unlike The Benjamin School College Guidance Department, Sam is focused on providing clear and actionable advice to help his students differentiate themselves from the competition and gain admission to top schools. My Benjamin School guidance counselor was working with ~50 other senior students besides me and so it was basically impossible to meet more than a few times senior year and get the individualized attention that I got with Sam starting in my sophomore year. Sam's advice allowed me to focus on what really mattered in preparing the best application possible and greatly reduced the stress of the process as he was always there to answer questions and remove any guesswork on my part. He also helped me identify scholarships that I could apply for and I received thousands of dollars in scholarship awards as a result. There is no doubt that if I had to do it again, I would work with Sam, and I would highly recommend him to other students who want personal advice and are looking to attend competitive colleges/universities."

—*Alexandra (Florida), Admitted to Harvard University*

We were impressed with Sam. He is a sharp, thoughtful young professional with impeccable academic credentials. To say we were pleased with the work and advice Sam provided would be an understatement. Our son was a challenging student to work with. He had very high SAT and AP scores but his GPA reflected a student who wasn't particularly engaged. In his junior year, he decided Southern Methodist University (SMU) would be his first choice. The college counselors at his high school thought SMU would be a reach for him due to the difference between his grades and his test scores. They didn't particularly encourage him to apply, and they suggested a number of weaker schools. I always felt conversations with his school counselors were rushed with formulaic advice. Sam, by way of contrast, was extremely attentive. His guidance was thoughtful. There was never a question in my mind that my son's best interests were Sam's top priority.

My son ultimately applied as an early-decision applicant to SMU, choosing to follow Sam's guidance over the guidance offered by his school counselors. The school counselors suggested his essay was inappropriate because he discussed a summer working for a US Congressman running for the US Senate. The school counselors felt the essay didn't say enough about him. Sam believed the essay, which focused on the political process in the United States and his feeling with respect to how it was failing its citizens, said more about him than any typical college essay.

My son was not only accepted at SMU, he was offered a $44,000 Cornerstone Scholarship for academic excellence and leadership. In the acceptance letter, SMU specifically referenced how impressed it was with his essay and what he took away from his internship experience. Had he not worked with Sam, I suspect he would not be at SMU today and certainly would not have been awarded a prestigious scholarship. I would certainly work with Sam again and have recommended him to close friends. In today's environment, I don't believe you can gain the type of insight and guidance Sam provides if you rely entirely in-house school college placement offices.

—*Parent (Florida), Son Admitted to Southern Methodist University (SMU)*

"Dear Sam, Fred and I just wanted to send you a heartfelt thank you. You have been an enormously positive influence on Harrison, already. We notice a big change in his attitude. We are really grateful for the time you are spending with him. Thank you so much!! Please feel free to let us know how we can support your efforts."

—*Parent (New York), Son Admitted to Duke University and Washington University in St. Louis*

Appendix IV:
Letters of Recommendation for Ivy League Prep

Yvette Trelles

███████████████

North Palm Beach, Fl 33408

███████████████

Samuel B. Silverman
Ivy League Prep
3801 PGA Blvd., Suite 902
Palm Beach Gardens, FL 33410
www.IvyLeaguePrep.com

January 13, 2015

To Whom It May Concern:

I am still on cloud nine: my daughter, Alexandra Murray, a senior at The Benjamin School, was recently admitted via the Early Action application program to Harvard College, her top choice.

This would not have been possible without the advice and personal guidance of Sam Silverman over the past several years. Not only did Sam get our oldest daughter into Harvard, but he also removed the stress and confusion from the college application process that my family and I would have gone through otherwise.

To put this in context, over a dozen students from Alexandra's Benjamin School Class applied through Early Action / Decision programs to Ivy League schools and other top tier schools including Stanford, Duke and Georgetown. Alexandra was the only one offered early admission to any of these schools — a testament to Sam's personalized strategy and approach to the college application process.

I first met Sam in 2011 after learning of his college admission consulting services from fellow parents at Benjamin and through an informational mailing that he does each year.

After meeting with Sam and speaking with other parents who had engaged him, I decided he would be a great fit to work with Alexandra, my oldest daughter. This was several years ago when Alexandra had just transferred from another school and was a freshman at Benjamin.

Alexandra was always a strong student academically, but her standardized test scores had room for improvement and she needed a creative idea or "edge" and

1

the expertise to develop, emphasize and maximize her potential. Over the past several years, Sam worked closely with our family to develop a custom theme for Alexandra's college application that would help her stand out from the worldwide competition. Sam has always been extremely accessible and reliable and willing to answer all of our questions about the application process.

Sam also went above and beyond, helping Alexandra seek out unique ways to gain third-party recognition for leadership in her extracurricular activities, identify scholarship opportunities, and strengthen her overall application to college. Beyond helping us through the application process, Sam has additionally become a close friend and mentor for Alexandra and today we consider him part of the family.

Sam's approach to the college application process is strategic, logical, and above all made sense to our family. Sam works with a select clientele who are passionate about providing their children with the best opportunities to attend top colleges and universities.

Alexandra and I could not be happier with our experience working with Sam and are so grateful for his support and guidance toward Alexandra during a crucial time in her life. If we had to do it again, we would work with Sam without a moment's hesitation.

I enthusiastically recommend Sam to any parent who feels that their child's school's college guidance department may not appreciate their child's special needs, talent or desire to gain admission to their "reach" school. Dreams do come true with proper planning, guidance and enthusiasm provided by knowledgeable and experienced college counselors like Sam Silverman. If you would like to speak with me about our experience, please feel free to contact me at the number above.

Sincerely,

Yvette Trelles, Esq.

2

Alexandra Murray

Palm Beach Gardens, Fl 33410

Phone: ███████████ • E-mail: ███████████████████

April 21, 2015

Sam Silverman
Managing Partner, Ivy League Prep
3801 PGA Boulevard, Suite 902
Palm Beach Gardens, Florida 33410
www.IvyLeaguePrep.com

RE: Letter of Recommendation for Sam Silverman, Ivy League Prep

To Whom It May Concern:

I am Alexandra Murray, and I am a graduating senior this year at The Benjamin School. A few months ago, I gained admission to my dream school—Harvard College. Working closely with Sam Silverman the past three years helped turn this childhood dream into a reality.

Sam is focused on providing clear and actionable advice to help his students differentiate themselves from the competition and gain admission to top schools. My Benjamin School guidance counselor was working with ~50 other senior students besides me and so it was difficult to meet several times senior year and get the individualized attention that I got with Sam starting in my sophomore year.

During one of our first meetings, Sam explained his approach to the admissions process, which I believe has been the key to his success working with me and other Benjamin students.

Sam's approach is based on two main ideas:

i. Personal involvement: Sam is personally involved in every decision related to high school academics and extracurricular activities during the year and over summers. I was in constant communication with Sam through e-mail and text with any questions that I had.

ii. Strategic decision making: Every decision is made with the goal of creating the strongest possible application to colleges/universities when the time comes to fill out and submit applications in the fall of senior year. Sam helped me focus the limited time I had outside of academics on the key elements that really matter in admission decisions.

Looking back, I think what was most valuable was Sam's help on what the overall "theme" of my application would be and what extracurricular activities, honors, and awards would support that theme and differentiate my application.

Sam also helped me with my SAT/ACT/SAT II preparation by providing specific materials and prep programs that helped me focus on areas of improvement and boost my scores. Every summer, we talked about what activities I would focus on and how those activities would help advance my application overall.

When it came time to actually putting together my application, Sam provided me with a template that helped me present all my accomplishments and activities in a professional, intuitive format. He also provided samples of other successful Ivy League applications to help give some context as to what a successful finished application looked like.

During the writing of the application itself, Sam provided me with ideas on what topics to focus on in each of the main essays and short-answer questions and then reviewed all final drafts prior to submission.

In summary, I greatly enjoyed working with Sam in the past three years. His advice allowed me to focus on what really mattered in preparing the best application possible and greatly reduced the stress of the process as he was always there to answer questions and remove any guesswork on my part. He also helped me identify scholarships that I could apply for and I received thousands of dollars in scholarship awards as a result.

There is no doubt that if I had to do it again, I would work with Sam, and I would highly recommend him to other students at The Benjamin School who want personal advice and are looking to attend competitive colleges/universities.

If you need any additional information, please do not hesitate to contact me.

Sincerely,

Alexandra Murray
The Benjamin School, Class of 2015
Harvard College, Class of 2019

Sandra Reinhard
. Vero Beach, FL 32968

Home: Mobile:

September 15, 2014

Sam Silverman, Managing Partner
Ivy League Prep
3801 PGA Blvd. Suite 902
Palm Beach Gardens, Florida 33410
RE: Letter of Recommendation - Ivy League Prep/ Sam Silverman

Dear Parent(s):

My name is Sandi Reinhard and my daughter, Leah Reinhard, was recently admitted to her top (college) choice, Georgetown University, where she has just begun her first semester of Freshman classes.

I have known Sam Silverman since 2012 when I engaged him to help Leah (a high-school junior at the time) navigate the college admissions process and develop a compelling and unique student profile to help her stand out.

Looking back, I am so thankful that I found Sam because not only did his advice and approach to the application process result in my daughter getting into her dream school, but it also removed a significant amount of stress and confusion for my family. Navigating through the maze of application questions and never-ending essay requirements can be quite overwhelming for a college applicant. It is very reassuring to have a professional consultant, like Sam, on hand for advice since even the simplest components of a college application can become confusing. It is far more challenging than it seems to summarize various accomplishments and scholastic achievements in the limited available space on a college application!

When we first met Sam, it was clear that he was not only well accomplished and highly intelligent, but also that he had a very strategic and action-oriented approach to the application process – a component which had been clearly lacking from the College Guidance Department at Leah's high school. Sam made it clear from our first meeting that the majority of our time working together would be done over the phone/e-mail given the digital nature of the application process. As a business professional who is accustomed to doing business in person, this made me a bit nervous at first; but it soon became clear that this was the best possible arrangement given our busy schedule and need to get answers quickly. Sam gave us his personal cell phone number and was always available during and after business hours or via e-mail. I was most impressed by his prompt response time during Leah's essay writing process. His expert guidance on topic guidelines along with his proof-reading feedback and suggestions were extremely helpful throughout the entire college application process.

In addition to the normal college/university applications, Sam encouraged Leah to explore summer programs during her junior year summer and reviewed her applications to several highly competitive summer programs. Leah ended up attending a summer program at Brown University and it was this experience, I believe, that helped further solidify her academic credentials when it came time to apply to colleges/universities later that year.

Ultimately Sam was able to refine Leah's overall marketability, for lack of a better term, to highlight the individual aspects of her Student Resumé. Sam's knowledge and history of college acceptance practices provided the necessary guidance for Leah to assemble her application and draw attention to her unique talents and abilities. The limited available space at leading institutions has created an extremely competitive environment with many top schools reporting only single digit acceptance rates. Since private *and* public universities must turn away thousands of highly qualified applicants each year, it is essential to submit an application that will stand-out among the rest. Sam helped Leah achieve this goal by organizing and showcasing her academics, community involvement, leadership and extra-curricular activities. He also provided suggestions to compliment her existing portfolio to create a more well-rounded application. I firmly believe that Sam's input in this regard was a critical component of Leah's acceptance to Georgetown.

Finally, Sam brought to our attention several college scholarships that were available to Leah. Sam helped assemble, edit and review her applications for these programs even though it was totally beyond the scope of our original engagement. As a result, Leah received thousands of dollars in scholarship funds.

Simply put, I cannot recommend Sam enough as an Advisor to you and your child in the difficult/ competitive college admission process. I encourage you to seriously consider making an investment with him in your child's future and for your own peace of mind.

Please contact me directly if I can provide any further information or a more detailed perspective of my personal experience. If I could impart any additional words of wisdom, I would simply say to begin planning for the college application process early. My only regret is that I didn't meet Sam Silverman sooner. Best of luck!

Sincerely,

██████████

Sandi Reinhard

LYTAL, REITER, SMITH, IVEY & FRONRATH

TRIAL ATTORNEYS — FOR YOUR RIGHTS

www.ForYourRights.com

March, 2013

RE: Letter of Recommendation - - Sam Silverman, Ivy League Prep

To Whom It May Concern:

  I have known Sam Silverman since 2008 when he became involved in preparing my daughter, Jaclyn, for the SAT test and in helping her keep her grades up at The Benjamin School. Sam unselfishly spent whatever time was necessary to prepare her for her tests - - he was available 24/hours per day and was able to accommodate our busy schedule and meet with Jaclyn on short notice over weekends and holidays.

  Sam also put together her college applications, reviewed her college essays and engineered her college application profile as a whole. Sam was so innovative, unique and impressive in preparing her applications that she was accepted to all seven (7) of the schools that she applied to. Jaclyn is presently at her top choice, Babson College, [Ranked #1 for Entrepreneurship by U.S. News & World Report 2013] pursuing an undergraduate degree in Business in Boston, MA.

  When my stepson, Jacob, was getting ready to begin the college process, there was no one else I would consider to guide me and my wife, Melissa, [and help Jacob] through the college admission process.

  Jacob is a junior this year and Sam is once again working his magic. He has already helped Jacob: (i) develop a unique community service project, (ii) pursue innovative extracurricular activities outside of school that will reinforce his admissions profile, (iii) gain recognition through third-party service and leadership awards that will help him stand out against the competition, and (iv) plan out a summer schedule that will further solidify his profile.

  Despite the fact that my daughter and stepson have completely different backgrounds, strengths, weaknesses, and interests, Sam formulated a successful plan for each that maximizes their strengths and makes them "shine" in the eyes of college admissions committees.

Northbridge Center • 10th Floor • 515 N. Flagler Drive • West Palm Beach, FL 33401 • Tel (561) 655-1990
P.O. Box 4056, West Palm Beach, Florida 33402-4056 • (800) 654-2024 • Spanish Line (561) 833-1964 • Fax (561) 832-2932

417

Sam teaches his students how to think independently and act confidently in their approach to standardized test-taking. With college admissions counseling, Sam knows all the tricks of the trade to place your child in the best possible position to gain admission to their desired college or university. Sam brings the "edge" that your child will need to be competitive in today's highly selective admissions process. Equally importantly, he has taken the stress, uncertainty and confusion out of the college admission process for my wife and I, since we know Jacob is getting the best help available - - help that we would have no idea otherwise how to provide for him.

In short, by hiring Sam, you will help your child gain admission to colleges/universities that otherwise would be out of reach, and remove all of the stress that comes down on involved parents who want to give their child the best possible education, but are not sure where to begin.

For those parents who are not sure where to begin, or what to do in general, Sam Silverman is the answer. With his individualized advice and customized planning techniques, your child will have the best chance of seeing their collegiate dreams come true.

Sincerely,

Joseph J. Reiter

JJR:aaw

GUNSTER
PRIVATE WEALTH SERVICES

Writer's Direct Dial Number: ▮
Writer's E-Mail Address: ▮

March 18, 2013

Re: Letter of Recommendation - - Sam Silverman, Ivy League Prep

To Whom It May Concern:

My husband and I first met Sam in 2005 when my older son was in 7th grade and needed guidance in using the computer to help organize his class work for school. Sam worked with him to set up study guides and class files, and this individualized attention helped my son succeed at the middle and high school level. A couple of years later we again turned to Sam for individualized SAT coaching. Sam offered not only a positive study system, but also many ideas regarding how to expand my son's experiences outside the classroom which benefited the community in addition to adding to the depth of his college applications. Recently I approached Sam again when my younger son was facing the college application process. I have been very pleased with the results thus far, as Sam is able to maximize study time and provide invaluable pointers during the college preparation process.

Sam's personalized and focused SAT tutoring helped both of my sons substantially increase their SAT scores. Sam also worked closely with my older son to help him differentiate himself among other applicants when it came time to put together his college applications. Sam helped my son best present his athletic, academic and community service accomplishments to the colleges of my son's choice. Today, my older son is currently enrolled in a top undergraduate business school and still connects with Sam to better navigate business school opportunities.

Sam uses a pragmatic, "work-smarter" approach to all that he does - an approach that is extremely effective in helping to develop a student's profile for college admission. It is not only about the amount of time one spends to prepare for college, but also the quality of that preparation that counts.

There are many SAT/ACT/academic tutors out there, but Sam has the ability to look beyond standardized tests and to help pave a path that leads to success. Sam is extremely committed to the future of his students and is 110% invested in their application process. He takes the time to understand his client's interests and to locate and recommend the next steps needed to help his client accomplish his or her goals. I continue to be impressed by Sam's

800 S. E. Monterey Commons Boulevard, Suite 200   Stuart, FL 34996   p 772-288-1980   f 772-288-0610   GUNSTER.COM
Fort Lauderdale | Jacksonville | Miami | Palm Beach | Stuart | Tallahassee | Tampa | The Florida Keys | Vero Beach | West Palm Beach

419

To Whom It May Concern
March 18, 2013
Page 2

constant dedication to his students and his ability to not only prepare them for the SAT/ACT exam, but also to help guide them towards new opportunities that are within their reach.

Sincerely,

Lisa A. Schneider
Shareholder
LAS/csm

420

NICKLAUS BROWN & CO

February 18, 2015

Sam Silverman
███████████████
Jupiter, Florida 33477

Re: Ivy League Prep

Dear Sam,

Ryan and I really appreciate the unbelievable responsiveness and professionalism you portrayed during the college admission process.

I believe that your guidance, professionalism and accessibility have given Ryan the opportunity to attend some of the best schools in the country.

Your skill and experience in project management exemplifies excellence and has been a great lesson for my son.

He was notified this week that NYU Abu Dhabi is interested in him attending and they have selected him to participate in a fully paid candidate weekend prior to admission.

Without your guidance we believe that this wouldn't have been possible.

Thank you for everything,

███████████████

Rory Brown
Managing Partner
Nicklaus Brown & Co.

Jaclyn Ann Reiter

Babson College, 231 Forest St, Babson Park, MA 02457

Email Address: ███████████████ Cell Phone ██████████

April 15, 2015

Samuel B. Silverman, Ivy League Prep
3801 PGA Blvd, Suite 902
Palm Beach Gardens, FL 33410

Re: Thank You – Letter of Recommendation

Dear Sam,

I want to take this opportunity to thank you for all your advice and support these past seven years.

It seems like it was just the other day when we first worked together on my college application strategy and application materials when I was a sophomore at The Benjamin School. Your logical, tailored advice provided the foundation for my college applications, and our work together paid off as I gained admission to my first choice, Babson College, where I am about to graduate next month.

When I began preparing my law school application materials, I was thrilled to find that you had expanded to graduate school admissions as well. Your comments and suggestions on my law school application, resume, and personal statement were invaluable, and they helped me tell my story to law schools across the country. This week I heard back from several law schools and again was admitted to my top choice, Stetson University College of Law where I will be starting law school in the fall.

I cannot thank you enough for all of your help and support. You are the first person I think of when I need advice on important decisions and I am very grateful that you have always been there for me. I look forward to returning back to North Palm Beach after Babson graduation next month and catching up with you in person over the summer.

All the best,

███████████████

Jaclyn Ann Reiter
Benjamin School, 2011'
Babson College, 2015'
Stetson University College of Law, 2018'

422

Louis and Cynthia Benedetto

███████████████ Palm Beach Gardens, FL 33418

Email: ████████████ Phone: ████████████

June 9, 2015

RE: Letter of Recommendation: Sam Silverman, Ivy League Prep—www.IvyLeaguePrep.com

To Whom It May Concern:

We received a letter from Ivy League Prep (ILP) prior to our daughter's sophomore year at The Benjamin School, and our interest was piqued. We had a few phone conversations regarding the services ILP offered; Sam was patient and never frustrated with any of our questions regarding the process. Clearly, Sam had the credentials and experience—he graduated from Benjamin and Yale, and he worked with many Benjamin families we knew—but we still wondered if he could help our daughter, Kiyo, achieve her potential. From the very beginning, Sam had a clear vision for Kiyo. He was organized in his ideas for moving the process forward, and his message resonated with us. We had friends in the Northeast who had gone through the college process two years earlier—it was stressful, tearful, and a full-time job for the parents, with uncertain and often disappointing results.

It was always our hope Kiyo would visit some universities before she began high school so that she could see what she would be working toward. We hoped she would remember the feeling of being on a college campus and that it would motivate her to work hard in high school and achieve her full potential. Kiyo always had an obsession with California, so when she was in eighth grade, we traveled to the West Coast; we visited USC, Stanford, UC Berkeley, University of San Francisco and UCLA. We returned from the trip with Kiyo wearing a USC sweatshirt; it was clear where she wanted to attend.

By Kiyo's sophomore year it was becoming evident USC would be a reach for her. Her grades, ACT scores, and extracurricular activities were solid, but not exceptional. USC is a high-profile university with an acceptance rate below 20 percent and is a top 25 school. After meeting with Sam and hearing what his approach would be, we took a leap of faith and handed over our child's college application strategy/process to Ivy League Prep. True to his word, Sam got the job done. Sam was able to make Kiyo's message and voice heard through her application. We could not have had a better experience with the college process, and Kiyo's acceptance to USC was one of the best days of our family's life.

In addition to Sam's help from start to finish, we felt we had "boutique" service every step of the way. The college counselors at The Benjamin School are spread too thinly (with about 50 senior students *each*) and barely have time to meet with (let alone get to know) underclassmen. To build the strongest application, Kiyo needed personalized attention early on as a sophomore, not in the last few months before applications were due in the fall of senior year. We did not want to take a chance on this once-in-a-lifetime process, given we were not equipped to help our child in this competitive arena.

Ivy League Prep is not inexpensive, and working with Sam will require your child to work hard and challenge himself/herself, but the results will be worth it. Not to mention, it will keep your sanity throughout the process.

Sincerely,

████████████████

Louis and Cynthia Benedetto
Parents of Kiyo, The Benjamin School, class of 2015

Kiyo Vigliotti

███████ – Palm Beach Gardens, Florida 33418

E-mail: ███████████   Phone: ███████

June 1, 2015

RE: Letter of Recommendation: Sam Silverman, Ivy League Prep, www.IvyLeaguePrep.com

To Whom It May Concern:

My name is Kiyo Vigliotti, and I graduated from the Benjamin Upper School in May of this year. A few months ago, I gained admission to my top college choice—the University of Southern California.

Knowing that all USC acceptance letters arrive in a yellow envelope, I was brought to my knees upon opening my mailbox, and seeing my "golden ticket" to Los Angeles. My heart soared, and after many tears of joy and hugs with my parents, the first person I called to share my news with was Sam Silverman.

Sam has been my academic mentor and coach for the past three years. Together, we executed a well-thought-out plan that allowed me to gain acceptance into well-respected and high-ranking schools, including NYU, University of Miami, Occidental College, Boston University, and Fordham University.

To help me get into my dream school, USC, and all of these other competitive schools, Sam devised a brilliant plan based on my academic and career interests. He helped me focus my effort and time on the activities that really mattered and allowed me to assemble a strong and very unique college application. Our hard work paid off, and I got into many schools, including USC.

To elaborate on Sam's resourcefulness, I must tell you about our first meeting. When we began this process, Sam astutely asked for my background and family ties. Given my interest in exercise science and food, and with a long lineage of chefs and agricultural science majors in my family, Sam recommended a strategy to focus on improving knowledge and access to high-quality food at the Benjamin School and within the local community.

Following this strategy, I brought in organic snacks for the Upper School, raised thousands of dollars for Feeding South Florida, conducted an intricate food survey for the Upper School, and completed a full college course about food production from the University of Florida during the summer of my junior year. Sam also helped me add personal touches to each application that showed my passion and deep connection to agriculture and food in general. In sum, Sam helped me brainstorm and grow a unique service project that helped me showcase my leadership skills in the local community and differentiate my college applications.

Once our strategy was in motion, Sam and I sat down together and we chose the list of schools that I would apply to. I probably applied to the most schools out of anyone in my grade, and I did it with ease. Others struggled to get five to eight applications out, while I easily completed more than fifteen.

When I met with the Benjamin School college counselors and shared this list of target schools, they told me that given my GPA and ACT scores, almost all of the schools were "reach" schools and USC in particular was beyond my reach. The college counselors encouraged me to apply to more "safety" schools that had much higher admission rates. Had I not been working with Sam, I would have been very discouraged and unsure of what I could do to improve my chances. Sam always had faith in my capabilities and our plan, and he never questioned or wavered from the list of schools that we had picked.

-1-

424

For my parents and myself, Sam was the right investment. He made the college application process bearable; in fact, I would dare to say enjoyable. The best part about working with Sam was not working with my parents. I have heard countless horror stories from my peers about the many arguments that had occurred over where to apply, how to approach each supplement, sending in test scores, and of course their parents forcing them to stay in on Friday nights to complete applications that were due the next day.

With Sam, I felt more secure in the supplements that I had submitted and I was always ahead of my classmates in terms of deadlines for applications and testing (AP, ACT, SAT tests). For example, many of my classmates did not even know which common application question they were going to answer at the beginning of our senior year—I had already fully completed it. It was polished and beautifully written; so the only thing that I had to do after that was write supplements, which was a breeze because of Sam.

If I had any questions, Sam got back to me within 12 hours, if not sooner. Most of the questions I had were technical ones once I got to the application process, because we had worked out all of the kinks for the information that I was going to use for my applications during the summer of my junior year (again placing me far ahead of my peers).

Sam was personal, and he devoted so much time specifically to my application, my supplements, my parents, and me. And because of this close relationship, Sam was able to impart individualized college-counseling wisdom that surpassed the generalized answers that I had found elsewhere.

If I could go back in time, I would hire Sam again without question. In fact, I know that I will work with Sam again when I apply to graduate school in a few years. I firmly and whole-heartedly believe that I would not have gotten into the schools that I did without Sam's help.

He set me apart from my fellow applicants. This year, USC had over 52,000 applicants, and I was one of the 9,000 students who were accepted. That is a 17.3% acceptance rate. The sheer chance of getting into a top 25 school these days is slim at best. Knowing that, Sam is absolutely worth the investment. In addition to the acceptances that I received, many schools offered me merit scholarships. For example, Fordham University offered me over $21,000 off a year, one of the many scholarships I was offered.

With Sam's help, I was able to raise my ACT score by 8 points, create an impressive schedule, and get accepted to the university that I truly wanted to attend. In addition, Sam went above and beyond and even helped me with the additional application to the honors writing/journalism program at USC months after I had already been admitted and our agreement had clearly been fulfilled. Thanks to Sam, I will be attending the 25th best school in the country and studying at the 5th best writing/journalism program nationwide.

For all parents who see their child wearing the college sweatshirt of the school they dream to get into, know that I was one of those children. I have worn the same USC sweatshirt for five years, and I will wear that same sweatshirt four years from now when I graduate from USC. I have wanted to attend USC since the summer before my freshman year of high school, and this dream has become a reality because of my hard work and partnership with Sam.

Sincerely,

Kiyo Vigliotti
The Benjamin School 2015
University of Southern California Honors 2019

-2-